An Introduction To
Scholarship in Music

An Introduction To
Scholarship in Music

by Cornelia Yarbrough
Louisiana State University

University Readers™
San Diego, CA

First published in the United States of America in 2009 by University Reader Company, Inc.

13 12 11 10 09   1 2 3 4 5

Printed in the United States of America

ISBN: 978-1-934269-28-2 (paper)

University Readers™
800.200.3908 l www.universityreaders.com

Contents

Figures

TABLES

Introduction

Introduction

As musicians we are constantly engaged in forming musical ideas and translating those musical ideas into musical behaviors. How we form our ideas, how we communicate them, and the effects of our communication upon listeners are areas from which questions arise to motivate and stimulate research. Research concerning these questions proceeds from various philosophical bases regarding the issues of how we know music and how we give meaning and value to it.

One purpose of this book is to introduce methods and materials of musical scholarship as it is practiced in the United States today. Music may occur in many forms, cultures, and situations. Likewise, it may be approached and subsequently examined through various modes of inquiry, both systematic and casual. Music may be studied in the presence of or in the absence of human interaction. In any case, the subject matter of music and the methodology of musical scholarship are inseparable.

Otto Kinkeldey has said, "In the widest sense musical scholarship may be fairly said to include any scholarly activity directed toward the investigation and understanding of the facts, the processes, the developments and the effects of the musical art."[1] Today's music scholars must read and understand a variety of research methods. New disciplines for the musician, such as voice science, are demanding different and expanded research skills and understanding. Research degrees in music education and pedagogy are becoming increasingly popular.

A second purpose of this book is to introduce graduate music students to the diverse methodologies of research in music. Specifically, the objectives are to introduce basic research materials and aids, to present a procedure for gaining bibliographical control of a research topic, to discuss the most efficient and effective

---

[1]Otto Kinkeldey, "Musical Scholarship and the University," *Journal of Renaissance and Baroque Music*, 1 (1946): 11.

ways to use library facilities, and to lay a foundation for the understanding of historical, philosophical, ethnomusicological, qualitative, descriptive, experimental, and behavioral research methodologies or modes of inquiry. Above all, there is an emphasis on doing research.

Chapter 1, "The Art of Bibliographical Control," explains the use of the library and other sources to gain bibliographical control and gives techniques for evaluating sources. Chapter 2, "Philosophical Foundations for Research in Music," introduces the student to some major questions and techniques of philosophical inquiry: knowing music; exploring the meaning of music; and sources and development of values. Techniques for logically analyzing and arguing a musical premise are presented. Chapter 3, "Music Historiography," presents the traditional techniques of discovering, editing, compiling, documenting, and annotating the music, composers, performers and musical artifacts of the past. In addition, issues of external and internal criticism of information are presented and techniques for doing research and writing in this mode of inquiry are explained. Chapter 4, "Ethnomusicology and Qualitative Research in Music," introduces the student to current methods, tools, and techniques of ethnomusicology and qualitative research in music education. Chapter 5, "Describing Musical Events and Behavior," presents techniques and tools for the systematic observation of musical events and behavior. Chapter 6, "Statistical Concepts," introduces some very basic statistical concepts to enable the student to better understand quantitative research reports. Chapter 7, "The Logic of Experimental Design in Music Research," analyzes the process of isolating cause and effect relationships in music and presents applications of statistical and behavioral designs.

At the end of each chapter, research applications are outlined to provide experiences in completing projects using the techniques of a particular mode of inquiry. Each chapter also has a bibliography for further reading. Appendices include annotated bibliographies, both general and music related, a comprehensive list of music and music related serials, and an outline of library classification systems.

This book has been in progress since 1986. It has been used in its various forms by graduate students, at both master's and doctoral levels, and in all areas of music, that is, performance, theory, composition, musicology, music therapy, and music education. A number of people have made this book better. Anne Edwards, Patricia Flowers, Jan Herlinger, Clifford Madsen, Judy Marley, Harry Price, Carol Prickett, and hundreds of graduate students at Louisiana State University and A & M College in Baton Rouge, the University of Alabama at Tuscaloosa, Syracuse University, and the Ohio State University. Finally, I am thankful for the positive support and daily feedback of my colleagues at LSU: Jim Byo, Jane Cassidy, Katia Madsen, and Evelyn Orman. Their careful attention and candid remarks were and are appreciated.

Cornelia Yarbrough
July 2008

 **Chapter One**

The Art of Bibliographical Control

Chapter One

The Art of Bibliographical Control

The history of music scholarship, as described in the introduction to this book, shows that research in music has expanded. Music scholarship now includes the study, analysis, and editing of music, the study of other musical artifacts, such as instruments, logical inquiries regarding how we know and value music as well as what music is and means, and systematic analysis and observation of music behavior.

No matter what mode of inquiry is selected to study a particular topic, the music scholar must begin with a complete, thorough knowledge and understanding of past treatments of that topic. Ignorance of past scholarship is a mistake, which leads ultimately to confusion and may result in delay of significant progress in research. Suffice it to say that every research project must begin with history.

Today, most of the fruits of music scholarship may be located in libraries, museums, or through historical societies. Most graduate students will need an excellent working knowledge not only of a research library but also of other avenues of locating materials and resources in order to begin any scholarly activity.

Traditionally, a research library has been an extensive storehouse of information classified for quick retrieval. As such it does three things: (1) it provides depth of information; it keeps many books on a subject, including all scholarly works; (2) it provides an historical view by keeping one copy of most works as a permanent record; and finally (3) it aims at comprehensiveness; it collects all forms of publication. In contrast, the branch library is restricted to collecting materials that can circulate and selecting only a small reference and periodical section to meet the needs of the local community it serves.[1]

Because of increasing costs and the availability of computer services, libraries are now moving away from the concept that the library acquires and stores material. Instead they are moving towards the concept of access to materials regardless of their physical location.

Although books are still the mainstays of most libraries, the "collection" represents a wide variety of print and non-print information. For the musician and researcher, non-print materials include the contents of audio archives, original manuscripts, and recordings. In addition to books which are housed in the main collection, musicians must not overlook collections of rare books, printed sheet music and collected works of various composers, serials (periodicals, for example), government documents, technical reports, maps, pictures, drawings, newspapers, and microforms (microfilm and microfiche).

The art of bibliographical control involves the observation and scrutiny of the evidences of history, both records and relics. *Records* are the intentional transmitters of facts. *Relics* are unpremeditated transmitters of facts.[2] Evidences of music history *records* include: chronicles, annals, biographies, genealogies, dictionaries, encyclopedias, histories, chronologies, catalogs of collections, memoirs, diaries, letters, original manuscripts, periodical publications and unpublished papers, dissertations, theses, ballads, anecdotes, tales sagas, phonograph and tape recordings, portraits, historical paintings, certain kinds of films, and kinescopes. Evidences of music history *relics* include: letters, literature, public documents, business records, certain kinds of inscriptions, language, customs, institutions, and musical instruments. Music scholars, regardless of the method of inquiry (i.e., historiography, ethnomusicology, quantitative, qualitative methods) selected, may be required to work with both of these categories of materials.

The subsequent development of an inventive bibliography might stimulate an organization of the results producing an original conclusion or explanation of some aspect of music history or musical behavior. This original conclusion or explanation must be the goal of serious research in music. Simply gathering information, formulating an outline, and rewriting what has already been said should not be considered significant research. Beginning researchers in music are encouraged to seek out heretofore unexplained musical events, phenomena, or artifacts and to contribute to our knowledge of music and music behavior through a creative research product.

---

[1]David Beasley, *How to Use a Research Library* (New York: Oxford University Press, 1988), 18.

[2]Jacques Barzun and Henry F. Graff, *The Modern Researcher*, 3rd ed. (New York: Harcourt Brace Jovanovich, Inc., 1977), 127.

Bibliographical Control: A Definition

The foundation for all research methodology is bibliographical control of the subject to be studied. To gain bibliographical control of a subject means to systematically develop a list of writings about it and to gather other evidences of history related to it. The result will be a bibliography, a formal list, of references and resources including information concerning authors, editions, publishers, dates of publication, page numbers, and so forth. In other words, a bibliography contains everything one might need to locate the reference or resource. The following steps are suggested as a process for gaining bibliographical control. It is important to note that returning to previous steps is a requirement as the search for all materials on a given topic unfolds. New keywords and the refinement of the topic for study will demand another visit to previously searched resources.

Step 1.   Select, define, and delimit a research topic or music artifact.

A most important step occurs when one selects a topic or a music artifact for research. The topic or artifact should be of such great interest that it would continue to entertain and inspire throughout the sometimes tedious process of gaining bibliographical control, reading and taking notes, writing and word processing the paper, and, finally, proofreading the final draft prior to submission of the research project. Throughout the process of controlled inquiry, the development of bibliographical control and the selection and delimitation of a research topic or artifact should take place in tandem. The researcher should avoid premature closure concerning the final bibliography and the specificity of the approach. A goal at this stage of the controlled inquiry should be to open as many bibliographical doors as possible.

One may discover a musical artifact in the rare books collection of a library, the special collections section, or even in your grandparent's attic. Once an artifact has been selected and before proceeding to **Step 2**, the researcher must complete an external criticism of the artifact. For guidance in this step, see Chapter 3 Music Historiography. The remainder of this section will describe the process to follow in developing a research topic.

Before the selection of a specific topic, it may be useful to select a broader area of interest. For example, "singing" may be the area of choice. To determine what aspect of singing one might finally decide upon, an exploratory analysis of it might be necessary. The purpose of this type of analysis is to use one's own experiences to list and categorize all aspects of the area of interest. For example, an initial exploratory analysis of "singing" resulted in a list of categories including performance characteristics, vocal techniques, physiological aspects, and teaching methods which included the terms, breathing, phonation, resonance, diction, range, tessitura, vocal pedagogy, voice, interpretation, intonation, posture, voice break, falsetto, chest voice, glottal attacks, passagio, bel canto, vibrato, and so forth. Now, one must decide whether to cover one, some, or all of the above characteristics.

For the purpose of providing an extended example of gaining bibliographical control, a tentative decision was made to search for all resources concerning "vocal pedagogy." This term may be a narrower term for the subject, "singing," or it may not be a term at all. Instead of approaching the subject directly, it may be necessary to approach the topic through separate aspects (breathing, resonance, phonation, diction) of vocal pedagogy. The topic, "vocal pedagogy," may change, grow or diminish, and be refined as the research effort proceeds. However, the exploratory analysis procedure has opened up key words for gaining bibliographical control of the topic and has provided a limited review of the entire area of interest. Exploring a topic through brainstorming, skimming books and journals, talking with others, integrating interests and experiences, and finally choosing a topic from a larger area of interest are valuable approaches to beginning the search.

After one has brainstormed and categorized or organized this experiential information, other resources can be used to further explore and refine the area. General and subject encyclopedias, books concerning singing, subject handbooks, music dictionaries, and articles in periodicals provide information, which will explain and define this topic. In addition, these resources will identify the authorities and better known works on the subject.

Step 2.   **List keywords and subject headings you will use for your search. Use the *Library of Congress Subject Headings Guide*, the Permuterm section of the *Arts and Humanities Citation Index*, the *Music Index*, and your own creativity for this step.**

The second step begins with identifying a general area for research, such as "vocal pedagogy." In determining subject headings and key words for it, several sources are most helpful. The ***Library of Congress Subject Headings (LCSH)*** is an accumulation of headings established and applied by the Library of Congress since 1897.[3] ***LCSH*** headings are valuable because they provide a hierarchy of terms, which are and are not related to the major term.

---

[3]***Library of Congress Subject Headings***, 30th ed., 5 vols. (Washington, D. C.: Cataloging Distribution Services, Library of Congress, 2007). Many libraries throughout the United States use LC headings for subject access in both manual and online catalogs. Copies of the latest edition of ***LCSH*** may be found in the reference

In addition to identifying approved subject headings for use in manual and online catalogs, musicians and researchers may find that the *LCSH* volumes can be used for narrowing and focusing a topic. These volumes are a most valuable bibliographical tool, since knowledge of the subject headings used to catalog the library's collection is often a prerequisite to locating all materials for a given topic.

There are a few overall points to remember about subject headings. Subject terms must be found that are acceptable to the library cataloging system. These terms may or may not be the terms the researcher is using. One way to find the right term is to use *LCSH*, the standard used by libraries in the United States. In addition, many other catalogs, indexes, bibliographies, and databases use essentially the same *LCSH* list of terms while others have their own thesaurus.

In using *LCSH* one must pay particular attention to the **NT** or **Narrower Term** cross-references, which lead to the *most specific* headings. Books are entered only under the most specific headings applicable to them and not also under larger generic headings. A second way to find the right subject headings is to use the tracings at the bottom of any catalog card or online record representing the relevant book. These notations will indicate the terms to be used to find similar books.

Examination of *LCSH* under the term, "Music," showed the narrow term (**NT**), "Voice." Looking under the term, "voice," led to another narrow term (**NT**), "voice culture." The term, "voice culture," revealed the uniform terms (**UT**) "vocal culture," "voice training" and "singing." Therefore, in searching bibliographical sources in library catalogs, we might concentrate on the subject headings, "singing" and "vocal or voice culture."

It is important to note first that the term, "vocal pedagogy," was not listed in **LCSH**. This does not mean that we should discard it. On the contrary, this term, and others we will discover as we progress, will continue to be important keys to unlocking information about our topic. Secondly, we have not yet selected nor fully defined and delimited our specific research topic.

The importance of key words in the development of a working bibliography cannot be overstressed. As bibliographies are explored and as references are read, the number of key words will again expand and may even change dramatically. George Bragg, founder and former director of the Texas Boys Choir, related the following story regarding the importance of key words in his own research:

> As an adult looking for histories of boy choirs and their origins, I came to realize that there were certain techniques, procedures, standards, phrases, and sounds that were inherited from past masters of boychoir choral art. Hence, it seemed what all of us, as boychoir

---

sections of most libraries. The set is kept up-to-date by quarterly cumulative microfiche editions and an annual compilation in paper. These supplements reflect the constant updating of headings to conform to current cataloging practices.

directors, had to do to comprehend the full extent and depth of our art was to obtain an historical foundation and become practitioners of an historical art.

This historical connection and understanding were missing from many of the authors whose writings had been collected earlier. Thus, I began to search for material on this unique, nebulous subject. Without knowing the range and extent of the subject of boychoir, I began to look for any information, which might lead me to a more valid strata of historical source. I could find nothing which had been written in any country of Europe telling of a national history of boychoir. Not even England, one of the best chronicled and documented countries in the world, had a composite history.

In my pursuit, quite naturally, I turned to the Library of Congress in Washington, D. C. Surprisingly, under the category of "Boy Choir," I found only thirty entries: four in Russian, three in Spanish, three in German, five in English (British), the rest were "how-to" books of American origin. I was disheartened, to say the least, for I had thought this "bibliotheca cornucopia" to be the most complete center on any subject in the world. So, finding the thirty volumes seemed to indicate my search was over.

However, at the end of the section there was a reference: "see Seises." The word had no meaning to me, but since I was at the end of my known source, I dutifully followed directions, knowing that I had nothing to lose, and possibly something to gain. As luck and scholarship would have it, the word "seises" became the "key" which unlocked the historical "vault" telling of boychoir and civilization as it was affected by a long and noble lineage of boy singers.

"Seises" referred to the "sixes" in Spain, that number of trebles transported to the Court of Spain from Burgundy in Flanders to supply the upper voices for the Choir of the Royal Chapel. Additional words, just as obscure: "maitrise," "Cambrai," "seeckmester," "chapel," became keys that opened a 14th century door which, also, led toward the 20th century, as well as backward in time. The limited view, so far, has given me some insight into the practices in vocal performance, beyond the Romans, the Greeks, the Hebrews, all the way back to the Egyptians of the Middle Kingdom, c. 1500 B. C.[4]

The above account demonstrates the importance of identifying subject headings and key words for developing a working bibliography. If there is no subject heading for a selected area of interest, an unconventional method for developing

---

[4]George Bragg to Cornelia Yarbrough, July, 1985.

key words may be useful. The ***Arts & Humanities Citation Index*** contains a "Permuterm" Subject Index for each annual issue. This is an alphabetical list of all significant or key words from the titles of all journal articles covered by that issue. This used in tandem with the more conventional ***Music Index*** should enable the development of key words. However frustrating the search becomes, it should be remembered that enormous patience and persistence are needed to explore and re-explore as keywords change and grow.

**Step 3.   Find an overview article if possible. For example, the
New Grove Dictionary of Music and Musicians might
provide a good general overview for most topics.**

The next step might be to see if someone has written an overview article or book that outlines the most important facts on the subject and provides a bibliography. This is precisely the purpose of an encyclopedia, such as ***The New Grove Dictionary of Music and Musicians***.[5] The article on "Singing" in ***The New Grove Music On-Line***[6] gives the history of singing and a brief treatment of theory and pedagogy. The article on "Voice" refers one to "Acoustics, Part VI."[7] Here, the treatment is more scientific and seemingly more in line with three subtopics of interest, breathing, resonance, and diction as outlined in our initial exploratory analysis.

Perusal of these overview articles increased the number of key words to be used in further developing bibliographical control. Now, in addition to those terms and headings listed above there are, for example, "formant," and "register." Second, there is a bibliography at the end of each of the articles.

Step 4.   Rethink, redefine, and further delimit the topic.

After an exploratory analysis of the area of interest, a check of ***LCSH*** and a perusal of overview articles, it may now be possible to select, define and delimit a more specific research topic. The interest and creativity of the researcher should always govern the selection of a topic. The task of piecing together bits of

---

[5]Do not be misled by the term "dictionary." In library and publishing terminology it refers simply to the alphabetical arrangement of articles without regard to their length, so it is often synonymous with "encyclopedia."

[6]Laura Macy, ed.*, Grove Music On-Line*, s.v. "Singing" by Owen Jander, Ellen T. Harris, David Fallows, and John Potter <http://www.grovemusic.com> (accessed 9 May 2008).

[7]Laura Macy, ed.*, Grove Music On-Line*, s.v. "Acoustics, Part VI The Voice" by Johan Sundberg <http://www.grovemusic.com> (accessed 9 May 2008).

knowledge into the typical "term paper" is not what advanced students should have as their goal. Instead, the ultimate goal for every scholar should be to contribute new knowledge.

Before continuing the search, it is wise to rethink the topic for more focus, and then to plan the search procedure so that one can proceed in as systematic a way as possible. The terms, "vocal pedagogy" and "voice science," appeared to represent the most recent developments in the teaching of singing. The question, "How has research in singing influenced the teaching of it?" seemed to generate the most interest in the researcher. In addition, it seemed to be the most promising question to pursue in order to contribute new knowledge.

Having further specified the topic, the following limitations were developed before proceeding to the next step in the process of bibliographical control: (1) a substantial bibliography is the primary objective of the search; (2) the search is limited to the specific time span, 1975-2008, the period during which most modern scientific research in singing has been conducted; (3) due to time considerations and lack of a second language, the search is limited to references in the English language;[8] and (4) the materials gathered are limited to the scientific methodology of teaching voice excluding vocal literature and the adolescent voice. With a firmer and more specific definition and delimitation of the research topic and with key words in hand, we were ready for the next step.

Step 5. **Using the subject headings and keywords listed as a result of steps 1, 2, 3, and 4, conduct searches in prominent bibliographies of bibliographies such as Sheehy, Duckles and Reed and others cited in Appendices A and B of Yarbrough.[9]**

The first method for discovering all possible references and resources is to explore bibliographies of bibliographies. Bibliographies of bibliographies are references containing extensive lists of other references containing bibliographies. Many bibliographies of bibliographies were eliminated at the outset because they were

---

[8]Given more time, the writer would include articles in French, Italian, and German, taking time for translations. Caution is recommended in this regard. Without consideration of foreign language sources, one might miss consequential information.

[9]Appendices A and B are annotated bibliographies of bibliographies. References in Appendix A are general reference books selected from Sheehy's *Guide to Reference Books*. Those in Appendix B are music reference books selected from Duckles and Reed, *Music Reference and Research Materials* and other music bibliographic resources.

retrospective in nature (published before 1975). Beginning with Sheehy's **Guide to Reference Books** (1986) and Baylay's supplement to the **Guide** covering the years 1975-1999 (see Appendix A), a search through current general bibliographies was initiated. Sheehy lists general and subject area references. There were several general and music bibliographies of bibliographies, which might prove helpful. The following paragraphs demonstrate the use of these references.

In search of current bibliographies, the **Bibliographic Index** was consulted using the terms, "singing" and "voice." The **Bibliographic Index** is a cumulative bibliography of bibliographies contained in books, pamphlets, and periodicals. There were two bibliographies listed here that are contained in the books, **Training the Singing Voice** (1979; MT 820 F43) by Victor A. Fields (pp. 267-328) and **English, French, German, and Italian Techniques of Singing** (1977; MT 823 M55) by Richard Miller (pp. 216-237). Fields has compiled sixty-one pages of annotated listings of books and magazine articles on vocal methodology and pedagogy. These span the years 1928-1945 and so are retrospective in nature. Miller's bibliography is less substantial (21 pages) and includes citations up to 1971. Since the search procedure established limited the time span to 1975-1999, these references may or may not be useful. Rather than discard these at this early stage, the decision was made to keep them for possible clarification of later materials and resources.

Two dissertations were discovered in later volumes of the **Bibliographic Index** which may prove invaluable: one by Owen Lloyd Duggan entitled, "A Research and Reference Guide for the Study of Vocal Pedagogy; Selected Works from 1967 to 1991" (University of Texas, Austin, 1992; UMI No. AAI9239198); and another by Karen Davis Bernard entitled, "A Bibliography of Current Research in Voice Science as Related to Singing and applied Vocal Pedagogy; A Doctoral Essay" (University of Miami, 1995, AAI9536852).

To continue the investigation of general reference materials listed in Sheehy, the **Cumulative Book Index** was inspected and found to be helpful in obtaining information concerning recent publication of books about singing, voice training, and pedagogy. The indices for 1980 and 1982 listed four books; those for 1983-1996 listed none. Finally, **Books in Print** was consulted using the subject guide and the terms, "singing," and "voice." Three current books were found here: **The Science of the Singing Voice** (1987; MT 821 S913) by Johan Sundberg; **The Science of Vocal Pedagogy** (1967) by Ralph D. Appelman; and **The New Voice Pedagogy** (1995) by Marilee David. Although Appelman's book was published in 1967, it was decided to keep it in the developing bibliography for possible future clarification of terms and other ideas.

After completing the investigation of the general reference material, which might lead one to materials concerning vocal pedagogy, a search for specific music bibliographies was begun by consulting **Music Reference and Research Materials** by Duckles and Reed. Under the subject heading, "voice," in the index, was one listing: *A Dictionary of Vocal Terminology: An Analysis* by Cornelius L. Reid (NY: Joseph Patelson Music House, 1983). This listing includes a bibliography, which may be helpful. A search under other subject headings (vocal, voice, pedagogy, and singing) yielded no other sources.

Step 6.   Conduct searches of electronic databases such as *RILM, The Music Index Online*, and *Dissertation Abstracts.*

Electronic databases require the use of Boolean Logic to formulate search queries while others offer it as an option for more detailed searching. In a Boolean search strategy, the operators (<u>and</u>, <u>or</u>, and <u>not</u>) are used to create a compound subject by combining topics. For example, a search query might request "Music <u>and</u> Therapy," "Music Aptitude <u>not</u> Achievement," or "Symphon? <u>or</u> Concerto Grosso." The question mark in the expression, "Symphon?" will tell the system to retrieve all words beginning with the root "symphon," for example, symphony, symphonic. The <u>or</u> operator is often used when an idea can be expressed by synonyms in order to broaden the search; an <u>and</u> links ideas to create a compound subject, limiting the search to those items which include both subjects; and <u>not</u> restricts the search. The best searches combine the operators. For example, consider the following logical search query: Music <u>and</u> Conductors <u>not</u> Electrical.[10]

Access to computer databases is now a common feature of most university libraries. Whether on a CD ROM system or via telecommunication lines to a distant database, the online searcher can locate a variety of materials in a wide range of disciplines. For the musician, *RILM,* the *Music Index, and Dissertation Abstracts* are familiar reference sources that, like hundreds of others, are now available for computer access either on-line or via CD-ROM. Because of the high cost of computer-based systems, many libraries may not have all these resources on-line.

RILM indexes research-based articles and dissertations including many that will be found also in the *Music Index.* The keyword, "vocal pedagogy," yielded 75 articles and dissertations in English. The keyword, "voice science," resulted in 17 entries.

The *Music Index* indexes several music periodicals that are important in the field of voice and vocal pedagogy. They include the *Journal of Research in Singing* and *NATS Bulletin.* Also, by looking under the subject heading, "singing," the researcher found book review citations as well as articles. A book review of *Profiles in Vocal Pedagogy* by Whitlock and an article, "Checklist of Recent Research, No. 3: Vocal Pedagogy," by T. M. Otto in the *Journal of Research in Singing* may

---

[10]Donald B. Cleveland and Ana D. Cleveland, *Introduction to Indexing and Abstracting* (Littleton, CO: Libraries Unlimited Inc., 1983), 24-26.

be useful. Searching under the keywords, "vocal pedagogy," and "voice science," resulted in 193 and 12 citations, respectively.

For this project in the influence of voice science on vocal pedagogy, we also searched *Dissertation Abstracts*. This search yielded 84 dissertations under the keyword, "vocal pedagogy," and 10 under the keyword, "voice science."

Step 7.   Search the *World Wide Web* for organizations, which might have information on your topic.

For this search, many search engines, such as Google, Dogpile, Mamma, Excite, WebCrawler, and others are available. We chose to search through Google and entered the term, "vocal pedagogy." This yielded over 73,000 hits containing sites in the .edu, .org, and .com domains. As expected, many of the entries cannot be used as they are listings of vocal pedagogy curricula at universities or advertisements. Other sites must be evaluated carefully for validity and reliability. Sorting through the high volume of information can be time consuming and, in many cases, disappointing in that the information gained is not valid.

Many music libraries in research universities have webliographies that are very helpful in regards to current information. The webliography for music resources at Louisiana State University contains links to many web resources that might be helpful in our search for information concerning vocal pedagogy and voice science.

Step 8.   First, search the electronic, standing, or published card catalogs in your own library; then, search the electronic catalog of the Library of Congress (www.loc.gov).

The collection of a research library may be cataloged in four ways. First there may be a card catalog in which each card represents a separate publication. Cards are printed and sold by the Library of Congress to many libraries throughout the world. These or similar cards make up the catalogs of most libraries. Most cataloging systems contain bibliographic material (authors name, title, publisher, date), the number of prefatory and text pages, the height of the resource in centimeters (used to plan shelving of it), the **LCSH** headings to be used in the subject catalog, the Library of Congress call number, the Dewey classification number, and the serial number of that particular card.

A second way a collection may be cataloged is through a book catalog also called a union catalog. Here the entries are sometimes printed and other times the cards from the card catalog are photocopied. Book catalogs of the music collections of the New York Public Library, the Boston Public Library, and the Library of Congress are available in most research libraries. These book catalogs may reside in a third form of cataloging, microform catalogs, which can be used with a microform viewer.

On-line computer catalogs are to a great extent replacing the three forms of catalogs mentioned above. It is often tempting to use the computer solely to complete the bibliographical control process. Caution is advised since the on-line catalog of a particular library may contain only those publications held by that library. Some also access other catalogs and databases. In addition, the library may be in a transition period during which they have been converting the card catalog to online. In this case, both on-line and card catalog searches are advisable.

First, note all the ways that the particular library can be searched on-line. Usually these will include searches by subject heading, keyword, call number, title, and author. Using the subject heading, "voice," resulted in 3,856 citations, the subject heading, "singing," gave 746, and that of "voice culture," 123 resources. Secondly, using the keywords, "vocal pedagogy," and "voice science," yielded only about 20 citations. Finally, a call number search using the call numbers provided by the *LCSH Guide* and others discovered through other searches revealed that the call numbers MT 820, MT 821, and MT 845 contained the most resources for our topic.

Armed with what we learned in the above searches, we then searched the *Library of Congress* and found that the entries revealed duplicated those we found in our own library.

Step 9.   With call numbers in hand, systematically browse the shelves.

The next searching strategy is systematic browsing. The practice of shelving books in a classified arrangement so that books on the same subject are placed next to each other in convenient groups predates the invention of the card catalog.[11] Thus, the card catalog and the shelf arrangement scheme are complementary. The card catalog and now the online catalog correct the weaknesses of the classified stacks by providing multiple points of access to works that can have only one position in the classes and by grouping under one subject heading works that are scattered among many classes. The shelf-browsing system in turn corrects the defects of the catalogs "by providing in-depth access to full texts, free of the constraints and filters of an artificial vocabulary

---

[11]Thomas Mann, *A Guide to Library Research Methods* (New York: Oxford University Press, 1987), 27. The development of classification schemes such as the Library of Congress and Dewey Decimal systems were devised in the early twentieth century. Few libraries had card catalogs then; so much effort went into the creation of precise categories and subcategories to reveal subtle relationships among subjects.

of subject headings arranged alphabetically rather than logically."[12] For our topic, the effect of voice science on vocal pedagogy, we might use call numbers for all books and periodicals located in our search for bibliographies to locate other sources of bibliography on the shelves. In the Dewey Decimal system, the call number 784 is used for "voice and vocal music;" in the Library of Congress system, MT 820-949 are the classification numbers for "singing and voice culture" (see Appendix D for keys to library classification systems). The call numbers most appropriate for our search are MT 820, MT 821, and MT 845.

Step 10.   Read and take notes using a self-developed system of bibliographic and note files while at the same time evaluating your sources.

Having completed the initial process of bibliographical control, the task of finding the reference and resource materials that have come to light, reading, taking notes, preliminary writing, and constructing the final paper should begin. This task is one of artful craftsmanship. It is artful in the sense that creative construction and organization of the materials should take place. However, craftsmanship, which demands the re-searching through bibliographical resources for additional supportive materials and for items, which insure thorough coverage, must also be present.

The process of reading and taking notes may be simplified and made more efficient by preparing large index cards, one containing the bibliographical and footnote citations in their correct forms according to the style manual chosen; and a set of cards containing notes with page numbers. The bibliography, footnote, and note cards should be keyed with a number for each set, for example, for the first reference examined, the bibliography and footnote card, and all note cards would be keyed by placing the number "1" in the upper right corner of the card. This procedure enables the researcher to shuffle note cards into a variety of orders without losing sight of the source of the material. In addition, the final typing or processing of the paper is made easier by the ability to use the key numbers with pages for footnotes (which already appear in the correct format), the ability to alphabetically arrange bibliography cards, and the ability to order note cards either topically, chronologically, or however the researcher chooses. Now with cards in hand, we begin the process of establishing a bibliography for the topic we have chosen.

First, a return to those bibliographical sources where citations were found which were thought to be valuable. Create a numbered bibliography card for each source. On the same card, create a footnote entry for that reference. Once all bibliographical

---

[12]Mann, 31.

cards have been completed and numbered, the sources must be located either in the library or through interlibrary loan.

One of the most important aspects of the research process is evaluating the quality of the sources in order to determine which provide reliable and useful information and which do not. The following questions should be asked as each source is examined:

1. Is this a primary or a secondary source? A primary source is the first or original source; a secondary source is another account derived from primary sources. The important question is how many intervening and interpretive sources there are between the researcher and the original observation or data. Each interpretation, even if objective and accurate, shapes the information through the analysis of the writer. Also, each intervening source represents a possibility for error or misinterpretation.

2. What are the author's or editor's qualifications? Is the author an expert in the subject matter or knowledgeable in the field? Check the title page and the preliminary pages to find out the author's credentials, by noting the author's degrees, experience, and the academic or other positions held. Also, look in biographical dictionaries and other reference books that give information about authors. Begin with the *Biography and Genealogy Master Index* which will indicate which sources such as *Who's Who in America, Who's Who in American Women,* and *International Who's Who in Music* contain biographical information. In addition to the author or editor, notice the name of the publisher, which may suggest expected standards. Many firms are associated with particular subjects, or certain types of books.

3. How current is the information? Check the copyright date. Some subjects change quickly and up-to-date information is needed. Other subjects may be covered adequately in earlier materials. Often the most current information on a particular topic is in periodicals.

4. What are the scope and treatment of the information? Examine the table of contents to get an overview of the subjects covered. Read the preface and introduction to determine the author's purpose, the intended audience, the scope of the work, and the author's treatment of the subject. Does the book or article attempt to cover more than is possible in a work of that size? Is the work written for a general reader, or the specialist in the field? Is the content of the book complete or partial, exhaustive or condensed? Can the work be associated with any school of thought or serve as a vehicle for a philosophical or ideological viewpoint? Is there any indication of bias in the treatment of material, and, if so, does it distract from the usefulness of the source? Is other material needed to give opposing ideas?

5. What is the format of the book? Are there illustrations, graphs, or drawings, if needed? Does the book provide bibliographies, reading lists, and footnotes? Is there an index to give easy access to specific information? Are other features provided which amplify the material, such as appendices or a glossary of terms? Does the source lack features that would be useful?

6. How was the book reviewed? Book reviews can be found in professional journals, *Book Review Digest*, *Book Review Index*, and *Choice*.

Advice commonly given to young researchers bears repeating. Simply because a book or article exists in print does not mean that it is accurate and reliable, nor does it mean that it is well suited for a particular purpose. The ability to evaluate each source is essential for academic and scholarly integrity.

Before reading a book, give it an inspectional reading. Read the title, subtitle, table of contents, the preface or introduction by the author, and the index. Secondly, determine what kind of book it is.

Step 11.   Do a citation search in the Arts and Humanities Citation Index.

Another method of locating materials is citation searching. Three unconventional indexes are used for this task. These are the *Science Citation Index (1955 -)*, *the Social Sciences Citation Index (1966 -)*, and the *Arts & Humanities Citation Index (1975 -)*. Each issue of these indexes contains a "Permuterm" Subject index, a Source index, and a Citation index. The first of these is an alphabetical list of all significant or key words from the titles of all journal articles covered by that issue. Collectively, these three indexes cover thousands of journals in all fields for use on any subject of interest.

In citation searching, one must begin with a known source - a book, journal article, conference paper, dissertation, or technical report. It can be any kind of knowledge record, published last year or centuries ago. A citation search will indicate whether someone has written a subsequent journal article, which cites that source in a footnote. It is often the case that a later work, which cites an earlier one, is probably talking about the same subject. Once the first tier of articles that cites the original source has been found, then articles that cited the first tier can be found, thus creating a second tier. Then citations for the second tier can be found, and so on, until a large amount of bibliographical information has been collected.

Because one must begin with a known source, citation searching should be done late in the search process after a significant amount of information has been gathered. This method is seldom used, but it is an excellent tool for locating well-hidden source materials.

**Step 12.   After completing the above steps, interview an expert
on the topic.**

The final search strategy, talking to people, is somewhat controversial. However, this writer agrees with Mann when he writes:

> Genuine learning should obviously be a broadening rather than a limiting experience; and in doing research the most important lesson to learn is that <u>any</u> source is fair game. One should always go to wherever the information needed is most likely to be, and very often this will be in someone's head rather than in a book. (Remember, too, though, that you can travel 'full circle' from talking to an expert to get back into the literature - for usually the expert will know the <u>best</u> written sources, and can thereby offer valuable shortcuts that will make library research much more efficient.)[13]

The Directory of Music Faculties in Colleges and Universities has an index which identifies each faculty member's expertise by a numerical code, for example, 32 is "Voice Instruction." Most beginning researchers are intimidated by the prospect of talking to an expert in the field or calling someone on the telephone to interview them. The fact is that most interviewees are flattered that they are considered knowledgeable in some area and will most often respond helpfully. Finding these experts is sometimes difficult. Other than faculty of local universities, experts may be found in several directories. The ***Directory of Directories*** describes approximately 10,000 sources in sixteen broad subject categories such as "Fine Arts Marketplace," "International Directory of Published Market Research," "National Directory for the Performing Arts/Educational," "Information Market Place," and "Toll Free Digest: A Directory of Toll Free Telephone Numbers." Another helpful directory is the ***Writer's Resource Guide***, edited by Bernardine Clark. This is a directory of sources (with telephone numbers) for authors who need facts in any field. Other experts are, of course, the authors of books or articles that have been read on the subject of interest.

One should begin the process by doing considerable background reading to prepare for the interview. Second, explain the purpose of the project and how the information will be used (a research paper, publication, broadcast, program notes, etc.). Third, ask specific questions. Fourth, respect the expert's intellectual property rights. Give credit to the expert in a footnote and in the bibliography. Fifth, ask for additional contacts to obtain more than one spoken viewpoint. Finally, after talking to someone who has been helpful, write a thank-you note.

---

[13]Mann, 120.

Bibliographical and Footnote Citation Formats

A bibliography contains a citation for every work consulted whether cited or not. A reference list contains only those works cited in the paper. There are two kinds of notes, reference and content. As such they have four main uses: (1) to cite the authority for statements in text - specific facts or opinions as well as exact quotations; (2) to make cross-references; (3) to make incidental comments upon, to amplify, or to qualify textual discussion - in short, to provide a place for material which the writer deems worthwhile but which would in the writer's judgment interrupt the flow of thought if introduced into the text; and (4) to make acknowledgments.

Note that in a footnote the superscripted number of the footnote, the author's first name followed by his last, the indentation of the first line, and the use of commas. If the word processing software will not superscript footnote numbers, new software must be purchased. Footnote numbers should not be written in by the author. Number footnotes consecutively throughout the paper.

Note that in a bibliography, the family name of the author is followed by the first, the use of periods instead of commas, and the hanging indent of the second and subsequent lines.

Most universities recommend specific style manuals for dissertations and theses. Journals contain a page detailing instructions to contributors that must be followed. It should be noted that the publisher decides what style the author should follow.

Summary

At this point in time the research process will have three aspects. First, the process of opening up a bibliography will continue and expand. Second, the process of writing bibliography cards and locating the materials in the library or through inter-library loan will continue. Third, as materials are located the researcher will read them, take notes, and begin writing.

Thus, the research process may be outlined as a twelve-step procedure:

1. Selection, definition, and delimitation of a research topic through exploratory analysis;
2. Listing of keywords and subject headings for the topic;
3. Finding and reading an overview article;
4. Rethinking, redefining, and further delimiting the research topic;
5. Using subject headings and keywords to search general and music bibliographies of bibliographies;
6. Conducting searches of electronic databases;

7. Searching the World Wide Web;
8. Searching the card catalogs of your own and other research libraries;
9. Browsing the shelves with call numbers in hand;
10. Reading, examining and evaluating resources while taking notes;
11. Completing a citation search procedure; and
12. Interviewing an expert in the field.

Remember that the process of research is an undulating one. That is, after selection of an area of interest, one may proceed to step two, the exploratory analysis. This step may require a return to step one in order to state more clearly the research topic. Likewise, step four (the formulation of research questions), may require a return to step three, step two and, subsequently, step one. The process, therefore, is one of constant redefinition and refinement. The patience and care with which this process is undertaken will determine the beauty of scholarship demonstrated in the final product.

There is no one magic formula for producing that research which will significantly influence the study of music for generations to come. History is fluid, ever changing. Only time gives us the perspective to evaluate our efforts and to select those musical events, products, and people, which are those true creative milestones.

RESEARCH APPLICATIONS

1. Select two reference books from each category in Appendices A and B. Review each reference and make notes regarding how this source might be useful to you in the future.
2. Select a topic of interest and write a brief description of how one might gain bibliographical control of that topic by following the twelve steps listed and explained in this chapter.
3. Submit a typed or word processed bibliography in Turabian style on a topic of choice. The bibliography must reflect an approach to the topic through a variety of sources, e.g., collections, encyclopedias, dictionaries, catalogs, discographies, histories, biographies, periodicals. It must also demonstrate facility in using all facets of the library including (where appropriate) audio archives, university archives, computer searches, inter-library loan, microfilm, and so forth.

BIBLIOGRAPHY

Barzun, Jacques and Henry F. Graff. *The Modern Researcher*, 3rd ed. New York: Harcourt Brace Jovanovich, Inc., 1977.

Beasley, David. *How to Use a Research Library*. NY: Oxford University Press, 1988.

Booth, Wayne C., Gregory G. Colomb, and Joseph M. Williams. *The Craft of Research*. Chicago: The University of Chicago Press, 1995.

The Chicago Manual of Style: The Essential Guide for Writers, Editors, and Publishers. 14th Ed. Chicago: The University of Chicago Press, 1993.

Cleveland, Donald B. and Ana D. Cleveland. *Introduction to Indexing and Abstracting*. Littleton, CO: Libraries Unlimited, Inc., 1983.

Druesedow, John E. *Library Research Guide to Music*. Ann Arbor: Pierian Press, 1982.

Duckles, Vincent H. and Ida Reed. *Music Reference and Research Materials: An Annotated Bibliography*. 5th ed. NY: Schirmer Books, 1997.

Gibaldi, Joseph and Phyllis Franklin. *MLA Handbook for Writers of Research Papers, Theses, and Dissertations*. 5th ed. NY: Modern Language Association of America, 1999.

Hitchcock, H. Wiley and Stanley Sadie, eds. *The New Grove Dictionary of American Music*. London: Macmillan Press Limited, 1986. S. v. "Bibliographies" by D. W. Krummel, v. 1, 205-213.

————————. S. v. "Discographies" by David Hall, Gary-Gabriel Giscondi, and Edward Berger, v. 1, 627-632.

————————. S. v. "Libraries and Collections" by Mary Wallace Davidson and D. W. Krummel, v. 3, 44-84.

————————. S. v. "Periodicals" by Imogen Fellinger and John Shepard, v. 3, 505-535.

Holoman, D. Kern. *Writing About Music: A Style Sheet from the editors of 19th-Century Music*. Berkeley: University of California Press, 1988.

Irvine, Demar and Mark A. Radice. *Writing About Music: A Style Book for Reports and Theses*, 3rd ed. Amadeus Press, 1999.

Library of Congress Subject Headings. 16th Ed. Washington, D.C.: Cataloging Distribution Services, Library of Congress, 1993.

"Man: Memo from a Publisher." From *Guidelines for Equal Treatment of the Sexes in McGraw-Hill Book Company Publications*, version published in *New York Times Magazine*, October 20, 1974.

Mann, Thomas. *A Guide to Library Research Methods*. New York: Oxford University Press, 1987.

Publication Manual of the American Psychological Association, 5th ed. Washington, D. C.: American Psychological Association, 2001.

Sheehy, E. P., Ed. *Guide to Reference Books*, 10th ed. Chicago: American Library Association, 1986.

Strunk, William and E. B. White. *The Elements of Style*. 4th Ed. Boston: Allyn & Bacon, 1999.

Turabian, Kate L. *A Manual for Writers of Term Papers, Theses, and Dissertations*, 7th ed. Chicago: University of Chicago Press, 2007.

Van Leunen, Mary-Claire. *A Handbook for Scholars*. 2nd Ed. New York: Oxford University Press, 1992.

Waddell, Marie L., Robert M. Esch, and Robert R. Walker. *The Art of Styling Sentences*. 3rd Ed. Hauppauge, NY: Barron's Educational Series, Inc., 1993.

Walvoord, Barbara F. *Writing: Strategies for all Disciplines*. Englewood Cliffs, NJ: Prentice-Hall Inc., 1985.

Williams, Joseph M. *Style: Toward Clarity and Grace*. Chicago: The University of Chicago Press, 1990.

Wingell, Richard J. *Writing About Music: An Introductory Guide*. 2nd Ed. Englewood Cliffs, NJ: Prentice Hall, 1996.

 **Chapter Two**

Philosophical Foundations for Scholarship in Music

Chapter Two

Philosophical Foundations for Scholarship in Music

Our musical beliefs and our ideas about life in general shape our understandings and our research approaches to the art and science of music. Philosophers have examined the phenomenon of music as it impacts human life. Music is not essential for explicit communication nor for survival purposes, yet it continues to be a central part of human experience. Why?

As musicians engaged in the formation of musical ideas and the translation of those musical ideas into musical performance, we may wonder about the "basic stuff" of music. What about music is beyond its natural occurrence? What is its ultimate reality? How we form our ideas, how we communicate them, and the effects of our communication upon listeners are areas from which questions arise concerning how we know music. What are the paths through which we may discover and know music? From what sources can we get reliable musical knowledge?

Secondly, we may question what music means. Is the meaning of music in the music or do people bring their own meanings to the music? Is music a universal language? Must music be studied in cultural context to uncover its true essence? Does notation fully impart the true meaning of music? Can a performer understand the essence of the composer's meaning in the performance of a work?

Another important question in the realm of philosophical inquiry concerns the value of music. Is music valuable for its own sake or must it serve extrinsic needs and uses? Who decides the value of music? Who chooses the music we perform and hear? Can we teach all musics or must we choose? What should we choose? In a more aesthetic sense, what music is good, beautiful, and worthwhile? Does "good" music always elicit an emotional response? What characteristics of music are necessary for lasting appeal? What role do imitation, repetition, tension, release, and nuance play in creating an aesthetic experience that is always defined as good?

These questions are those most often discussed in philosophical inquiry in music. To provide a basis for further analysis by the beginning philosopher, each of these three areas - knowing, meaning, valuing, - will be further explored and developed later in this chapter.

At the outset, there must be a clarification of what is meant by the terminology, "philosophy of music" and "musical aesthetics." While the two have the same fundamental meaning, musical aesthetics represents an extension of philosophies of music. Etymologically, the term, "philosophy," comes from the Greek, "philos," meaning love and "sophia," wisdom - "love of wisdom." It has been defined as "the rational explanation of things." In contrast, the term, "aesthetics," comes from the Greek, "aisthesis," meaning "sense perception." Although aesthetics has been regarded as a branch of philosophy, it has now become an independent mode of inquiry concerned exclusively with the phenomena of art and its place in human life. Thus, while philosophy deals with the thoughtful examination of ideas concerning music, aesthetics deals with the examination of sensual responses to music. The two areas overlap and join at times in the pursuit of a common goal, understanding.

Music philosophies have included careful, deliberate, and systematic analyses of musical ideas. These ideas may be categorized as those regarding (1) how we know music; (2) how we value it; and (3) how we realize the meaning of music. While contemporary musical aesthetics may also deal with philosophical issues concerning knowing, valuing, and meaning, it places far more emphasis on the sensual aspects of human behavior and experience in the presence of music.

Thus, the subject matter of philosophy of music may include questions concerning the epistemological analysis, the methods and limits of our knowledge, of music. For example, do we know music through intuition, through reason and by the system of rationalism, or do we know it experientially, through sense experience, and by the system of empiricism? In addition, can we fully know music perceptually, conceptually, or through a combination of perception and conception.

Secondly, the subject matter of philosophy of music may include questions concerning the meaning of music, or, the logic, semantics, signs and symbols, and language of music. For instance, is the meaning of music embodied in it or is it designated by the listener? Also, questions may be asked regarding whether the meaning of music is absolute and universal, or whether the meaning is relative to the culture and experience of the listener? Still other questions might concern what particular aspects of musical language give meaning to music, what in music is transmitted and what is received, and whose intentions (the composer, the performer, or the listener) give music meaning.

Finally, a philosopher might examine aesthetic values of music. What are our behavior and experience in the presence of and through the process of artistic expression? What effect does music have on people under various conditions? How does musical taste develop? What musical styles do we prefer and why? How do variations in the combinations of musical elements, such as pitch, dynamics, timbre, rhythm, instrumentation, affect our preferences or aesthetic experiences? How do these elements contribute to beauty of artistic expression? What is the relationship between emotional responses and aesthetic experiences? Indeed, what is an aesthetic experience?

These subject matters of a philosophy and aesthetics of music - knowledge, meanings, values, musical experiences - are apparent in an examination of the history of philosophical ideas concerning music. Philosophical inquiry is a method through which one may examine in a formal way, through systematic logic, the ideas within these various topics.

The early Greeks were concerned with the physics and mathematics of music as well as composition and vocal or instrumental performance. Early Greek and medieval theories of music were based on the conviction that the same numeric harmony [e.g., the tuning systems of Pythagoras (perfect fifths) and Aristoxenus (equi-temperament)] that becomes audible through music determines the order of the universe as well as that of the soul. Plato, the heir to the Pythagorean theory of music, contributed idealism in a philosophy which proposed that true art is a sensuous manifestation of eternal ideas, can reveal divine truths, and point the way to higher values in the next life. St. Augustine continued to develop both the ideas of Pythagoras and Plato. Of the six books of St. Augustine's *De Musica*, five were devoted to questions such as meter, rhythm, scale, all directed toward discovering numerical relationships as the basis of musical delight. The sixth book sought to lift the reader from the audible, visible and mutable numbers to the immutable numbers through which the invisible things of God were revealed.

Throughout the Medieval and Renaissance periods those who wrote about music reflected the philosophies of the time during which they wrote whether scholastic, rationalistic, or empirical. A philosophical approach questioning the meaning of music, the ultimate reality of it, and the method of knowing it was the mode of inquiry for early scholars such as Boethius (d. ca. 524), Cassiodorus (d. ca. 580), and Isidore of Seville (c. 570-636).[1] In the Middle Ages, the principles of Greek philosophy were maintained. The more science there was in an art, and the less work it required the services of the body for its execution, the higher it ranked and the better founded was its claim to be classed as "liberal."

It was not until the Renaissance that the emphasis shifted from the art object (the music itself) to the person as listener or creator. While the Greeks celebrated the works of artists, as a slave-holding society they had contempt for manual labor and therefore no regard for artists as creators. In the feudal society of the Middle Ages,

---

[1] Glen Haydon, *Introduction to Musicology* (Chapel Hill, N.C.: The University of North Carolina Press, 1941), 4-6.

artists were kept in a lowly but respected position. With the growth of the new Italian city-states and a new urban society, the artist was given a chance to throw off the social limitations of membership in a guild and demand a more dignified place in society. "Art" was now more and more frequently coupled with the predicate, "Fine."

It was the work of Alexander Baumgarten in the mid-eighteenth century which foreshadowed the beginning of aesthetics, a new branch of philosophy which eventually was to become its own field. Its name was chosen from terms he had used in two of his treatises.[2]

From this time on, other philosophers applied their methods to aesthetics. Kant's approach to beauty and art, in his *Critique of Aesthetic Judgment* (1790), demonstrated a transcendental devotion to the search for *a priori*, universal principles. Schelling (1775-1854) described beauty as "the ideal informing the real." Hegel (1770-1831) in his *Lectures on Aesthetics* distinguished three phases of a universal history of artistic creation: (1) the "symbolic art" as produced by the nations of the ancient Orient; (2) Greek art as a perfect equilibrium of the ideal and the sensuous form; and (3) art in the Christian era as a spiritual comprehension of the idea resulting in a new form of art, called "romantic." Schopenhauer (1788-1860) saw art as a substitute for religion.[3]

Music theorists and composers have been the chief practitioners of philosophical inquiry in music although there are some philosophies of music education.[4] Philosophies of music, specifically, have been approached from an aesthetics point

---

[2]Alexander Baumgarten, *Meditationes philosophicae de nonullis ad poema pertinentibus*, 1735*; Aesthetics*, 1750*.*

[3]Monroe C. Beardsley. *Aesthetics from Classical Greece to the Present*, (Tuscaloosa, AL: The University of Alabama Press, 1975); Frederick Coppleston, S. J., A *History of Philosophy,* 9 vols. (New York: Image Books, a Division of Doubleday & Co., Inc., 1953-); Katherine E. Gilbert and Helmut Kuhn*, A History of Esthetics,* (New York: The Macmillan Company, 1939); Edward A. Lippman (Ed.*), Musical Aesthetics: A Historical Reader,* v. 1 (New York: Pendragon Press, 1986); Martin J. Walsh*, A History of Philosophy* (London: Geoffrey Chapman, 1985).

[4]Bennett Reime*r, A Philosophy of Music Education*, 2nd ed. (Englewood Cliffs, NJ: Prentice Hall, Inc., 1989); Abraham A. Schwadron*, Aesthetics: Dimensions for Music Education*, (Washington, D.C.: Music Educators National Conference, 1967); David Elliott, *Music Matters* (NY: Schirmer Books, 1994); Clifford K. Madsen, ed., *Vision 2020: The Housewright Symposium on the Future of Music Education* (Reston, VA: MENC-The National Association for Music Education, 2000).

of view. Eduard Hanslick's ***The Beautiful in Music*** (1854),[5] and Edmund Gurney's, ***The Power of Sound*** (1880)[6] were pioneer works in which music was explored as an art object in its own right. Hanslick's *reductio ad absurdum*, music means itself, opened the door for many supportive treatises as well as counter arguments. One of those counter arguments was contained in Halbert Britain's, ***The Philosophy of Music***.[7] Britain stated, "The secret of the versatile power of music over the emotions lies in the fact that the symbolism of music conforms so closely to the dynamics of the emotional conscious." Thus, the stage was set for the argument concerning whether music should be judged for its intrinsic merits or for its effects on the mood of the listener.

Thus, philosophical inquiry involves questioning of any and all ideas regarding music and musical experience. The process is one which does not rely solely on the expression of opinion, but one which demands formal, logical procedure. First, it may be a literary procedure requiring thorough analyses of *a priori* premises concerning music or musical experiences by the systematic delineation of thesis and antithesis information. Alternately, it may be a compositional procedure requiring symbolic realization of relationships or interactions among musical ideas.

KNOWLEDGE

The customary sources of knowledge have been intuition, custom, experience, sensation, and reason. In its more precise philosophical sense, intuition is an immediate apprehension of the external world, of values, of truths. Intuition, by this definition, has no mediating factor such as sensation, experience, or ideas between the mind and what is known. It is a kind of self-evidence, an innate sense, or extrasensory perception.   We often describe a moving musical performance as magical and count ourselves lucky to have been a part of an intuitive event in which everything immediately and mysteriously peaked to provide a musically and emotionally rewarding experience. In addition, we permit ourselves the luxury of not studying the characteristics of these outstanding events because the act of studying them might subtract from the art of their occurrence.

Custom as a source of knowledge is closely related to folklore and common sense. Customary knowledge is that of prevailing beliefs and practices. An appeal to custom is basically an appeal to the status quo. Custom is also closely related to tradition. The argument for custom as a source of knowledge is fortified by the

---

[5]Eduard Hanslick, ***The Beautiful in Music***, trans. by Gustav Cohen (New York: Liberal Arts Press, 1957).

[6]Edmund Gurney, ***The Power of Sound*** (London: Smith, Elder, & Co., 1880; New York: Basic Books Publication Co., Inc., 1967).

[7]Halbert H. Britain, ***The Philosophy of Music*** (New York: Longmans, Green, & Co., 1911).

argument for tradition, or "it has always been that way." The apprenticeship method of learning to sing or to play an instrument is the customary way to acquire this type of musical knowledge. To study with someone, who studied with someone, who studied with someone, who studied with Brahms is a much sought after musical credential.

Experience as a source of knowledge can be viewed in several ways. For example, experience can involve direct interaction with an object or with the environment. Direct experience requires learning by doing, necessitates accurate feedback to correct mistakes, and may be counterproductive without a second type of experiential learning characterized as vicarious. Vicarious experience involves learning from the mistakes or successes of others. Watching a master teacher play a musical passage that has been directly experienced may be a valuable path toward knowledge that will ultimately result in a better musical performance.

Intuition, custom, and experience as sources of knowledge are less formalized and more subject to whimsical occurrence and attention. For researchers in music, indeed in any field, more systematic modes of inquiry are essential. For illumination of these more systematic modes of inquiry, we must look to those experts in critical and reflective thinking, philosophers.

Perhaps the best way to organize our thinking concerning philosophical inquiry is to examine a series of contrasting ideas: rational (conceptual) versus empirical (perceptual) paths to knowing; embodied versus designated meanings; and intrinsic versus instrumental values. To begin we will briefly explore two streams of philosophical inquiry: rationalism, associated most closely with the philosophy of Plato; and empiricism, associated most closely with John Locke.

For the rationalistic philosopher, reason is the fundamental factor in knowing. The human mind has the power to know with certainty some truths about the universe that observation and sense experience cannot give. For example, we know every event has a cause. We know this not through observation and sense experience but rather through intuition. Moreover, we have knowledge prior to experience and not by or through experience. Knowledge is, therefore, *a priori*. According to Plato, the realm of appearance is the ordinary world of happening, about which we can never have more than an opinion. In contrast, the realm of intelligible reality is the timeless system of mathematical objects and of forms such as goodness and justice, or in other words, the realm of ideas.

As a rationalist philosopher contemplating the ultimate reality of music, one may begin with Plato's allegory of the cave. Plato asks us to imagine an underground cave that has an opening towards the light. In this cave are living human beings with their legs and necks chained from childhood in such a way that they face the inside wall of the cave and have never seen the light of the sun. Above and behind them, between the prisoners and the mouth of the cave, is a fire, and between them and the fire are a raised way and a low wall, like a screen. Along this raised way men pass by carrying statues and figures of animals and other objects in such a manner that the objects they carry appear over the top of the low wall or screen. The prisoners, facing the inside wall of the cave, cannot see one another nor the objects carried behind them, but they see the shadows of themselves and of these objects thrown on to the wall they are facing. They see only shadows.

These prisoners, says Plato, represent the majority of mankind, beholding only shadows of reality and hearing only echoes of the truth. Their view of the world is most inadequate, distorted by "their own passions and prejudices, and by the passions and prejudices of other people as conveyed to them by language and rhetoric." However, if one of the prisoners who has escaped grows accustomed to the light he will after a time be able to look at the concrete sensible objects, of which he had formerly seen but the shadows. He is converted from the shadow world of prejudices and passions to the real world though he has not yet ascended to the world of intelligible, nonsensible realities. He sees the prisoners for what they are, namely prisoners in the bonds of passion and sophistry. Moreover, if he perseveres and comes out of the cave into the sunlight, he will see the world of sun-illuminated and clear objects (which represent intelligible realities), and lastly, though only by an effort, he will be able to see the sun itself, which represents the Idea of the Good, the highest Form, "the universal cause of all things right and beautiful - the source of truth and reason."[8]

Thus, in considering Plato's allegory one may transfer the understanding of its meaning to an understanding of music's ultimate reality. For Plato, earthly music was a shadow of the Ideal. Is there something about music, an ultimate reality, which continues in constant procession around, above, and beyond our ordinary experiences of it?

Pythagoras and other early Greek scientists and philosophers proposed a doctrine of harmony in which numbers, ratios, proportions and acoustics were symbols of universal order. Aristotle commented that, "They supposed the elements of numbers to be the elements of all things, and the whole of heaven to be a musical scale and a number."[9] By the early Middle Ages the doctrine of harmony was firmly in place as demonstrated by the threefold classification of music proposed by Boethius: *musica mundana*, the music of the spheres, unheard by man; *musica humana*, the harmony that exists within man, between soul and body; and *musica instrumentalis*, the music made by man, an imperfect imitation of the higher kinds

---

[8]Plato, **The Republic**, book 7, trans. Francis MacDonald Cornford (London: Oxford University Press, 1945), 227-235.

[9]Aristotle, **Metaphysics**, trans. W.D. Ross (Oxford: The Clarendon Press, 1924), A. 5. 985b-986a. Aristotle did not totally agree with this idea that through mathematical deduction we might know truth. He was empirical in his approach to knowledge and, as one of the first natural scientists, emphasized induction through direct observation as the primary source of truth.

of music.[10] Thus, a direct parallel may be seen between Plato's allegory of the cave and the logic through which these rationalists arrived at the ultimate reality of music.

The five senses (seeing, tasting, touching, hearing, smelling) are the most obvious sources of knowledge. Some philosophers have considered the senses the primary source of knowledge; others have rejected them. Plato, for example, made it very clear that he believed the senses are not the source of knowledge, but the source of error and falsehood. His theories of an immortal soul and of innate ideas are cases against sense perception as a source of knowledge.

However, for the empiricist there can be nothing in the intellect that was not first in the senses. Therefore, there is no *a priori* knowledge. John Locke, an empirical philosopher, theorized that the human mind was at birth a *tabula rasa*, a blank tablet, which gained all knowledge from experience. According to Locke, experience has twin sources: sensation (the sense experience of the external world) and reflection (the introspective experience of the mind's own operations). Locke says, in the ***Essay concerning Human Understanding***:

> Let us then suppose the mind to be, as we say, white paper, void of all characters, without any ideas. How comes it to be furnished? Whence comes it by that vast store which the busy and boundless fancy of man has painted on it with an almost endless variety? Whence has it all the materials of reason and knowledge? To this I answer, in one word, from EXPERIENCE. In that all our knowledge is founded; and from that it ultimately derives itself. Our observation...is that which supplies our understandings with all the materials of thinking.[11]

Two streams of philosophical thought are apparent. Those philosophers who stress reasoning or thought as the fundamental factor in knowledge are known as rationalists; those who stress the role of observation or experience or the senses are known as empiricists. For classical rationalists like Plato, the foundation of knowledge consists of a set of first principles, the universal *a priori* principles known intuitively. From these self-evident first principles, other truths can be deduced, by the unerring methods of mathematics. For empiricists the foundation of knowledge consists of direct observation. By recording, classifying, and describing observable behavior and events, truths can be induced, by the procedures of natural science.

---

[10]Oliver Strunk, ed. ***Source Readings in Music History*** (New York: Norton, 1950), 84-85.

[11]John Locke, ***Essay concerning Human Understanding***, Book II, Chapter 1, Section 2, Abridged and ed., Raymond Wilburn (London: J. M. Dent & Sons, Ltd., 1947), 26.

From a different perspective, one might say that one arrives at knowledge perceptually or conceptually or both. Perceptual knowledge has been described as that gained through immediate awareness or sensation. Conceptual knowledge, on the other hand, is ideational. While perceptual knowledge involves immediate sensation and concerns the direct apprehension of the environment through the five senses, conceptual knowledge involves memory, imagination, abstraction, symbolization, and reasoning. The disagreement among philosophers concerning sense perception versus innate ideas as the source of knowledge is the basis for the distinction between empiricism and rationalism. Empiricists generally agree upon sense experience as a primary source of knowledge and rationalists generally agree upon some form of knowledge independent of experience.

The perception and discrimination (seeing or hearing) of pitch, tempo, dynamics, and other musical elements have been described by various researchers in psychology and music. The arguments concerning musical aptitude (innate musicality) and musical achievement (learned musicality) are echoes of arguments between those who would declare innate ideas as the source of knowledge versus those who would declare the environment as the source.

It is in analytical approaches to music that philosophical inquiry plays a significant role. The analysis of musical masterpieces is preceded by a definite philosophical system. Bent dichotomizes analytical methodologies as either inductive or deductive in approach. An empirical (or inductive), discovery-procedure approach may be observed in Jeppesen's *Palestrina and the Style of the Dissonance*, Jan LaRue's *Guidelines for Style Analysis*, and probably all computer-assisted analytical projects. For example, Jeppesen located and listed occurrences of specific intervals within specific melodic patterns, thus presenting the entire data for each conclusion induced from that data. Alternately, according to Bent, deductive procedures may be observed in Riemann's phrase-structure analysis, Réti's thematic process analysis, and Schenker's structural analysis. For example, Schenker begins with an *a priori* premise that musical compositions are tonal and are projections of the tonic triad. In deducing, or proving, his theory, Schenker devised a graphic notation whereby the various layers of the fundamental structure of a composition are laid out. He then accompanied these graphs with reasoned narratives and further musical examples.[12]

MEANING

Some philosophical arguments regarding music concern whether the meaning of music is contained within it (embodied meaning), whether meaning is brought to it

---

[12]Stanley Sadie, ed., *The New Grove Dictionary of Music and Musicians* (London: MacMillan Publishers, Ltd., 1980), s.v. "Analysis" by Ian Bent, 340-88.

from outside by individuals participating in it (designated meaning), or whether its meaning may be approached through a combination of these two ways.

Discussions of embodied meaning in music have explored variables which give the most meaning to music.

> Of the variables which give meaning to music, tempo plays the largest role. According to Hevner, who has carried on numerous experiments in this area modality is probably second in importance. Pitch level seemingly ranks third. Harmony and rhythm are of far less importance, and whether the melody is ascending or descending carries relatively little meaning to the listener. In other words, the listener is most likely to change the affective terms with which he describes a piece of music whenever its tempo is appreciably slowed or hastened. Other alterations of the musical matrix change less strikingly how he will describe the music.[13]

Farnsworth mentions other notions of embodied and designated meaning in his discussion of alleged mode and key effects:

> In Grecian times, long before the day of free modulation and tempered scales, a melody was supposed to reflect the unique psychological character of the mode in which it was written. If it was in the Dorian mode with its arrangement of a half tone, three whole tones, a half-tone, and two whole tones (as in e,f,g,a,b,c,d,e) dignity, manliness, courage, and self-dependence were the qualities thought to be expressed. But if the Lydian mode was used, the melodic message was considered one of softness and self-indulgence. Because he believed that hearing the Lydian mode could be harmful to man's character, Plato banned it from his 'Ideal Republic'. It should be noted that the internal arrangement of the Lydian scale is that of our current major scale![14]

An interesting approach to a discussion of meaning in music may be seen in Moore's "A Programmed Guide To Closed Systems."[15] Here musical examples are presented and analyzed as containing the closed systems of titles, composers, tempo indications, staffs, clefs, meter symbols, key signatures, notes, rests, dynamics, metronome markings, and so forth. In exploring how much meaning each of

[13]Paul Farnsworth, *The Social Psychology of Music*, 2nd Ed. (Ames, Iowa: The Iowa State University Press, 1969), 83-84.

[14]Farnsworth, 72.

[15]C. K. Madsen and R. S. Moore, *Experimental Research in Music: Workbook in Statistics* (Raleigh, N.C.: Contemporary Publishing Co., 1978),1-11.

these closed systems might give to music, the question, "What closed systems must be present on a musical score in order that it might be 'sounded' or performed?" is asked. In other words, does the absence of any one of the closed systems change the meaning of music or our ability to experience the true meaning of the music?

Philosophers of the latter 16th, the 17th, and the early 18th centuries, regarded the principal aim of music as being to arouse the passions or affections. For example, in the "doctrine of affections" (*affektenlehre*) music was viewed as an expression of human temperaments, passions, and moods and in the "doctrine of figures" (*figurenlehre*) music's structural and stylistic elements (repetition, fugue, climax) were related to corresponding rhetorical devices thus giving music designated meaning as an oratorical art.[16]

Further examples in which concepts of embodied versus designated meaning may be illustrated are found in programmatic and allegorical musical descriptions of the Romantic period. Here music was thought of as psychological drama and explained in terms such as "desperate struggle," "the knocking of fate," "threatening fortissimo," or "gloomy minor." Other designated or embodied meanings are those described by chromesthetics (people who hear music as colors) and those who espouse hermaneutic theories interpreting musical motifs as expressions of human emotions.

Leonard B. Meyer in **Emotion and Meaning in Music** explored two premises. First, he posited that music must be understood in terms of learned responses within some established musical style. Secondly, he defined these learned responses as being within a culturally determined stylistic norm where one musical event implies others. Therefore, according to Meyer, emotion and meaning result when the listener's learned expectations are satisfied, delayed, or frustrated. Thus, Meyer's philosophical theory is oriented toward the listener who experiences emotion and meaning rather than the music or the composer as sources of musical meaning.[17]

According to Susanne Langer's **Philosophy in a New Key**, the principles of musical form are structurally the same as those patterns of human feelings. A phenomenon is often understood through symbolic transformation, that is, through constructing an object analogous to the phenomenon. Music, in a similar way, has meaning because of the symbolic transformation of human feelings into musical form. The recognition of this identity between human feelings and musical form is what makes music so interesting. It is necessary to note that Langer does not think that music necessarily describes, expresses, or evokes anyone's actual feelings.[18]

---

[16]Don M. Randal, ed., *The New Harvard Dictionary of Music* (Cambridge, Mass.: Belknap Press of Harvard University Press, 1986), 16, 698-700.

[17]Leonard B. Meyer, *Emotion and Meaning in Music* (Chicago: The University of Chicago Press, 1956).

[18]Susanne Langer, *Philosophy in a New Key* (Cambridge, Mass: Harvard University Press, 1942).

The contrasting viewpoints regarding whether meaning resides in the music or is brought to the music by those interacting with it (listeners or performers) may also be observed in the differing underlying philosophical positions within the field of ethnomusicology. The view of Mantle Hood is that ethnomusicology "is directed toward an understanding of music studied in terms of itself and also toward an understanding of music in society."[19] Hood's approach is one of understanding the musical product first and foremost. Another viewpoint held by Alan Merriam is "that music sound is the result of human behavioral processes that are shaped by the values, attitudes, and beliefs of the people who comprise a particular culture. Music sound cannot be produced except by people for other people, and although one can separate the two aspects [the sound aspect and the cultural aspect] conceptually, one is really not complete without the other. Human behavior produces music, but the process is one of continuity; the behavior is shaped to produce music sound, and thus the study of one flows into the other."[20]

For example, Schenker's underlying philosophy presupposes that music is never concerned with metaphors of feeling or expression but only with the internal relationship of musical elements.[21] For Schenker, "performance directions are fundamentally superfluous, since the composition itself expresses everything that is necessary...Performance must come from within the work; the work must breathe from its own lungs—from the linear progressions, neighbouring tones, chromatic tones, modulations...About these, naturally, there cannot exist differing interpretations [Auffassungen]."[22]

Another viewpoint regarding meaning that is interesting to explore is that found in existential philosophy. An existentialist philosopher in music might propose that music is indefinable except as individuals might make it definable; that is, it turns up; it has no meaning except that which we as individuals might choose to give it. These philosophers stress the premise that existence precedes essence. Jean Paul Sartre says:

---

[19]Mantle Hood, "Music, the Unknown," in *Musicology*, gen. ed. Richard Schlatter (Englewood, Cliffs, N. J.: Prentice-Hall, 1963; reprint Westport, CT: Greenwood Press, Publisher, 1974), 217-326.

[20]Alan Merriam, *The Anthropology of Music*, (Evanston, Ill: Northwestern University Press, 1964), 8.

[21]Schenker, *Harmonielehre*, Trans. E. M. Borgese, Ed. and Annotated by Oswald Jonas (Chicago: University of Chicago Press, 1954); *Kontrapunkt*, Trans. John Rothgeb and Jurgen Thym, Ed. John Rothgeb (New York: Schirmer Books, 1954); Allen Forte, "Schenker's Conception of Musical Structure," *Journal of Music Theory*, 3, No. 1 (April 1959): 1-30.

[22]Quoted in Rothstein, "Schenker as an Interpreter of Beethoven's Piano Sonatas," *19th Century Music*, 8 (Summer 1984): 10.

What is meant here by saying that existence precedes essence? It means that, first of all, man exists, turns up, appears on the scene, and, only afterwards, defines himself. If man, as the existentialist conceives him, is indefinable, it is because at first he is nothing. Only afterward will he be something, and he himself will have made what he will be.[23]

VALUES

A third question with which philosophers wrestle is, "What is the good?" Aristotle was probably correct when he said, "All men seek the good, but by different routes." The expression, "the good," suggests something of value. Most of us would agree that we all seek the best in every aspect of life. Philosophical discussions revolve around whether the good constitutes an absolute or a relative value, that is, whether the good is set apart from and quite unrelated to the routes through which we might seek it or whether the different routes to seeking it determine the good. We may transfer this argument to musical values and judgments of value. Is the good in music inherent or is music given value by groups or individuals? Is music that is chosen, bought, listened to, performed by most groups or individuals better than music that is not chosen by most? Does classical music represent the good despite the fact that few people choose it?

Value terms both positive and negative suggest meaning. Values, regardless of the objects in question, can be classified as intrinsic or instrumental. Intrinsic value is the inherent worth of an entity or object. An instrumental value, on the other hand, is the value of the consequences or product of an entity or event. An intrinsic value is good for its own sake, while an instrumental value must be good for something else. Music (both good and bad) has the potential for both intrinsic and instrumental values. Compare the inherent worth in the music of the complete works of Bach to the consequential value of the use of music to teach a mentally retarded child to spell her name. Whether music of intrinsic value is better than music of instrumental value is another philosophical discussion that often occurs among musicians. Thus, value issues regarding music have been addressed both in terms of the value of a musical object or event and expressions of value for a musical object or event.

In the first case, three approaches have evolved in determining the value of music. First, there are those who approach music from a purist, isolationist, or formalist point of view. Composers and philosophers present this viewpoint by stating that

---

[23]Jean Paul Sartre, *Existentialism and Human Emotions* (Secaucus, N.J.: Castle, a division of Book Sales, Inc., n. d.),15.

music is primarily formal design;[24] that music is an external tonal representation not involved with feelings or situations;[25] that music is conceived in terms of only the elements of sound and time;[26] and that the supreme creative process and "mysterious source of artistic work...must always remain hidden from human comprehension."[27] For these purists, absolutists, and formalists, value criteria for music may be developed only from objective musical organization. Therefore, differences in value are the result of differences in musical structure.

Secondly, there are those who believe the value of music lies in its uniqueness as a medium for artistic expression within the context of life's experiences. These philosophers' viewpoints have been described as contextualist or expressionist. To them, music is not an isolated art that exists for its own sake. Schwadron summarized this viewpoint very aptly.

> On the contrary, it exists for our sake, enriched by and giving meaning to all forms of human behavior. Education, psychology, morality, religion, economics, politics– all are crucially involved in artistic interpretation and judgment...Values should be socially recognized and pragmatically constructed along broad humanistic lines. Not the expert, but the mass of men should judge the worth of musical art.[28]

Finally, there are those who approach the value of music from the viewpoint of relativism. These philosophers support the idea that critical judgments may be justified on the bases of personally derived value criteria. Thus values are relative to and conditioned by cultural groups and historical periods. From a relativistic view, both isolationist and contextualist value criteria depend upon learning and conditioning. Moreover, relativism recognizes the desire for improvement, the need for the cultivation of musical taste, the reality of a plurality of values, and the need for qualitative standards.

---

[24]Hanslick, *The Beautiful in Music*, Trans. G. Cohen (New York: Liberal Arts Press, 1957).

[25]Hermann L. F. Helmholtz, *On the Sensations of Tone as a Physiological Basis for the Theory of Music*, trans. Alexander J. Ellis (London: Longmans, Green, 1875).

[26]Igor Stravinsky, *The Poetics of Music, trans*. by A. Knodel and I. Dahl (New York: Random House, 1947).

[27]Paul Hindemith, *Craft of Musical Composition, trans*. by A. Mendel, Book I (New York: Associated Music Publishers, Inc., 1942), 11.

[28]Abraham A. Schwadron, *Aesthetics: Dimensions for Music Education* (Washington, D.C.: Music Educators National Conference, 1967), 37.

One of the most influential discussions of the value of music has been that provided by Leonard B. Meyer in his article, "Some Remarks on Value and Greatness in Music." Meyer makes the point that

> Value refers to a quality of musical experience. It is inherent neither in the musical object per se nor in the mind of the listener per se. Rather value arises as a result of a transaction, which takes place within an objective tradition, between the musical work and a listener. This being the case, the value of any particular musical experience is a function both of the listener's ability to respond - his having learned the style of the music - and of his mode of response."[29]

Through attention to the listener's ability to respond and his mode of response, we come to issues regarding the development of values for music. Philosophical questions concerning values for music have been discussed using a variety of terms.

The definition and development of musical taste, or value for music is ongoing. Theoretical discussions of the development of value for music have included LeBlanc's proposed model for the development of music preferences,[30] Berlyne's experimental aesthetics theory,[31] Roederér's neurophysiological theory,[32] and Skinner's operant behavior theory of emotional responses.[33] Most of us would agree that the ability to value music is a top priority. Ultimately, as professional musicians, we would want a person to be a consumer of music, a performer, and a listener to music. Indeed,

> The degree to which our students can actively participate in a musical experience may be the indicator of musical affect defined as relevancy, affinity, relationship, association, and liking/love/fondness.[34]

[29]Leonard B. Meyer, "Some Remarks on Value and Greatness in Music," *Journal of Aesthetics and Art Criticism*, 17 (June 1959): 486-500.

[30]Albert LeBlanc, "An Interactive Theory of Music Preference," *Journal of Music Therapy*, 19 (1982): 28-45.

[31]D. E. Berlyne, *Studies in the New Experimental Aesthetics: Steps Toward an Objective Psychology of Aesthetic Appreciation* (New York: Halstead Press, 1974).

[32]J. G. Roederer, "The Psychophysics of Musical Perception," *Music Educators Journal*, 60 (1974): 20-30.

[33]B. F. Skinner, *Science and Human Behavior* (New York: The Free Press, 1953).

[34]C. Yarbrough, "Indicators of Affect for School Music Teachers," *Update: Applications of Research in Music Education*, 4 (1985): 3-5.

Thus, philosophical inquiry in music might interpret musical experience from various viewpoints or approaches such as rationalism, empiricism, or existentialism. From these philosophical bases, one might explore questions concerning the meaning of music, judgments of the good in music, and the intrinsic and instrumental values of music. Regardless of the question one chooses to explore or the philosophical basis of the argument, there are basic techniques for the conduct of philosophical inquiry.

WRITING TECHNIQUES FOR PHILOSOPHICAL INQUIRY

Philosophy organizes and interprets experiences by analysis, synthesis, and projection. The goal of analysis is to define completely the characteristics of a concept or problem through a method of writing called, "Argument." At the beginning of the argument, the writer must state the problem or concept in clear terms and, if necessary, define terms or concepts to be used in the development of the final definition of the problem. The analysis of problems through argument reveals agreements, inconsistencies, and contradictions in the forms of model instances, borderline instances, and contrary instances of the problem. To find principles, philosophers often make assumptions and evolve principles from them. From assumptions and principles in the light of analysis, hypotheses can be formed. Hypotheses are "if-then" statements made with regard to the analysis of the problem and further conclusions or consequences.

After agreements, inconsistencies, and contradictions have been located and defined by analysis, the philosopher will seek some principle of explanation, one that will resolve the inconsistencies and conflicts so as to give meaning and understanding. This is the synthetic phase that is viewed as the opposite of analysis. Unlike the structure of analysis, which consists largely of supporting a thesis, the synthetic phase demands that opposing viewpoints be disposed of using logic, facts, statistics, and so forth. In this kind of argument, borderline and contradictory cases are dealt with carefully toward the goal of further definition of the problem. The structure of synthesis requires sets of prior assumptions and basic principles. These prior assumptions and basic principles may be established during the analytical phase of the argument. However, during the synthetic phase, they form a frame of reference that is normative rather than analytical. Value judgments will most probably be included as well as logical relations.

All the techniques discussed above - analysis, synthesis, projection, deduction, induction, definition of terms, dialectic - may be useful in writing a philosophical essay. The organization of the essay should include an introduction, a reconstruction of the argument, a critical assessment (thesis and antithesis), and a conclusion (or synthesis).

An effective introduction should convey the importance of the critical discussion to follow. It should relate the argument to some broader issue by proceeding from more general ideas and then focusing on the specific premise.[35] The introduction should end with the statement, "Therefore, the premise of this essay is that ..."

Techniques for writing the introductory paragraph are as follows:

1. Begin with a brief history, or overview, of the subject. Move from past to present, ending with the thesis statement.
2. Begin with a short summary of the controversy of different schools of thought on the subject under discussion, ending with the thesis statement.
3. Begin with a list of statistics or details, ending with the thesis statement.
4. Begin with an amusing or relevant anecdote dealing with the topic and end with the thesis statement.

A clear, concise statement of the premise of the paper (the thesis) is essential. The thesis statement should not be confused with the first sentence of the paper. The four points outlined above are suggestions for leading the reader to accept the thesis as a natural resolution of the preceding sentences. The purpose of the thesis statement is to crystallize the main idea.

The second section of the essay should begin with a paraphrase or quotation conveying both sides of the argument. This should be followed by a careful definition of the issues, definition of terms, and the introduction of implicit ideas in the argument. The terminology used should, of course, suit the audience for whom the essay is being written.

The concepts or ideas discussed in the main body may demand clear definition of terms used to explain them. Definition helps make individual words, concepts and abstractions easier to understand by focusing on concrete or specific aspects of them. This often entails more than simply the dictionary meaning of a word. This method can be particularly helpful when dealing with an abstract concept such as "good music." This idea could be defined by examining it from many different angles (personal, historical, psychological, spiritual, aesthetic).

There are several ways to formulate a good definition:

1. Definition by synonym - giving another term that quickly specifies the single meaning for the concept.

---

[35]A *premise* is a first statement of an assumption that one has prior to a philosophical argument, or speculation, or analysis of a problem.

2. Definition by function - defining meaning by describing what the word or concept does.
3. Definition by example - illustrating with examples that broaden the definition.
4. Definition by comparison - beginning with a topic sentence stating the comparison and going on to expand and explain it.
5. Definition by contrast - contrasting the given term with others that are close in meaning, or contrasting the ideal meaning with the real.

A critical assessment (thesis and antithesis) of the argument should follow the definition section. Reasons for accepting the argument should be presented by using examples of model cases. Next, reasons for rejecting the argument should be presented using contrary cases or using the opposite view for the model cases. Also, borderline cases might be introduced and discussed in this section.

Good writing necessarily revolves around one's understanding of and ability to reason both deductively and inductively. In deductive reasoning one begins with a general truth and tries to connect it with some individual case by means of a middle term or class of objects known to be equally connected with both. The connection is called a syllogism. Until the time of the Renaissance, insight into most problems was sought by means of deductive logic, a methodology associated with Plato and developed artfully by Aristotle. Deductive logic relied on logical reasoning and began with a major premise. This was a statement, similar to an axiom, which seemed to be a self-evident and universally accepted truth: Man is mortal; God is good; the earth is flat.

For example, the terror that gripped Columbus's sailors was a fear supported by deductive logic. To them the earth was flat. That was their major premise. Then they began reasoning. If the earth were flat, then flat surfaces would have boundaries. The boundaries of flat surfaces would be the edges of those surfaces. If a ship passed across a flat surface, it would come to the edge of it. There, they reasoned, it would fall off. The logic was sound; the reasoning, accurate; the conclusion, valid. Where the whole proposition went wrong was that the major premise was incorrect. The reasoning began with a preconceived idea, an *a priori*, that seemed to be true.[36]

With the Renaissance came a new approach to the discovery of knowledge. The emphasis was upon this world and an intense interest in its phenomena. Through inductive reasoning, the process of reasoning or drawing a conclusion from particular facts or individual cases, empirical writers arrived at general principles or laws. An example of inductive reasoning may be drawn from an actual research project. A group of neurologists sought an answer to a problem in medicine. How

---

[36]It should be noted that unlike Columbus's sailors, most learned people of the time knew or suspected that the world was round, not flat.

long can a person have a "flat EEG" (an isoelectric brain tracing indicating cerebral death) and still recover? Silverman and his associates observed actual cases - 1,665 of them. They noted that in all cases when the flat EEG persisted for 24 hours or more not a single recovery occurred. All the facts pointed to the same conclusion. It is tragically unlikely that a recovery might take place with those who exhibit flat EEG tracings of 24 hours or more duration.[37] One cannot, of course, rule out the unexplored cases, but from the data observed the conclusion reached was that recovery seems impossible. The line from each case led to that one conclusion.

Many modern researchers employ a combination of inductive and deductive reasoning termed "scientific method" involving the collection of data under controlled laboratory conditions or testing hypotheses through controlled experimentation. Through a process of deductive reasoning, *a priori* hypotheses are logically analyzed and criticized. During the process of deductive reasoning, the forms of dialectic and syllogism may be used. These *a priori* hypotheses are then tested through the process of inductive reasoning, by observing many particular cases, some of which may be model cases, some borderline, and others, contradictory. From the analyses and synthesis of these data, one may draw conclusions, develop further hypotheses, collect more data, and so forth.

The technique of achieving intellectual insight through deductive logic includes practice of a special method called dialectic. Zeno of Elea invented dialectic as a method of refuting an opponent's opinion by accepting it hypothetically and then forcing the opponent to admit that it led to contradictory conclusions. In Plato's account, Socrates' dialectic became the art of eliciting satisfactory definitions (or rejecting unsatisfactory ones) by the systematic use of question and answer. Later, among the Stoics and again in the Middle Ages, the word, Dialectic, was often used as a general name for logic.

Another deductive technique that may be used is the syllogism, an argument or form of reasoning in which two statements or premises are made and a logical conclusion drawn from them. The form of a syllogism is as follows:

Major Premise: All graduate music students are human beings;
Minor Premise: Students enrolled in Intro to Research are graduate music students;
Conclusion: Students enrolled in Intro to Research are human beings.

---

[37]Daniel Silverman, Michael G. Saunders, Robert S. Schwab, and Richard L. Masland, "Cerebral Death and the Electroencephalogram," *Journal of the American Medical Association*, 209 (Sept. 1969): 1505-1510.

Here "graduate music students" is the subject of the major premise; "human beings" is the predicate. In the minor premise, the subject of the major premise becomes the predicate. In the conclusion, the subject of the minor premise becomes the subject of the conclusion and the predicate of the major premise becomes the predicate.

Logic, therefore, is the systematic study of the structure of propositions and of the general conditions of valid inference by a method that abstracts from the content or matter of the propositions and deals only with their logical form. The most elementary form of logic is propositional calculus. Propositional calculus deals with sentence connectives such as "and," "if," "or," "not," "if and only if," and so forth. To exhibit and analyze the logical properties of the connectives, it employs propositional variables such as p, q, and r, which are to be thought of as variables replaceable by sentences. In strictness, the sentences by which the propositional variables are replaceable should be sentences of some appropriate formalized language. An excellent example of this technique may be found in *Music and Mind* by Harold Fiske.[38] Here, axioms are presented and propositional variables concerning those axioms are structured formally using logical connectives.

The conclusion or synthesis section should begin with a brief restatement of the argument. Then there should be a return to ideas in the introduction. Finally, the position that now seems reasonable should be stated.

Doctoral students may find the techniques outlined above very useful in two ways. First, the techniques are useful in developing a rationale and need for study for the thesis, dissertation, or monograph. This section of the final document for the doctoral degree may be the most consequential section because it requires systematic analysis of the topic of study. Second, junior or senior faculty will find these techniques useful in writing justifications of the need for new courses or new curricula.

SUMMARY

There are various approaches to and philosophical bases for acquiring knowledge, through more informal means involving experience, intuition, and custom, and through the more formalized approaches of empiricism and rationalism. An understanding of and appreciation for these approaches will provide a better foundation for future philosophical inquiry in music and for a more substantive approach to critical analysis of research.

What do these philosophical approaches offer to those who propose philosophical inquiry into, "How we know music?" A rationalist philosopher in music might

---

[38]Harold E. Fiske, *Music and Mind* (Lewiston, NY: The Edwin Mellen Press, 1990).

approach music with various sets of *a priori,* or prior assumptions about music. Music will then be examined in light of these prior assumptions. On the contrary, an empirical philosopher in music might approach music by analyzing its content and defining what is directly observed.

The importance of understanding these various approaches to knowing music may be illustrated by the problems researchers have encountered in studying preferences for music. How does one know preferences for certain tempos? Might it be because there is a standard *takt* (beat) for that music to which we compare variations in tempo (rational approach)? On the other hand, might it be because there is agreement among many individuals that this is the correct tempo (empirical approach)? Could there be many correct tempos from which a choice might be made any of which would be correct for the individual making that choice (existential approach)? Thus, philosophical inquiry requires a knowledge and understanding of the advantages and limits of various approaches to and philosophical bases for acquiring knowledge. It requires a procedure of analysis, synthesis, and projection as well as the ability to reason both deductively and inductively. Philosophical inquiry is laden with many choices that can only honestly be chosen from a position of broad understanding. Once a broad base of understanding has been established, one can confidently choose whatever path of novel narrowness one wishes.

A scholarly approach may be characterized as one that allows an objective presentation of knowledge. It is a scholar's responsibility to understand various viewpoints and to present them regardless of personal biases. While it may be true that each researcher's interests may color his or her final research product, it may be equally true that the final research product, if approached objectively, may change those initial biases.

Acquiring knowledge is a lifelong pursuit. To advance the art of music, musical scholarship must persist. True musical scholars are those who continue to perfect their empirical and rational approaches to musical research and inquiry. Those who know are those who have not only carefully, objectively, and systematically pursued truth, but also those who have done so frequently.

RESEARCH APPLICATIONS

1. Locate the guidelines for the preparation of theses and dissertations published by your university. Note the paper requirements (8.5" x 11" white 100% cotton paper with watermark), margins (left, top, bottom, and right, 1"; margins set by word processing software many not ensure correct margins and must be carefully checked by printing a sample page), spacing (standard double spacing, three lines per inch; single spacing for long quotations, long tables, multiline captions, and bibliographic entries (double spacing between bibliographic entries); type size (10-point or larger), print quality (computer printers should yield letter-quality; use double strike dot matrix or laser), and pagination (do not number the first page; place page numbers in the upper right corner no less than one-half inch from the top and right side of the page). Set the computer software for these parameters and begin now to use them for all assignments.

2. State a philosophical premise and present a formal argument for or against it using classical philosophical techniques.

3. Take two seemingly opposite philosophies of music performance, instruction, composition, or listening and analyze, criticize, and synthesize them to one.

BIBLIOGRAPHY

Abeles, Harold F. "Responses to Music." In *Handbook of Music Psychology*, ed. D. A. Hodges. Lawrence, KS: National Association of Music Therapy, 1980, 105-140.

Adorno, T. W. *Philosophy of Modern Music*. Translated by A. G. Mitchell and W. V. Blomster. New York: Seabury Press, 1973.

Allen, Warren Dwight. *Philosophies of Music History*. NY: Dover Publications, Inc., 1962.

Anderson, W. D. *Ethos and Education in Greek Music: The Evidence of Poetry and Philosophy*. Cambridge: Harvard University Press, 1966.

Aristotle. *Metaphysics*. Translated by W. D. Ross. Oxford: The Clarendon Press, 1924.

Artz, F. B. *From Renaissance to Romanticism: Trends in Style in Art, Literature, and Music, 1300-1830*. Chicago: University of Chicago Press, 1962.

Baumgarten, Alexander. *Theoretische Aesthetik*. Hamburg: F. Meiner, 1983.

——————————. *Meditationes philosophicae de nonullis ad poema pertinentibus*. Translated by Karl Aschenbrenner and William B. Holther. Berkeley: University of California Press, 1954.

Beardsley, Monroe C. *Aesthetics from Classical Greece to the Present*. Tuscaloosa, AL: The University of Alabama Press, 1976.

Bent, Ian. *Analysis*. With a Glossary by William Drabkin. NY: W. W. Norton & Co., 1987.

Berlyne, D. E. *Conflict, Arousal, and Curiosity*. NY: McGraw-Hill, 1960.

Berlyne, D. E, ed. *Studies in the New Experimental Aesthetics: Steps Toward An Objective Psychology of Music Appreciation*. NY: Halstead Press, 1974.

Blume, Friedrich. *Two Centuries of Bach, An Account of Changing Taste*. Translated by Stanley Godman. London: Oxford University Press, 1950.

Boretz, B. and E. T. Cone, eds. *Perspectives On Contemporary Music Theory*. New York: W. W. Norton, 1972.

Bosanquet, Bernard. *A History of Aesthetic*. NY: Macmillan & Co., 1892.

Britain, Halbert H. *The Philosophy of Music*. NY: Longmans, Green, and Co., 1911.

Cedarblom, Jerry and David W. Paulsen. *Critical Reasoning*, 2nd ed. Belmont, CA: Wadsworth Publishing Co., 1982.

Chavez, C. *Musical Thought*. Cambridge, MA: Harvard University Press, 1961.

Churchland, Patrica S. *Neurophilosophy: Toward a Unified Science of the Mind-Brain*. Cambridge, MA.: MIT Press, 1986.

Cone, E. T. *The Composer's Voice*. Berkeley and Los Angeles: University of California Press, 1974.

——————————— *Musical Form and Musical Performance*. NY: W. W. Norton, 1968.

Coppleston, F., S. J. *A History of Philosophy*, 9 vols. Garden City, NY: Image Books, 1946-1974.

Dahlhaus, Carl. Translated by W. W. Austin. *Esthetics of Music*. Cambridge, UK: Cambridge University Press, 1982.

Descartes, René . *Discourse on the Method of Properly Conducting One's Reason and of Seeking the Truth in the Sciences*. Translated by F. E. Sutcliffe. Harmondsworth, Middlesex, UK: Penguin Books, Ltd., 1968.

Elliott, David. *Music Matters*. NY: Schirmer Books, 1994.

Epperson, G. *The Musical Symbol: A Study of the Philosophic Theory of Music*. Ames, IO: Iowa State University Press, 1967.

Fechner, G. T. *Vorschule der Ästhetik*, 2 vols. Leipzig: Breitkopf & Hartel, 1897-98.

Fiske, Harold E. *Music and Mind: Philosophical Essays on the Cognition and Meaning of Music*. Lewiston, NY: The Edwin Mellen Press, 1990.

Forte, Allan. "Schenker's Conception of Musical Structure. *Journal of Music Theory* 3 (April 1959): 1-30.

George, F. H. *The Science of Philosophy*. New York: Gordon and Breach Science Publishers, 1981.

Gilbert, Katherine E. and Helmut Kuhn. *A History of Esthetics*. NY: The Macmillan Company, 1939.

Gurney, Edmund. *The Power of Sound*. London: Smith, Elder & Co., 1880; NY: Basic Books Publishing Co., Inc., 1967.

Hanslick, E. *The Beautiful in Music*. Translated by G. Cohen. NY: Liberal Arts Press, 1957.

Helmholtz, Hermann von. *On the Sensations of Tone as a Physiological Basis for the Theory of Music*, trans. A. J. Ellis. NY: Dover, 1954. Originally published, 1862.

Hegel, G. W. *The Phenomenology of the Mind*. Translated by J. B. Baillie. NY: Macmillan & Co., 1931.

Hindemith, Paul. *A Composer's World: Horizons and Limitations*. Cambridge, MA: Harvard University Press, 1952.

——————————. *Craft of Musical Composition*, Book I. Translated by A. Mendel. NY: Associated Music Publishers, 1942.

Hospers, John. *Meaning and Truth in the Arts*. Chapel Hill, NC: University of North Carolina Press, 1946; Hamden, CT: Archon Books, 1964.

Katz, Ruth and Carl Dahlhaus, Eds. *Contemplating Music: Source Readings in the Aesthetics of Music*. NY: Pendragon Press, 1987.

Kivy, P. *The Corded Shell: Reflections on Musical Expression*. Princeton, NJ: Princeton University Press, 1980.

Krathwohl, D. R., B. S. Bloom, and B. B. Masia. *Taxonomy of Educational Objectives, the Classification of Educational Goals, Handbook II: Affective Domain*. NY: David McKay Company, 1956.

Langer, Susanne. *Philosophy in a New Key*. Cambridge, MA.: Harvard University Press, 1942.

LeBlanc, Albert. "An Interactive Theory of Music Preference." *Journal of Music Therapy*, 19 (1982): 28-45.

Lippman, E. A. *A Humanistic Philosophy of Music*. NY: New York University Press, 1977.

_____, Ed. *Musical Aesthetics: A Historical Reader*. 2v. NY: Pendragon Press, 1986.

Locke, John. *Essay Concerning Human Understanding*. Abridged and ed., Raymond Wilburn. London: J. M. Dent & Sons, 1947.

Madsen, Clifford K., ed. *Vision 2020: The Housewright Symposium on the Future of Music Education.* Reston, VA: MENC – The National Association for Music Education, 2000.

Madsen, Clifford K., Ruth V. Britten, and Deborah Capperella-Sheldon. "An Empirical Method for Measuring the Aesthetic Experience in Music." *Journal of Research in Music Education*, 41 (1993): 57-69.

Meyer, Leonard B. *Emotion and Meaning in Music*. Chicago: The University of Chicago Press, 1956.

__. "Some Remarks on Value and Greatness in Music." *The Journal of Aesthetics and Art Criticism*, XVII, No. 4 (June 1959), 486-500.

Mill, John Stuart. *A System of Logic*, Book III, Chapter 8. NY: Harper and Brothers, 1873.

Munro, Thomas. "The Psychology of Art: Past, Present, Future." *The Journal of Aesthetics and Art Criticism*, XXI (Spring 1963).

Plato. *The Republic*. Translated by Francis MacDonald Cornford. London: Oxford University Press, 1945.

Pole, William. *The Philosophy of Music*. Boston: Houghton, Osgood, & Co., 1879.

Portnoy, J. *Music in the Life of Man*. NY: Holt, Rinehart and Winston, 1963.

_____. *The Philosopher and Music: A Historical Outline*. NY: Humanities Press, 1954.

Pratt, Carroll C. *The Meaning of Music*. NY: 1931.

Randal, Don M., ed. *The New Harvard Dictionary of Music*. Cambridge, MA: Belknap Press of Harvard University Press, 1986. S. v. "Theory" by Matthew Brown, 844-854.

Reynolds, R. *Mind Models: New Forms of Musical Experience*. NY: Praeger, 1975.

Reimer, Bennett. "Leonard Meyer's Theory of Value and Greatness in Music." *Journal of Research in Music Education* 10 (1962): 87-99.

_____. *A Philosophy of Music Education*, 2nd ed. Englewood Cliffs, NJ: Prentice-Hall, Inc., 1989.

Rothstein. "Schenker as an Interpreter of Beethoven's Piano Sonatas. *19th Century Music* 8 (Summer 1984): 10.

Rowell, L. *Thinking About Music: An Introduction to the Philosophy of Music*. Amherst, MA: The University of Massachusetts Press, 1983.

Sadie, Stanley, ed. *The New Grove Dictionary of Music and Musicians*. 1980. S.v. "Analysis" by Ian Bent, v. 1, 340-88.

Sartre, Jean Paul. *Existentialism and Human Emotions*. Secaucus, N. J.: Castle, a division of Book Sales, Inc., n.d.

Schenker, Heinrich. *Harmonielehre*. Translated by Elizabeth Mann Borgese. Edited and annotated by Oswald Jonas. Chicago: University of Chicago Press, 1954.

——————. *Kontrapunkt*. Translated by John Rothgeb and Jurgen Thym. Edited by John Rothgeb. New York: Schirmer Books, 1987.

Schwadron, Abraham A. *Aesthetics: Dimensions for Music Education*. Washington, D.C.: Music Educators National Conference, 1967.

——————. "Aesthetic Values in Music Education. *Music Journal* (May 1964): 42.

——————. "Musical Aesthetics: A Review and Critique.": *Music Educators Journal*, 51 (February-March 1965): 69-71, 181-183.

Walvoord, Barbara F. *Writing: Strategies for all Disciplines*. Englewood Cliffs, NJ: Prentice-Hall Inc., 1985.

Whitehead, Alfred N. *The Aims of Education and Other Essays*. NY: The Free Press, 1929.

——————. *Dialogues*. Recorded by Lucien Price. Westport, CT: Greenwood Press Publishers, 1954.

Zuckerlandl, V. *Sound and Symbol: Music and the External World*. Translated by W. R. Trask. Bollingen Series 44. Princeton, NJ: Princeton University Press, 1956.

Yarbrough, Cornelia. "Good Teaching May Be in Sonata Form." In *Applications of Research in Music Behavior* ed. Clifford K. Madsen and Carol A. Prickett. Tuscaloosa, AL: University of Alabama Press, 1987.

——————. "Indicators of Affect for School Music Teachers." *Update: Applications of Research in Music Teaching*, 4 (1985): 3-5.

Chapter Three

Music Historiography

# Chapter Three

Music
Historiography

I n Western musical culture the most important kinds of events have been the production of music by composers, its communication by performers, and the reception of it by listeners. Traditionally the function of music historiography has been to support composition and performance by discovering, editing, compiling, documenting, and annotating the music, composers, and performers of the past.

While the musical score certainly has been the most important artifact for study by historiographers, it has been necessary to look at other related artifacts in order to understand fully what is represented in the score (see Figure 1. Evidences of Music History in Chapter 1). The process of opening up the world of records and relics, which may solve the mysteries contained in the score, has been the goal of modern music history. The subsequent development of an inventive bibliography might stimulate an organization of the results producing an original conclusion or explanation of some aspect of music history.

HISTORICAL BACKGROUND

Harrison points out that it was not until the seventeenth and eighteenth centuries that historical treatises began to appear in increasing numbers. Prior to the late eighteenth century, music historiography was "interwoven with and inseparable from artistic activity." Composers like Palestrina and Corelli either reworked material by composers who had published music some forty to fifty years earlier or performed music almost entirely by contemporary composers. Musical history in the modern sense of the recovery and interpretation of past styles was considered unnecessary and irrelevant.[1]

Modern music historiography began during the second half of the eighteenth century with the appearance in 1776 of both the first volume of Dr. Charles Burney's *General History of Music* and all four volumes of Sir John Hawkins' *History of the Science and Practice of Music*.[2] There were, of course, other histories during this period: *De cantu et musica sacra* (1774) by the Abbot Martin Gerbert; *Storia della musica* (three volumes, 1757-1781) by the Franciscan Padre Giambattista Martini of Bologna; and *Allgemeine Geschichte der Musik* (two volumes, 1788 and 1801) by Johann Nicolaus Forkel.[3]

Characteristic productions of the nineteenth century were complete editions of composer's works, studies of their lives, and local and period histories almost all of which concerned the period from the sixteenth century to Mozart. These musical historians were for the most part gifted amateurs such as Raphael Kiesewetter, a civil servant; Carl von Winterfeld, a magistrate; August Wilhelm Ambros, specializing in law and public service; Otto Jahn, a professor of archaeology and philology; and Chrysander, who was musically self-taught.

In contrast to these musical amateurs was Francois Joseph Fétis (1784-1871), an historian, music lexicographer, theorist, composer, and director of the Brussels Conservatory. His unfinished *Histoire generale de la musique* was the first attempt at a history of music of all peoples, regarding Western music as the expression of one culture among many. Many regard this work as the forerunner of ethnomusicology.[4]

It was during the nineteenth century that the completion or initiation of some of the greatest projects in music editing and publishing occurred. Among these was a complete, critical edition of J. S. Bach's works.[5] The Bach Gesellschaft, founded in 1850 for this purpose, took 50 years and 46 volumes to accomplish it.[6] Other publications of massive anthologies during this period included the thirty-three-volume edition of Palestrina's works completed by F. X. Haberl and full-scale restoration

---

[1]Frank LL. Harrison, "American Musicology and the European Tradition," in *Musicology*, gen. ed. Richard Schlatter (Westport, CT: Greenwood Press, Publishers, 1963), 10-11.

[2]Burney completed publication of his four volumes in 1789.

[3]Harrison, 15–25.

[4]Harrison, 27–30.

[5]The first cantata to be printed after Bach's death was issued in 1821. In 1823, a copy of the *St. Matthew Passion* was made for Mendelssohn who, in 1829, conducted its first performance since Bach's death. This performance greatly accelerated the revival of Bach's music.

[6]Friedrich Blume, *Two Centuries of Bach, An Account of Changing Taste*, trans. Stanley Godman (London: Oxford University Press, 1950).

by the Benedictine monks of Solesmes of the most important early Gregorian chant manuscripts.[7]

It was during the years 1885 to 1930 that the general principles of transcription and the history of musical notation were established, largely through the work of Johannes Wolf.[8] The numerical index of Mozart's works by Ludwig Köchel[9] and the dictionary of musical sources of all periods compiled by Robert Eitner[10] were completed during this period. Numerous other complete editions of music of the Middle Ages were produced including a large repertory of English music for virginals and lutes, and ten volumes of Tudor church music as well as complete editions of single composers' works such as Mozart, Schumann, Schubert, Brahms, Praetorius, Sweelinck, Rameau, Berlioz, Couperin, Corelli, Monteverdi, Victoria, and Chopin.[11]

Beginning in the 1930s a number of European musical scholars emigrated to the United States including Apel, Bukofzer, David, Alfred Einstein, Geiringer, Gombosi, Hertzmann, Lowinsky, Nathan, Paul Nettl, Plamenac, Sachs, Schrade, and Winternitz. The presence of these European scholars, plus the fact that virtually all American born musicologists were trained in Europe at the time, resulted in the adoption of European ideas regarding the categorization of music historiography. Thus the categories became general history, period history, history of forms, biography, bibliography, and scholarly editions of music. Due to the almost total reliance upon European sources for original manuscripts, there was an increased use of photography.[12]

Between about 1930 and the early 1950s, textbooks giving a survey of the history of music for courses in liberal arts colleges, basic handbooks and monographs of music history, and doctoral dissertations in music were the major products of music historiography. Among these was Paul Henry Lang's *Music in Western Civilization* (1941) that contains not a single musical example and that demonstrates Lang's interest in music as an expression of the spirit of time and place. There were also several period histories and handbooks including The Norton series, *Music in the Middle Ages* (1940) and *Music in the Renaissance* (1954) by Gustave Reese, *Music in the Baroque Era* (1947) by Manfred F. Bukofzer, *The Rise of Music in*

---

[7]Harrison, 39–40.

[8]*Geschichte der Mensuralnotation 1250–1460*, 1905; *Handbuch der Notationskunde*, 1913–19.

[9]*Chronologisch-thematisches Verzeichnis sämtlicher Tonwerke Wolfgang Amade Mozarts*, ed. Alfred Einstein (Leipzig: Breitkopf & Hartel, 1958).

[10]*Biographisch-bibliographisches Quellon-lexikon der Musiker und Musikgelehrten der christlichen Zeitrechnung bis zur Mitte des 19. Jahrhunderts*, 10 vols., 1900–1904.

[11]Harrison, 45–48.

[12]Harrison, 56-57.

the Ancient World East and West (1943) by Curt Sachs, and *Music in the Romantic Era* (1947) by Alfred Einstein. Others were manuals of notation by Willi Apel and Carl Parrish, *Source Readings in Music History* (1950) by Oliver Strunk,[13] and *Studies in Medieval and Renaissance Music* (1950) by Manfred F. Bukofzer.

Four monographs were published by university presses, only two of which were written by American-trained scholars. *The Italian Madrigal* (3 vols, 1949) by Alfred Einstein required forty years to gather materials including original manuscripts, information concerning the social setting of Italian secular music, tastes of the time, life at princely courts, and the relations of musicians to each other and to their patrons from libraries throughout the world which had to be transcribed and translated from the original sources. *The Sonata in the Baroque Era* (1959) by William S. Newman was twenty years in the making. *A Short History of Opera* (2 vols., 1947) by Donald J. Grout was the first systematic survey of opera since 1919; and *Gregorian Chant* (1958) was written by Willi Apel. Other important works of this period were Donald J. *Grout's A History of Western Music* (1960), with an emphasis on history of style, and *The Art of Music* (1960) by Beekman Cannon, Alvin Johnson, and WilliamWaite that attempted for the first time to link up currents of philosophic and aesthetic thought with musical styles. Noteworthy editions or transcriptions by Americans during this time included *60 Sonatas by Domenico Scarlatti,* ed. Ralph Kirkpatrick (G. Schirmer, 1958) and *Mozart fantasias and sonatas for piano,* ed. Nathan Broder (T. Presser, 1956).

Two major post-World War II efforts were *Die Musik in Geschichte und Gegenwart (MGG)* and *The New Oxford History of Music. MGG* is a comprehensive music encyclopedia of the highest scholarly merit. It is in German, but is of international scope and coverage with complete listings of composers' works and detailed monographs. *The New Oxford History of Music* is an excellent resource for teaching as well as scholarship. There are ten volumes to date with an additional volume of chronological tables and a general index planned. There is an accompanying set of recordings issued under the title *The History of Music in Sound*.[14]

Succeeding *MGG* as the major reference work supporting and informing musical scholarship is *The New Grove Dictionary of Music and Musicians,* a 20-volume work edited by Stanley Sadie and published in 1980. The text of *The New Grove* was set by computer and parts of it have reappeared, revised, in a series of volumes

---

[13]A more comprehensive collection of writings on music is now available selected and edited by Ruth Katz and Carl Dahlhaus entitled *Contemplating Music: Source Readings in the Aesthetics of Music* (NY: Pendragon Press, 1987).

[14]Vincent H. Duckles and Ida Reed*, Music Reference and Research Materials*, 5th ed. (NY: Schirmer Books, 1997), 10 vols., 120-121.

since 1980.[15] Now ***Grove Music Online*** (www.grovemusic.com) allows constant addition of information to this monumental source.

Since the birth of American music historiography in the mid-nineteenth century, important periodicals have led the way by providing more current access to research. Among the first of these was J. S. Dwight's ***Journal of Music*** (1852-81) that, among articles appealing to a broad segment of the population, contained articles on music history.

The Musical Quarterly is this country's oldest musicological review, founded in 1915 by G. Schirmer. Until World War II contributors were mainly European musicologists who wrote articles on acoustics, psychology, physiology, aesthetics, and ethnographic and folk music in addition to articles concerning biographical, critical, theoretical, and historical subjects. From about 1937, the ***MQ*** has predominately published historical and ethnomusicological articles by American scholars.[16]

Claude Palisca observed the actual practice of musicologists through perusal of the initial ten years, 1950-60, of the ***Journal of the American Musicological Society.*** His observation revealed a predominance of articles in the fields of historical and ethnological musicology with an emphasis on medieval, renaissance, and baroque style periods.[17] In a recent content analysis of the ***Journal of the American Musicological Society,*** for the years, 1961-86, Yarbrough and Sharp noted that 63% of the articles published during this time period concerned the Middle Ages, Renaissance, and Baroque style periods. In addition, this analysis revealed that less than 1% of the articles concerned music in antiquity. Further analysis of the articles' subject matter revealed close parallels over time. A comparison of articles of 1961-1973 and those from 1974-1986, showed that liturgical music of the Middle Ages and vocal music of the Renaissance were the most frequent subjects in both periods of time. The largest difference with respect to era was the coverage given to Romantic music or drama; only one article in this era appeared from 1961 to 1973, while eight articles were published from 1974 to 1986.[18]

Periodicals such as ***19th Century Music*** and ***Perspectives in New Music*** have done much to stimulate research in later periods. In addition, ***The Musical Quarterly*** remains a scholarly source for all style periods and genres.

For articles related to music in America, four other periodicals have recently appeared on the scene, the ***Moravian Music Journal,*** 1958-; ***Popular Music and***

---

[15]Duckles and Reed, 120.

[16]Claude V. Palisca, "American Scholarship in Western Music," In ***Musicology,*** gen. ed. Richard Schlatter (Westport, CT: Greenwood Press, Publishers, 1963), 99-100.

[17]Palisca, 99, 196

[18]Cornelia Yarbrough and Michael Sharp, "A Content Analysis of the Journal of the American Musicological Society, Unpublished paper, Louisiana State University, 1987.

Society, 1971-; *The Black Perspective in Music,* 1973-; and *American Music,* 1983-. In addition, the research journals for music therapy and music education have published historical research related to those fields. Heller has compiled two excellent bibliographies, one for historical research in music education and the other, for music therapy. Entries include books, articles, dissertations, and masters' theses.[19] Most recently, the historians of the music education scholarly community have introduced the *Journal of Historical Research in Music Education* that replaces and continues the *Bulletin of Historical Research in Music Education.*

Perhaps the most notable step forward in American musicology is the recognition of the importance of American music history. H. Wiley Hitchcock has said that we know less about our own music than about that of Western Europe. Its conglomeration and assimilation of many styles, traditions, origins, and purposes characterize the history of American music. The sacred versus secular dichotomy drawn in discussing American music prior to 1820 has discouraged "serious" inquiry in the past. There is an introduction to two bodies of American music reflecting two attitudes toward it, the cultivated and the vernacular. Hitchcock says,

> On the one hand there continues a vernacular tradition of utilitarian and entertainment music, essentially unconcerned with artistic or philosophical idealism; a music based on established or newly diffused American raw materials; a 'popular' music in the largest sense, broadly based, widespread, naive, and unselfconscious. On the other hand there grows a cultivated tradition of fine-art music significantly concerned with moral, artistic, or cultural idealism; a music almost exclusively based on continental European raw materials and models, looked to rather self-consciously; an essentially transatlantic music of the pretenders to gentility; hopefully sophisticated and by no means widespread throughout all segments of the populace.[20]

Richard Crawford describes five American history books in terms of the balance they achieve between the coverage of traditions of American music that correspond to those of European art music and coverage of vernacular forms of special significance in American life. John Tasker Howard's *Our American Music* (1931 and later editions) emphasized the "cultivated tradition" with no musical examples. Howard

---

[19]George N. Heller, "Historical Research in Music Therapy: A Bibliography," and "Historical Research in Music Education: A Bibliography," Unpublished papers, University of Kansas, Department of Art and Music Education and Music Therapy, 1986 and 1988.

[20]H. Wiley Hitchcock, *Music in the United States: A Historical Introduction,* 2nd ed. (Englewood Cliffs, N. J.: Prentice-Hall, Inc., 1974), 52.

did include chapters on folk music of the American Indians, "Negro Music," and touched on music of the Broadway stage, Tin Pan Alley, and jazz.[21]

Crawford cites Gilbert Chase's ***America's Music from the Pilgrims to the Present*** (1955) as a text in sharp disagreement with Howard's "polite approach."[22] Chase demonstrates that both the techniques of musicology and ethnomusicology must be used to clarify and facilitate the study of American music.[23] According to Palisca, this is necessary because the musical past of this nation represents several strands: the "colonial" thread which includes the music of the Puritan pilgrims, the Germans, Moravians, Dutch, French, and other national groups that settled here, bringing with them their old-world musical culture; Black gospel music and jazz; American Indian music; and the music of the native composers, both serious and popular, and an additional layer of anonymous popular and folk music with mainly oral traditions.[24]

Three other texts mentioned by Crawford are Wilfrid Mellers's ***Music in a New Found Land*** (1966), H. Wiley Hitchcock's ***Music in the United States*** (1969 and later editions), and Charles Hamm's ***Music in the New World*** (1983). According to Crawford, Mellers was highly selective, omitting most of eighteenth- and nineteenth-century American music, most commercial popular music, and virtually all folk music. Hitchcock "set a high standard of compression and clarity of state-ment" in his book that omits (or rather he assigned to another author) folk music. Hamm, like Chase, favored vernacular music and was the "first academically trained historian of American music to embrace even the highly commercial genres of contemporary popular and country music with sympathy and enthusiasm."[25]

Finally, Crawford concludes that no event in the history of music in the United States "matches the importance of the publication, in 1986, of ***The New Grove Dictionary of American Music***."[26]

> Amerigrove marks a new beginning in the study of music in the United States. If not precisely a millennial event - scholarly monu-ments, however deeply longed for, are sure to be taken for granted and carped at as soon as they appear - the publication of Amerigrove establishes a Great Divide in American musical historiography. Before Amerigrove (B. A.), academic scholars could consider 'American

---

[21]Richard Crawford, "Amerigrove's Pedigree: On *The New Grove Dictionary of American Music*," **College Music Symposium**, 27 (1987): 172-186.

[22]Crawford, p. 181.

[23]Gilbert Chase, ***America's Music from the Pilgrims to the Present***, rev. 2nd ed. (New York: McGraw-Hill Book Co., 1966).

[24]Palisca, 212-13.

[25]Crawford, 181-182.

[26]Crawford, 172.

music' a congeries of varied enterprises, only some of them worthy of a scholar's attention. 'American music' was a selective label whose meaning depended entirely upon who was using it. (A New York Philharmonic program of 'American music' at Avery Fisher Hall would overlap not al all, for example, with television's annual 'American Music Awards.'In the post-Amerigrove age, however - 1987 A. D. is the Year 1 A. A. - the tag 'American music' resonates with a new ecological completeness. 'If we have erred,' the editors write, 'we hope it is on the side of inclusiveness.'[27] Here is the key to Amerigrove's importance. By publishing, with considerable public fanfare, under prestigious auspices, and in sumptuous physical trappings, so much data about so many different kinds of American music, the editors have created a single subject where before there were many. In something of the way each of the thirteen British colonies gained new strength when it joined the United States of America, so each branch of American musical endeavor can be contemplated more richly when viewed as part of a diverse, complex whole: *E pluribus unum.*[28]

At the present stage in the development of American music historiography, the most urgent task is to create modern editions for the vast quantity of music and primary literary sources of the period before 1800 that still exist only in manuscript and early printed editions. The editing and collating of manuscripts and rare editions have top priority. The most important documents are those that contain musical compositions or fragments of them. These are found in autograph versions, contemporary copies, other copies, and printed editions more or less contemporary with the composer. Next in importance are treatises, including all technical instructional writings relating to composition and performance, as well as speculative works. Then come letters of composers, musicians, or others that furnish descriptions of musical performances or organizations or that discuss music and musicians in some substantial way. Contemporary critical, aesthetic, and biographical writings and archival records are other documents that should be made accessible.

Scholarly editions of America's music, which should serve as excellent models, are those by Lowens and Marrocco and Gleason. Included in these editions is information on the character and content of all the sources, on variants, on neces-

---

[27] *The New Grove Dictionary of American Music*, ed. by H. Wiley Hitchcock and Stanley Sadie, with Susan Feder as editorial coordinator, 4 vols. (London and New York: Macmillan, 1986), 1:viii.

[28] Crawford, 173.

sary editorial changes, and information on the cultural context in which the music might have been performed.[29]

MODEL PROJECTS IN MUSIC HISTORIOGRAPHY

The activities of music historians include a wide variety of projects such as the compilation of comprehensive databases and bibliographies, writing program notes, biographies, cataloging collections, writing historical surveys, and writing articles for dictionaries and encyclopedias of music, to mention a few. One of the more interesting database projects is that of the ***Thesaurus Musicarum Latinarum***, an evolving database that will eventually contain the entire corpus of Latin music theory written during the Middle Ages and the early Renaissance. It is the project of a consortium of universities (including Ohio State University, Princeton University, Louisiana State University, University of Illinois, and the University of Colorado) and is centered at Indiana University. The data files of the ***TML*** contain the text of the source, printed or in manuscript, just as it stands and without editorial intrusions. The database will display text alone; musical examples, charts, and figures alone on machines with graphic capabilities; or text and graphics simultaneously in separate windows on machines with multitasking capability. The ***TML*** will make it possible for scholars to locate and display in a matter of minutes on their personal computers every occurrence of a particular term, a phrase or passage, or a group of terms in close proximity in any published edition contained in the ***TML*** database.[30] This is a good example of how computers are being used to sort through and combine information thereby saving scholars countless hours of searching and increasing the amount of time spent on the critical and analytical aspects of historiography.

An example of bibliographical work in music is the ***Bibliographical Handbook of American Music*** by Donald W. Krummel. Krummel begins his book with sections on "Chronological Perspectives" and "Contextual Perspectives" - the former divided into music before 1825, from 1826 to 1900, since 1900, and current; the latter citing regional, group, and personal bibliographies. Sections on "Musical Mediums and Genres" (concert music, vernacular music, popular song, and sacred music) and "Bibliographical Forms" (including source materials, writings about

---

[29]Irving Lowens, ***Music and Musicians in Early America*** (New York: W. W. Norton & Co., Inc., 1965); ***Music in America: An Anthology from the Landing of the Pilgrims to the Close of the Civil War: 1620-1865***, eds. W. Thomas Marrocco and Harold Gleason (New York: W. W. Norton & Co., Inc., 1964).

[30]Thesaurus Musicarum Latinarum: A Comprehensive Database of Latin Music Theory of the Middle Ages and the Renaissance. Project Director, Thomas J. Mathiesen. Bloomington, IN: Indiana University, School of Music.

music, and discography) complete this work. There is an index incorporating subjects, authors, and titles in one alphabetical listing, with title entries giving authors' last names.[31] Studying this model will provide insight into the various ways history might be organized and approached through bibliographical means.

It is a good idea to locate and study good models for the various forms of music historiography before attempting to craft the research product. Of course, one should gain bibliographical control of the subject before attempting the study of a model example. It is inappropriate to force information into a particular format for which it is not suited. On the other hand, it is helpful to study the work of other scholars so that one might better learn the art and craft of historical writing.

TECHNIQUES OF MUSIC HISTORIOGRAPHY

The techniques of music historiography require several steps. After selection of the music artifact, it must be subjected to external criticism. During the stage of external criticism, clues in the form of keywords and subject headings should be noted. The second step is the development of bibliographical control of all materials and resources related to the artifact. The third step occurs also during the first and second steps and is the on-going internal criticism of the resources and materials located. Finally, the craft of writing the final report begins.

Step 1.   **External Criticism: A complete description must be
developed which includes determination of author
(or composer, instrument maker) and date, exact
measurements, translation of script or notation,
examination of material or paper, and so forth.**

Simply defined, an artifact is a product of human workmanship. Musical artifacts, therefore, include musical scores, instruments, books, letters, diaries, periodical publications, recordings (phonograph, compact disc, audio-, and videotapes), public documents, inscriptions, and songs, anecdotes, or stories transmitted orally. Research applications by graduate students have included the study of such artifacts as their own instruments, editions of particular masterworks, unusual transcriptions, opera glasses, and the complete papers of an early nineteenth century parlor music composer. Other projects by graduate students examined diaries, first editions of music theory books, minutes of early American music organizations, and ladies'

---

[31]Krummel, Donald W., *Bibliographical Handbook of American Music* (Urbana, IL: University of Illinois Press, 1987.

plantation ball music books found in the Louisiana Collection of the Louisiana State University Libraries.

The first task of the music historiographer in dealing with an artifact is one of external criticism. It begins with a content analysis of the artifact. A complete description must be developed which includes determination of author (or composer, instrument maker) and date, exact measurements, translation of script or notation, examination of material or paper, and so forth. Physical properties such as color, weight, gloss, grain, watermarks, and measurement of age may be useful. After a complete and thorough description of the artifact has been made, it may be helpful to compare it to others of the same period, or by the same composer or maker. There should be a consideration of whether the object is a forgery or has been altered, whether a text has been ghost written, whether plagiarism (an acceptable practice in early Greece and Rome) has occurred, and whether mistakes in transcription or notation have been inadvertently made. Throughout this sometimes tedious process, the historiographer may need the assistance of other specialties, for example, linguistics, the study of language; paleography, the study of ancient handwriting and musical notation; epigraphy, the study of inscriptions; diplomatics, the study of official documents; seals, the study of their materials and legends; heraldry, the study of symbols on a shield; numismatics, the study of coins and metals; genealogy, the study of human pedigrees; chronology, the measurement of time and the placing of events in time; and many other specialties.[32] Palisca notes that,

> Once lists of all known manuscripts and printed editions of a work have been compiled and microfilms or photostats have been gathered, the work of sorting out authentic and usable sources begins. The age and provenance of each source must be ascertained, and the hand or printer identified. Handy as films are, they may turn out to be inadequate during this critical stage. The determination of dates, owners and history, and the proper order of items often depends upon watermarks, bindings, and the precise way gatherings are arranged and sewn together. Once the manuscripts have been analyzed, a family tree or stemma of traditions is derived. Finally, the editor decides upon his principal source or sources and on those to be referred to in the revisions-report . . . or footnotes. . . Often, after better acquaintance with all the sources, a single source from which an editor will have produced an early transcription may turn out to be less reliable than another. In this manner, a music historiographer proceeds.[33]

[32] Jones Shafer, ed., *A Guide to Historical Method* (Homewood, IL: The Dorsey Press, 1969), 99-130.
[33] Palisca, 180.

For example, the documents studied by Mendel and his associates for the *New Bach Edition* were principally performance parts and scores many of them composed in haste and preserved for the most part in practical form that allowed for performances in churches. In contrast, Beethoven's music was not composed in haste but rather sketched out ahead of time in great detail. A meticulous chronological description and analysis of Beethoven's sketchbooks provide a record of the growth of Beethoven's compositions from the earliest ideas to the final score.[34] Both of these studies used numerous evidences of history to unravel the secrets of Bach's and Beethoven's compositional procedures and chronology. The records used included biographies, autobiographies, chronologies, catalogs of collections, letters, diaries, memoirs, and, of course, the original manuscripts and sketchbooks.

An example of the difficulties encountered in external criticism may be seen in the work of Arthur Mendel in editing the full score of the *St. John Passion* for the *New Bach Edition* being published in Germany. He put his seminar at Princeton to work sorting out approximately 500 pages of parts. Twenty-one different handwritings were discovered. These results were compared with those of teams of investigators in Göttingen and Tübingen who had classified the handwritings in all Bach manuscripts. Some modifications in the seminar's conclusions resulted. The Princeton group also worked on the problem of relating the parts to particular known performances and of determining the earliest version. They spent almost a year on these questions. After further consultation, it became evident that the parts once considered duplicates were really the earliest known set.[35]

Another example of the problems of external criticism may be seen in the work of Douglas Johnson, Alan Tyson, and Robert Winter on the Beethoven sketchbooks. The sketchbooks were found in a wide variety of places and collections, many of them were mutilated with pages torn out and sold separately, and some presented special problems. Although Beethoven preserved his sketches throughout his lifetime "with an almost parental protectiveness," only two or three of the more than thirty large-format sketchbooks Beethoven used between 1798 and 1826 remain in their original condition.[36] To sort out the history and location of the sketchbooks, Johnson, Tyson, and Winter began their work with a survey of the principal collections including the Artaria, Landsberg, Grasnick, and Beer-Mendelssohn collections.[37] This is followed by a detailed description of the three types of sketchbooks studied: those with regular structure and professional stitching (type 1); those with

---

[34]Arthur Mendel, "Recent Developments in Bach Chronology," *Musical Quarterly* 56 (July 1960): 283-300; Johnson, Douglas, ed. with Alan Tyson and Robert Winter, *The Beethoven Sketchbooks: History, Reconstruction, Inventory* (Berkeley and Los Angeles: University of California Press, 1985).

[35]Mendel, 283-300.

[36]Johnson, et al., 13.

[37]Johnson, et al., 14-42.

regular structure and nonprofessional stitching (types 2A and 2B); and those with irregular structure and nonprofessional stitching (type 3). The authors discuss the possibilities and limits of reconstruction as follows:

> In books of type 1, both structure and overall size can be predicted, so that it is relatively easy to discover the number of missing leaves and the places at which they were removed. On the other hand, the absence of any predictable structure or size in books of type 3 sets severe limits to the possibilities of reconstruction; here losses cannot usually be inferred from interruptions in the gathering structure (although it is sometimes possible to identify fugitive leaves by other techniques shortly to be described). It is the sketchbooks of types 2A and 2B that are perhaps the most likely to prove deceptive. Because their internal structure is for the most part regular, we can usually detect the loss of single leaves or single bifolia. But the total number of leaves is not predictable, so pairs of bifolia may have slipped away without a trace, especially from the outside of a single large gathering. Moreover, since the paper for these books appears to have come from batches already in Beethoven's possession or from a copyist's shop, rather than in complete packets from a retailer, we must in principle allow for the possibility of an occasional irregularity in the structure - an unpaired bifolium, for example - and for the inclusion of leaves that had been partially used before the book was assembled.[38]

The subsequent accounts of their work on watermarks and the paper itself represent an excellent model for novice researchers. The remainder of this monumental book is a description of the desk and pocket sketchbooks, the sketches in score for the late quartets, and some particular problematical cases such as the sketches for the **String Quartets, Opus 59** (1806), sketches for the **Fifth Piano Concerto, Opus 73** (1809), and for the **Piano Sonata, Opus 106** (1817-1818).

Current controversies on editing medieval, Renaissance, and Baroque music center on problematic compromises between historical accuracy and modern methods of notation. It was the practice of not long ago to use as many as five clefs when scoring a five-part, sixteenth century composition because original parts were written this way. Original note values were also preserved even though they suggested very slow tempo when the composer really intended a fast one. Now the trend is toward making the scores of older works look like a contemporary one.

The appearance of music published since the 19th century has included pitch, tempo, meter, rhythm, accentuation, dynamic markings, phrasing, instrumentation, and so forth, explicitly indicated by the composer. Some early notations give only

---

[38]Johnson, et al., 49.

pitch, as in plainchant or early organum; others give pitch and suggest rhythm. In the thirteenth century, the relative time value of notes became definitive but tempo was not precisely indicated. Still later, in the fifteenth century, ratios were given to show changes of tempo and rhythm, but no basic rate of pulsation was defined. Barlines were absent in music written only in parts before about 1600 and often afterward; expressive marks and instrumentation indications were also rare at this time. Consequently, musical editors must reconstruct probable performance (for performers) and allow scholars to see the original state through the reconstruction. To give expression marks, tempi, phrasing, and instrumentation when the composer has not indicated them is now considered poor editorial practice.[39]

The chief problems of musical transcription occur for the period of about 1250-1600. Staff notation of one kind or another was not the only system used. A variety of musical notations can be found that vary not only over time but from country to country as well. Some systems were a mixture of staff and letter notation, as in Old German Organ Tablature. A tablature is a system of notation, which uses letters, numbers, or other symbols to represent the music. Lute music had its own Lute Tablature in French, Italian, Spanish or German types, all different and requiring special attention. All English lute composers wrote in French Lute Tablature. The problems involved in creating editions of early American hymn tunes necessitate knowledge of a variety of shape-note traditions.

The beginning researcher must realize that in general there are two types of editions of early music. First there is the edition that makes no distinction between the composer's own text and the editor's additions to it. Many of these editions appeared in the nineteenth century. These often reflected a performer's idiosyncrasies with considerable divergences from the autograph or first edition. The other type of edition is the *urtext* or original edition. The text appears clean and uncluttered, and any additions, corrections or amendments are made by the editor in the light of his or her researches based on the autographs, surviving copies, and early editions, are clearly distinguishable from the composer's own text. An editor will normally put some information in square brackets, some in small type, and other information in italics. How this is done depends upon the musical context.

**Step 2.   Bibliographical control of primary and secondary
                sources must be achieved.**

Music historiography requires meticulous attention to detail and enormous concern for accuracy. In addition to the examination of primary source material, the scrutiny of a wide variety of secondary source materials is necessary.

---

[39]Palisca, 182-83.

Primary sources for music historiography include documents such as autobiographies, letters, diaries, handbills, books, films, pictures, paintings, inscriptions, recordings, transcriptions, and research reports. Relics and remains are also primary sources and include musical instruments, paintings or other forms of iconography, and even the contents of ancient burial places which may reveal a good deal about the musical life of a culture. Finally, oral testimony is a valuable primary source because it is the spoken account of a witness of, or participant in, an event.

Secondary sources are the reports of a person who relates the testimony of an actual witness of, or participant in, an event. These sources are usually of limited worth for research purposes because of the errors that may result when information passes from one person to another. Most music history books and encyclopedias are examples of secondary sources for they are often several times removed from the original, first hand account of events.

At this point in the development of the historiography project, it is time to return to Chapter 1, The Art of Bibliographical Control. The steps for developing a comprehensive bibliography of resources related to the chosen artifact should be followed.

Throughout the research process, the researcher must maintain an attitude that the music or the musician being studied may be of great value. While it is clear that Bach and Beethoven are forever in the classical repertory, new discoveries are yet to be made. The challenge of music historiography is not only to study those geniuses of music history but also to study the institutions, chapels, churches, opera and theatre companies, and other individuals surrounding those geniuses. The music historiographer must demonstrate tenacity, commitment to long hours of tedious scrutiny of materials, and careful documentation of the results.

Step 3.   Internal criticism involves authenticating the historical artifact and evaluating their accuracy or worth.

After careful external criticism of documents or relics, it is the responsibility of a scholar to evaluate their accuracy or worth. Although the artifact in question may be genuine, does it reveal a true picture? What of the writers of source materials? Were they competent, honest, unbiased, and actually acquainted with the facts, or were they too antagonistic or sympathetic to give a true account? Did they have any motives for distorting the facts? How long after an event did they make a record of their testimony, and were they able to remember accurately what happened? Were they in agreement with other competent witnesses? Were facts uncovered without prior assumptions or personal biases? This is the purpose of internal criticism.

Francis Bacon, a great British philosopher during the Renaissance, examined the difficulties in the pursuit of internal criticism in his famous doctrine of "the idols."

He described four main types: the idols of the tribe, the idols of the cave or den, the idols of the market place, and the idols of the theatre.

The idols of the tribe are those errors, which occur when things, which are not directly observable, are neglected. Bacon says, "for what a man would like to be true, to that he tends to give credence." He thus draws attention to a danger of relying on appearances, on the untested and uncriticized data of the senses, to the phenomenon of wishful thinking, and to the mind's tendency to mistake abstractions for things. To avoid these pitfalls, one should apply a three step test to any conclusions reached: (1) is the conclusion probable considering all external factors examined above; (2) is the conclusion plausible; and (3) is it certain. The answers to these three tests may conclude the research or require that it continue.[40]

Barzun and Graff give two fundamental rules in avoiding the idols of the tribe: first, proof demands decisive evidence that confirms one view and denies its rivals; and second, truth rests not on possibility nor on plausibility but on probability. They cite an example of a scientific test on the paper on which a suspected document is written or printed.

> The reasoning goes: This paper is made from esparto grass. The document is said to have been written in 1850. But in 1850 esparto paper was not made, it having been introduced by Thomas Routledge in 1857. Therefore, the document is forged.[41]

As Barzun and Graff critically analyze this reasoning, the conclusion seems only highly probable. Things not directly observable, such as some other, unsung papermaker may have introduced grass into the batch before Routledge; or the tests applied may not be exact enough to differentiate between similar fibers that might have been in the paper at the earlier date. Here truth demands decisive evidence that denies the possibility of the alternative conclusions.[42]

The idols of the den are errors peculiar to each individual. Temperament, education, reading and special influences may lead a person to interpret phenomena according to the viewpoint of a personal cave or den. There have been many accounts regarding the inability of witnesses to observe accurately. In addition, lack of familiarity with subject matter may cause errors in reporting. Here, the scholar must examine the credentials of the individual who supplied the information in order to verify the facts obtained.

------

[40]Francis Bacon, ***Novum Organum***, edited with introduction and notes by T. Fowler (Oxford: 1950).

[41]Jacques Barzun and Henry F. Graff, ***The Modern Researcher***, 3rd ed. (New York: Harcourt Brace Jovanovich, Inc., 1977), 134.

[42]***Ibid***.

A third type of errors, according to Bacon, is the idols of the marketplace. These are errors due to the influence of the language. Because common usage may be inadequate, language may stand in the way of the expression of a more adequate analysis. Sometimes words are employed when there are no corresponding things, when there is no clear concept of what is meant, or without any commonly recognized meaning. Also, there are often two meanings with which to contend, a literal meaning versus a colloquial meaning; or an ancient meaning versus a current one.

The idols of the theatre are the philosophical systems of the past, which Bacon describes as false philosophies. First, there is sophistical philosophy corrupted by dialectic; second, empirical philosophy, based on a few, narrow observations; and third, superstitious philosophy characterized by the introduction of theological considerations. Regarding the first idol of the theatre, the Sophists were teachers of rhetoric in the 5th century B.C. who practiced the art of persuasion through dialectic, debate conducted in conformity with the laws of formal logic. Sophistical arguments were those intended to deceive and, as such, contained a subtle fallacy. The second idol of the theatre cautions us to remember those instances, which have not been observed. Finally, the third idol reminds us of the problems inherent in the acceptance of dogma.[43]

Thus, Bacon's idols are reminders of the attributes of good scholarship: careful, critical, and accurate observation; avoidance of bias in presenting research results; careful choice of words in reporting research; and an understanding of the varied philosophical systems, their advantages and their limitations.

Step 4.   Organize, write, edit, and submit the final report.

Historical writing is that which is most familiar to students. It is most often expository in technique. The final report should include an introductory paragraph or two setting the stage for the artifact to be examined. Then the external criticism of the artifact should be presented followed by a thorough internal criticism of the artifact and the sources consulted. It may be desirable to place the artifact in a larger context. For example, the examination of the works of a composer of parlor music might also include a discussion the social customs of the nineteenth-century and the music publishing industry at the time.

The format for the presentation of historical papers includes:

1. A title page on which the title of the paper, the author, and the date submitted appear;
2. The text, each page of which must be numbered;
3. Footnotes or endnotes; and
4. A comprehensive bibliography.

---

[43]Bacon, *Novum Organum*.

The style manual recommended by the instructor or the journal for which the paper or article is being written should be consulted for details concerning organization, format of tables and figures, abstracting if necessary, and other format issues.

The final paper should demonstrate controlled inquiry, creativity and imagination, and intellectual honesty. Questions to be answered regarding controlled inquiry are as follows: Does the paper have a single informing theme with its proper development and is the topic thoroughly covered? Is each of the paragraphs a division with a purpose, organizing a number of sentences into a treatment of one idea and its modifications? Are there transitional words and phrases to connect sentences and insure a good flow of ideas? Is the appearance of the paper neat, free of typographical errors and misspelled words? Does the paper faithfully and accurately follow a style manual?

The second area of concern in the final paper is creativity and imagination. Creativity and imagination may be measured in several ways. One way is to examine the number and variety of resources and source materials used. It may be that a paper that lists only books in the bibliography is not as creative and imaginative as a paper that uses original recordings, letters, diaries, books, interviews, dissertations, unpublished compositions, and other types of source materials. A second way to measure creativity and imagination is to examine the paper in light of the author's ability to transfer information learned in the research process beyond the specificity of the topic, or the ability to go beyond the observation of factual information toward personal commentary. The ability to synthesize past experiences, information from a variety of sources, and knowledge gained during the research process is necessary in the production of a truly creative product.

Finally, the research paper should be intellectually honest. Intellectual honesty requires scholarly documentation of sources for ideas or facts contained in the paper. Scholarly documentation demands the absence of plagiarism. In addition, intellectual honesty requires accuracy of information. Careful, painstaking attention to detail and striving for perfection are characteristics of respected scholars.

SUMMARY

To review the scope and function of music historiography, one must return to Chapter 1 for techniques in developing bibliographical control of a subject being studied. The techniques and problems of external criticism are, for the most part, objective and straightforward although tedious and time-consuming. On the other hand, the techniques of internal criticism are more subjective and therefore more difficult to control. It is all too easy for the beginner to assume rather than to test information, to reach a hasty conclusion before all the information has been examined, to respond to pressure for discovering something really important, or to overlook the importance of detail in favor of generalities.

There is no one magic formula for producing that research product which will significantly influence the study of music for generations to come. History is fluid, ever changing. Only time gives us the perspective to evaluate our historical efforts and to select those musical events, products, and people, which are those true creative milestones.

RESEARCH APPLICATIONS

1. Visit the special collections division of any library. Select any musical artifact (composition in manuscript form, rare book, instrument, etc.) and trace its origin, cultural context, use in musical performances, and discover any other pertinent facts about it. Write a short, well-documented report of your research.

2. Write program notes for the performance of a major classical work. Consider the characteristics of the audience for whom you are writing: educated, over 40 years old, non-musicians. Your goal is to assist the audience both in their understanding of and in developing a love for the work being performed. The program notes must be accurate both historically and musically.

BIBLIOGRAPHY

Chase, Gilbert. *America's Music from the Pilgrims to the Present*, rev. 2nd ed. NY: McGraw-Hill Book Co., 1966.

Crawford, Richard. "Amerigrove's Pedigree: On *The New Grove Dictionary of American Music*." *College Music Symposium*, 27 (1987): 172-186.

——————. *American Studies and American Musicology: A Point of View and A Case in Point.* Brooklyn: Institute for Studies in American Music, Brooklyn College of the City University of New York, 1975.

Harrison, F. L. "American Musicology and the European Tradition." In *Musicology*, pp. 1-86. Humanistic Scholarship in America Series: The Princeton Studies, Gen. ed. Richard Schlatter. Englewood Cliffs, NJ: Prentice Hall, 1963; reprint ed., Westport, Conn.: Greenwood Press, Publishers, 1974.

Haydon, Glen. *Introduction to Musicology*. Chapel Hill, N.C.: The University of North Carolina Press, 1941.

Helm, Eugene and Albert T. Luper. *Words and Music*. Hackensack, NJ: Joseph Boonin, Inc., 1971.

Heller, George N. "Historical Research in Music Education: A Bibliography." Lawrence, KS: The University of Kansas, Department of Art and Music Education and Music Therapy, 1988.

——————. "Historical Research in Music Therapy: A Bibliography." Lawrence, KS: The University of Kansas, Department of Art and Music Education and Music Therapy, 1986.

Hendrie, Gerald. *Mendelssohn's Rediscovery of Bach*. London: Oxley Press, Ltd., 1971.

Hitchcock, H. Wiley. *Music in the United States: A Historical Introduction*. 2nd ed. Englewood Cliffs, N. J.: Prentice-Hall, Inc., 1974.

Johnson, Douglas, ed. with Alan Tyson and Robert Winter. *The Beethoven Sketchbooks: History, Reconstruction, Inventory*. Berkeley and Los Angeles: University of California Press, 1985.

Leichtentritt, Hugo. *Music, History, and Ideas*. Cambridge, MA: Harvard University Press, 1946.

Lowens, Irving. *Music and Musicians in Early America*. NY: W. W. Norton & Co., Inc., 1965.

Marrocco, W. Thomas and Harold Gleason. *Music in America: An Anthology from the Landing of the Pilgrims to the Close of the Civil War: 1620-1865*. NY: W. W. Norton & Co., Inc., 1964.

Martindale, C. and A. Uemura. "Stylistic Evolution in European Music." *Leonardo* 16 (1983): 225-228.

Mendel, Arthur. "Recent Developments in Bach Chronology." *Musical Quarterly* 56 (July 1960): 283-300.

Randal, Don M., ed. *The New Harvard Dictionary of Music*. Cambridge, MA: Belknap Press of Harvard University Press, 1986. S. v. "Editions, Historical" by Harold E. Samuel, 264-276.

Strunk, Oliver, ed. *Source Readings in Music History From Classical Antiquity Through the Romantic Era*. NY: Norton and Co., 1950.

 **Chapter Four**

Ethnomusicology and Qualitative Research in Music

Chapter Four

Ethnomusicology and Qualitative Research in Music

Anthropology in the late 19th century was divided into two different specialties. Those who believed in the importance of nature in human development were physical anthropologists. Those who believed in the importance of nurture in the development of human society were cultural anthropologists. Cultural anthropology, more specifically ethnography, is the foundation for the two music research methodologies known as ethnomusicology and qualitative research.

Ethnography is the descriptive study of a particular human society. It is based almost entirely on fieldwork requiring complete immersion in the culture and everyday life of the people who are the subjects of study. Using a technique known as participant observation, the anthropologist usually selects and cultivates close relationships with individuals, known as informants, who can provide specific information on ritual, kinship, and other aspects of their society. There is a concentration on current events, rather than history.

Two influential cultural anthropologists of the early 20th century were Franz Boas and Bronislaw Malinowski. Boas, a professor of anthropology at Columbia University, and his now-famous students, Margaret Mead and Ruth Benedict, were immersed in the nature-nurture debate which was prominent throughout much of the first half of the century. Darwin's theory of evolution influenced the nature side of the debate while Kant's philosophy of idealism as well as Hegel's logical positivism influenced the nurture side. Boas's view was that culture controlled all human actions since birth. In the words of his student, Ruth Benedict: "The life history of the individual is first and foremost an accommodation to the patterns and standards traditionally handed down in his community; from the moment of his birth the customs into which he is born shape his experience and behavior."[1]

Before the late 19th and early 20th centuries, scholars did not travel to other cultures to study them. Instead they studied artifacts and diaries brought back from exotic lands by missionaries, traders, and adventurers. Malinowski was the first cultural anthropologist to spend long periods of time in a native village to observe the New Guinea culture. He also wrote about how he obtained his data and what the field experience was like. Malinowski believed that a theory of culture had to be grounded in particular human experiences, based on observations, and inductively sought.

Boas's idea was that the culture into which one is born is the context within which the study of the individual must take place. In his view, the culture shapes the individual. This is an important concept for both ethnomusicology and qualitative research in music education. In addition, both methodologies embrace Malinowski's idea of the importance of observation in the field in order to completely understand the culture.

The intellectual roots of both ethnomusicology and qualitative research lie in the idealist movement, in particular the philosophy of Immanual Kant. Kant claimed that immediate experiences and sensory observations are mediated by mind, and that all human intellect is imbued with and limited to human interpretation and representation. Therefore, we cannot assume that we know what things mean to others. Knowledge is a human construction. It starts with sensory experience of external stimuli; these sensations are immediately given meaning by the recipient.[2] "New perceptions mix with old, and with complexes of perception, some of which we call generalizations. Some aspects of knowledge seem generated entirely from internal deliberation, without immediate external stimulation – but no aspects are purely of the external world, devoid of human construction."[3]

ETHNOMUSICOLOGY

Ethnomusicology is the scientific study of music in any world culture or sub-culture in terms of its actual sounds and performance practices, but also in relation to its

---

[1]Ruth Benedict, ***Patterns of Culture*** (NY: The New American Library of World Literature, 1960), 18.

[2]Frederick Coppleston, ***A History of Philosophy***, Introduction to Volume IV and Volume VI (Garden City, NY: Image Books, A Division of Doubleday & Company, Inc.1985), 54-62; Volume VI, Part IV, 180-393.

[3]Liora Bresler and Robert E. Stake, "Qualitative Research Methodology in Music Education," in Richard Colwell, ed., ***Handbook of Research on Music Teaching and Learning*** (NY: Schirmer Books, 1992), 76.

cultural context and in comparison to other cultures. Historically, it has two broad applications: (1) the study of all music outside European art music, including survivals of earlier forms of that tradition in Europe and elsewhere; and (2) the study of all varieties of music found in one locale or region.[4]

Regarding the scope of ethnomusicology, Bruno Nettl explained that the ethnomusicologist deals mainly with three kinds of music. The first category is what he describes as "music of the non-literate societies, those, that is, which have not developed a system of reading and writing their own languages, and which accordingly have a relatively simple way of life."[5] The peoples included in this category are the American Indians, the African Negroes, the Oceanians, the Australian aborigines, and many Asian tribes. A second category is that of the cultures, which have developed music, having a considerable complexity of style, a professional class of musicians, notation, and a theory of music. Cultures representing this category are those of China, Japan, Java, Bali, southwest Asia, India, Iran, and the Arabic-speaking countries. Finally, a third category is folk music, or the music in oral traditions found in those areas, which are dominated by high cultures. Nettl says,

> ...Thus not only Western civilization but also the Asian nations such as Japan, China, etc., have folk music, but of course that of the West has played a much greater role in research. Folk music is generally distinguished from the music of nonliterate societies by having near it a body of cultivated music with which it exchanges material and by which it is profoundly influenced. It is distinguished from the cultivated or urban or fine art music by its dependence on oral tradition rather than on written notation, and, in general, by its existence outside institutions such as church, school, or government. And it has become accepted as part of ethnomusicology by many scholars because its styles, though related to Western art music, are yet sufficiently different to allow it to be classed among the strange, exotic manifestations of music which form the core of ethnomusicology.[6]

The earliest notable examples of attention to non-Western music are the *Dictionaire de musique* (1768) of Jean-Jacques Rousseau, which contains the first serious notation of Oriental and folk melodies, and a four-volume work, by F. Baltazard Solvyns, published in Paris from 1808-1810, under the title, *Les Hindous*.

---

[4]Bruno Nettl, *Reference Materials in Ethnomusicology* (Detroit: Information Service, 1961).

[5]Bruno Nettl, *The Theory and Method in Ethnomusicology* (New York: The Free Press of Glencoe, 1964), 5.

[6]*Ibid,* p. 7.

Mantle Hood points out that the subtleties of Eastern musical cultures - elusive even in the twentieth century - were insurmountable for most musicologists in earlier times. Hood further cautions that while their writings may accurately report some musical details, naive misunderstanding and misinterpretation nevertheless typically characterize them.[7]

Carl Stumpf (1848-1936) and E. M. von Hornbostel (1877-1935) represent the German tradition in ethnomusicology, *vergleichende Musikwissenschaft* (comparative musicology). Taking advantage of the invention of the phonograph in 1877 by the American, Thomas Edison, German ethnologists in distant colonial territories made recordings, which were subsequently studied by psychologists and acousticians of the Berlin Phonogramm-Archiv. Thus, the German interest was in acoustics, psychology, and physiology in an effort to understand principles of tuning systems, scales, and musical instruments, leading to a number of speculative theories. They rarely conducted fieldwork relying instead on the small, recorded samples and other artifacts brought to them by others.[8] German methods were developed under Hornbostel and introduced in the United States, in 1928, by his pupil, George Herzog.[9]

In contrast to the methods of the Berlin School, American scholars based their studies of the American Indians on fieldwork. Because they were afraid that Native American cultures were quickly vanishing, Americans used the phonograph to preserve Indian music. In 1890, the American archaeologist and ethnologist, J. W. Fewkes, made an important advance by using the recently developed phonograph to record the music of the Zuni Indians. He was assisted in the transcription and study of his recordings by Benjamin Ives Gilman who, in 1891, published an article on Zuni melodies in which he confidently asserted that "a collection of phonographic cylinders like that obtained by Dr. Fewkes formed a permanent music museum of primitive music, of which the specimens are comparable, in fidelity of reproduction and for convenience of study, to casts or photographs of sculpture or painting."[10]

At the end of the 19th century in Europe, nationalism stimulated the recording and notating of local folk songs. Béla Bartók (1881-1945) and Zoltán Kodály used the Edison phonograph to record folk songs in Hungary, Romania, and Transylvania. In England, Cecil Sharp (1859-1924) studied traditional English folk song. The

---

[7]Mantle Hood, "Music, the Unknown," In *Musicology*, gen. ed. Richard Schlatter (Westport, CT: Greenwood Press, Publishers, 1963), 218-222.

[8]Helen Myers, ed., *Ethnomusicology: An Introduction* (NY: W. W. Norton & Co., 1992), 4.

[9]Willi Apel, ed., *Harvard Dictionary of Music*, 2nd ed. (Cambridge, Mass.: The Belknap Press of Harvard University Press, 1969), s. v. "Ethnomusicology," by Mantle Hood, 298-300.

[10]Benjamin Ives Gilman, "Zuni Melodies," *Journal of American Ethnology and Archaeology*, ed. J. W. Fewkes, 1 (1891): 65-91.

Australian composer, Percy Grainger (1882-1961), emigrated to England where he recorded Lincolnshire folk song on wax cylinders in 1906 and issued in 1908 the first commercial recording of folk song, with the Gramophone Company, London.[11]

The most prolific collector of Native American music in the early 20th century was Frances Densmore (1867-1957) who was collaborator in the Bureau of American Ethnology at the Smithsonian Institution for 50 years and author of over a dozen monographs. She studied the Chippewa (1910-1913), Teton Sioux (1918), Papago (1929), Choctaw (1943), Seminole (1956), and others.

In the ethnomusicological research done before 1930, emphasis was placed on the collection, analysis, and description of the music itself (further discussion of the development of tools and techniques to notate and transcribe music collected appears later in this chapter). The earliest established phonogram archives began in the United States and collections now at the Library of Congress and major American universities comprise a gigantic museum.[12] An excellent collection of Canadian and Eskimo materials is housed in the National Museum at Ottawa. The oldest European archive was established in Vienna around 1900 and somewhat later, a rich archive was developed in Berlin. During World War II, the valuable collection at Berlin was dispersed, and by the early 1960's, less than one-fifth of the material had been recovered. The remainder is presumed to be in Russian hands.[13]

Since 1950, American ethnomusicologists, like Alan P. Merriam and Mantle Hood, have proposed that the primary understanding of music depends on an understanding of the people's culture. Merriam stressed the importance of fieldwork, that is, the need for the ethnomusicologist to collect his raw material himself and to observe it in its "live" state.[14] In addition, Hood felt it necessary to become bi-musical, or the equivalent of a native musician through totally immersing oneself into foreign cultures as an active musician.[15]

Today, ethnomusicologists have shifted their interests from pieces of music, or musical products, "to processes of musical creation and improvisation – com-

---

[11]Myers, p. 4-5.

[12]Archives of pre-"lp" commercial disc sound recordings now exist in the Library of Congress, the Rodgers and Hammerstein Archives of Recorded Sound of the New York Public Library, the Belfer Audio Laboratory and Archives of Syracuse University, the Stanford Archive of Recorded Sound of Stanford University, and the Yale Collection of Historical Sound Recordings of Yale University. *The Rigler and Deutch Record Microfilm Index* available in each of the archives, contains the photography of approximately 650,000 commercial sound disc recording labels.

[13]Hood, 1963, 228.

[14]Alan P. Merriam, "Ethnomusicology, Discussion and Definition of the Field," *Ethnomusicology*, 4 (1960): 107-114.

[15]Hood, 1963, 277-278; Myers, 8-11.

position and performance – and the focus shifted from collection of repertory to examination of these processes."[16] Fieldwork is considered of utmost importance.

The 1970s and 1980s were decades of fieldwork in societies largely untouched by Western traditions. Myers lists the examples of Anthony Seeger's research among the Suyá, a remote community of the Amazon (1987), Marina Roseman's study of the Temiar of the Malaysian rain forest (1984), Steven Feld's work among the Kaluli people of highland Papua New Guinea (1982, 1988), and Monique Brandily's study of the Teda of Chad (1982).[17]

The increasing interdisciplinary characteristic of ethnomusicological research is evident in the two major periodicals of the field, *Ethnomusicology* and *Yearbook for Traditional Music*. Recent articles describe musics of other cultures in terms drawn from linguistics, interactionism, phenomenological sociology, information theory, structuralism, cybernetics, and semiotics.[18]

QUALITATIVE RESEARCH IN MUSIC EDUCATION

As described earlier in this chapter, qualitative research in music education, like ethnomusicology, has its roots in cultural anthropology and, more specifically, ethnography. A researcher using this methodology enters the world of the people he or she plans to study, gets to know them, gets to be known and trusted by them, and systematically keeps a detailed written record of what is heard and observed. The researcher supplements this material by collecting other data such as school memos and records, newspaper articles, and photographs. The two primary methods of data collection are in-depth interviewing and participant observation.[19]

At the April, 2004 meeting of the Editorial Committee of the *Journal of Research in Music Education*, a sub-committee composed of three eminent researchers (Marie McCarthy, University of Michigan; James Daugherty, University of Kansas; and Wendy Sims, University of Missouri-Columbia) reported the criteria that should be considered when reviewing qualitative studies: describes clearly the purpose and the central research question/phenomenon to be studied; provides evidence that the topic is important; sets study within a theoretical framework; integrates a sufficient number of related studies into various parts of the paper; indicates clearly how sites and individuals are selected; demonstrates rigor in data collection and uses

---

[16]Myers, 12.

[17]Myers, 14.

[18]Myers, 12-15.

[19]Robert C. Bogdan and Sari Knopp Biklen, *Qualitative Research for Education: An Introduction to Theory and Methods,* (Boston: Allyn and Bacon, Inc., 1982).

appropriate protocols; demonstrates that high ethical standards were maintained; employs clear and effective methods of validation; accesses the complexity of the central question/phenomenon; and supports thematic exploration and conclusions with evidence.

METHODS, TOOLS, AND TECHNIQUES

Ethnomusicology has traditionally been concerned with both the music and the social context within which the music occurs. In contrast, qualitative research is more concerned with context than with musical content. This is due to the fact that qualitative research most often occurs in educational situations where the music is for the most part understood, while ethnomusicological research occurs more often where the music is not a part of the Western culture.

Both ethnomusicological and qualitative projects have certain features in common. First is the essential component of fieldwork or the observation of people where they are. Second is the informant or the person who supplies the information. Third are the performances, both musical and cultural (rituals or ceremonies of traditional life), as well as performances staged especially for the researcher (informal conversations, interviews and recording sessions). Fourth, is recording in the form of written fieldnotes, music recordings, cassettes of interviews, still photographs, film and video recordings, and items acquired in the field (books, records, musical instruments).

Analysis of the Music.
As mentioned earlier, in the ethnomusicological research done before 1930, emphasis was placed on the collection, analysis, and description of the music itself. By the end of the nineteenth century, it had become evident that sounds that could not be represented by the notation conceived and developed in the Western world posed a basic problem requiring the help of the physicist and the acoustician. In 1884 and 1885, the British mathematician and philologist, Alexander John Ellis, whose primary interest was phonetics, demonstrated that there were tuning systems and scales built on entirely different principles from those employed in the West, and that these were accepted by non-Western ears as normal and logical. Ellis also developed a method for expressing intervals between pitches in non-Western music in "cents" (e.g., 100 cents = one half step between pitches), so that they could be readily compared to the familiar tempered tuning system of the West.[20] In

---

[20]Alexander John Ellis, "Tonometrical Observations on Some Existing Non-Harmonic Scales,*" Proceedings of the Royal Society of London*, 37 (May-December

a summary of his findings, Ellis stated, "The final conclusion is that the Musical Scale is not one, not 'natural,' nor even founded necessarily on the laws of the constitution of musical sound so beautifully worked out by Helmholtz, but very diverse, very artificial, and very capricious."[21]

Another tool for the analysis of music of other cultures was the Stroboconn, an instrument essential to the study of tuning systems and scales. A panoramic sonic analyzer also was valuable for studies of the quality of sound as it was represented on an oscilloscope and photographed by a Polaroid camera. The most important instrument, the tape recorder, was developed commercially such that multichannel recording on a relatively small, compact machine powered by an easily replenished battery supply was possible.

Fewkes, a pioneer in recording non-Western music, recorded as many versions of songs as possible. These were later transcribed by Gilman, who included notes of mechanical deviation. However, no diacritical markings other than accents were added to the notation. Others, including Hornbostel and Stumpf, advocated that microtonal deviations in pitch and florid melodic embellishments would tend to obscure the principal flow of the tune. Thus, it seems that a number of investigators paid little attention to the refinements and subtleties of the melody.[22]

Others stressed the importance of highly detailed notation. In 1928, Milton Metfessel demonstrated how a specially designed movie camera could record a sound wave photograph that could subsequently be plotted and superimposed over a half-step musical staff and finally summarized in a type of pattern notation. This camera could register musical sounds objectively, showing subtleties of pitch, duration, attack, release, and other details of performance style that resist transcription in Western music. He also pointed out that the striking difference in perception of musical sound by the human ear varies according to conditioning.[23]

A few years later a different approach to graph notation was undertaken by Charles Seeger. Beginning with his first publication on this subject,[24] he continued the development and refinement of a scientific instrument called the melograph. His method of graph notation seemed to have several advantages over phonophotography: the notation was instantaneous; sensitivity to sound of the heated stylus recording on a special type of waxed graph paper could be controlled for as much or as little detail of the pitch line as was desirable; amplitude was reproduced by a

---

1884): 368-385.

[21]Alexander John Ellis, "On the Musical Scales of Various Nations," *Journal of the Society of Arts*, 33 (March 27, 1885): 485.

[22]Hood, 1963, 251.

[23]Milton Metfessel, *Phonophotography in Folk Music* (Chapel Hill: University of North Carolina Press, 1928).

[24]Charles Seeger, "An Instantaneous Music Notator," *Journal of the International Folk Music Council*, 3 (1951): 103-106.

separate stylus but on a graph moving in alignment with the pitch line; a separate one-second time marker aided in the study of rhythm and tempo.[25]

With the advent of digital recording and computerized analysis, examination of the music of other cultures has become quite detailed, so much so that there is almost too much information. Thus, over-analysis might prove to be a problem in processing the musical or cultural intent of the society being studied.

The techniques for the analysis of music may be applied by the qualitative researcher in music education to study the development of children's singing abilities, for example. This may be done using current technology to compare solo singing versus group singing. Also, a qualitative researcher might be interested in studying the influence of the group on children's musical participation.

Case Study Approach.

A case study is a detailed examination of one setting, or one single subject, or one single depository of documents, or one particular event. *Historical* organizational case studies focus on a particular organization over time, tracing the organization's development. Data sources for this type of study are, for example, interviews with people who have been associated with the organization, observations of the present situation, and existing written records. In *observational* case studies, the major data gathering technique is participant observation. These observations might be of a particular place in an organization (a classroom, a teachers' room, the cafeteria), a specific group of people (Navajo Indians, a particular high school choir, a Javanese instrumental ensemble), or some activity (religious ceremony, tribal celebration, courtship). *Life history* case studies can involve over one hundred hours of tape-recorded meetings and over 1,000 pages of transcripts. Some life history interviews attempt to capture the subjects' rendering of their whole lives, from birth to death. Others may be limited to a particular period in the person's life. *Multi-site* case studies have one of two purposes: (1) they are oriented toward developing theory and they usually require many sites or subjects; or (2) they use a constant comparative method whereby the formal analysis begins early in the data collection and is nearly completed by the end of data collection.[26]

Fieldwork.

Both ethnomusicologists and qualitative researchers consider their primary tool to be the "observation of people *in situ*; finding them where they are, staying with them in some role which, while acceptable to them, will allow both intimate observation

---

[25]Charles Seeger, "Toward Universal Music Sound-Writing for Musicology," *Journal of International Folk Music Council*, 9 (1957): 63; *Studies in Musicology, 1935-1977* (Berkeley, California: University of California Press, 1977): 168-81.

[26]Bogdan and Biklen, 58-72.

of certain parts of their behaviour [*sic*], and reporting it in ways useful to social science but not harmful to those observed."[27]

The earliest guides for fieldwork came from anthropology. The fundamental issues were outlined by Bronislaw Malinowski in his ***Argonauts of the Western Pacific***, written in 1922 as a result of his extensive fieldwork in New Guinea. These include inductive versus deductive research strategies, participant observation, the importance of open-mindedness and self-criticism, the linking of apparently unrelated data, the difference between observation and insight, the distinction between the scholar's observations and the ideas expressed by the native informant, the isolation of the anthropological adventure, and the frustration, anxiety and despair of culture shock.[28]

In-depth Interviews with Informants.
"The purpose of interviewing is to find out what is in or on someone else's mind. The purpose of open-ended interviewing is not to put things in someone's mind (for example, the interviewer's preconceived categories for organizing the world) but to access the perspective of the person being interviewed."[29] It is highly recommended that interviews be conducted using a tape recorder. The interviews can then be transcribed to reflect accurately what the subject said in response to the interviewer.

"Interviews must be phrased in culturally expressive terms, taking into account the concepts held in that society using the appropriate words and ways of talking."[30] For example, difficulty in phrasing questions may occur when cultures, like the Navajo, have no word for "music."

Participant Observation.
Using this method, the researcher observes, listens to, and sometimes converses with the subjects in as free and natural an atmosphere as possible. The assumption is that the most important behavior of individuals in groups is a dynamic process of complex interactions and consists of more than a set of facts, statistics, or even discrete incidents. The observer is a participant in the group and his or her observa-

[27]E.C. Hughes, "Introduction: The Place of Field Work in Social Science," In B. H. Junker, ed., ***Field Work: An Introduction to the Social Sciences*** (Chicago: 1960).

[28]Bronislaw Malinowski, ***Argonauts of the Western Pacific*** (New York: 1922).

[29]M.Q. Patton, ***Qualitative Evaluation and Research Methods***, 2nd ed., (Newbury Park, CA: Sage Publications, 1990), 278.

[30]Myers, 37.

tions are those of natural behavior in a real-life setting, free from the constraints of more conventional research procedures.

The observer must know the language of the subjects. While it seems obvious that one must know the language of non-Western cultures before a study of them can begin, it is less obvious that qualitative researchers in educational settings must be prepared for many different languages, both colloquial and formal, that are now present in American schools. In many schools, as many as fourteen or more languages are represented and used. To many researchers the use of American and African American slang by many school children poses a major difficulty in interpretation.

Another assumption of participant observation is that human behavior is influenced by the setting in which it occurs. The researcher must understand that setting and the nature of the social structure and its traditions, values, and norms of behavior. He or she must observe and interpret in terms of how the subjects view the situation, how they interpret their own thoughts, words, and activities as well as those of others in the group.

Participant observers begin without preconceptions and hypotheses. Using inductive logic, they build their hypotheses as they are suggested by observations. They periodically reevaluate them based on new observations, modifying them when they appear to be inconsistent with the evidence.

After returning from each observation, the researcher writes out what happened. These field notes consist of a detailed (often referred to as "thick") description of people, objects, places, events, activities, and conversations. In addition, the researcher will record ideas, strategies, reflections, hunches, as well as note patterns that emerge.[31]

Ethnomusicologists and qualitative researchers must be sensitive to the subjects they are studying. First, it is important to choose a receptive community to study. Take documentation about yourself and your project. Present your human as well as your professional self. If entering a new community it may be advisable to work through a chain of introductions, courtesy visits to government officials, through the bureaucratic hierarchy to the ministry of culture, through the school board, parents, principal, and teachers.

Personal and Official Documents.

The following documents are often used as sources of data: records, reports, printed forms, letters, autobiographies, diaries, compositions, themes or other academic work, books, periodicals, bulletins or catalogues, syllabi, and court decisions. One must bear in mind that data appearing in print are not necessarily trustworthy. Here the techniques of external and internal criticism used by the historian are crucial.

---

[31]Bogdan and Biklen, see pp. 75-83 for an extensive example of field notes.

The documents used in ethnomusicological and qualitative research may serve at least eight purposes. First, the documents may be used to describe prevailing practices or conditions. Second, they may enable the researcher to discover the relative importance of, or interest in, certain topics or problems. Third, fourth, and fifth, in qualitative examinations of educational practices, documents may be used to discover the level of difficulty of presentation in textbooks or in other publications, to evaluate bias, prejudice, or propaganda in textbook presentation, and to analyze types of errors in students' work. The final three purposes are historical in nature and include the use of documents to analyze the use of symbols representing persons, political parties or institutions, countries, or points of view; to identify the literary style, concepts, or beliefs of a writer; and to explain the possible causal factors related to some outcome, action, or event.[32]

Photography and Videography.
Photographs are those taken by the researcher and those provided by the informants. The researcher must be careful to get permission of the subjects to be photographed. Some cultures forbid photography because they believe it "steals the soul." Legal issues come into play when the researcher wishes to videotape school children in the classroom. Permission must always be requested and granted before these techniques may be used.

Coding Analysis of Data.
Particular research questions and concerns, theoretical approaches, and the academic disciplines suggest particular coding schemes. Bogdan and Biklen suggest some coding families that might be useful. *Setting/context codes* may be used for descriptive literature produced about the subject or setting and general statements people make describing the setting or the subject. *Definition of the situation* codes are used for data that tells how the subjects define the setting or particular topics and what is important to them. *Process* codes point to time periods, stages, phases, passages, steps, careers, and chronology. *Activity* codes are directed at regularly occurring kinds of behavior. *Relationship and social structure* codes direct one to cliques, friendships, romances, coalitions, enemies, and mentors/students.[33]

Some scholars in ethnomusicology code each page according to the 888 topics listed in the *Outline of Cultural Materials* by Murdock. For music, Murdock gives: 53: Fine Arts (533 – music, 534 – musical instruments, 535 – dancing, 536 - drama, 537 – oratory); 54: Entertainment (545 – musical and theatrical productions, 547

---

[32]John W. Best and James V. Kahn, *Research in Education* (Allyn & Bacon, 1998), 247-248.

[33]Bogdan and Biklen, 156-170.

– nightclubs and cabarets, 549 – art and recreational supplies industries). Myers states that, "The ethnomusicologist will need to devise a more detailed system suited to musicological research."[34]

EXAMPLES OF ETHNOMUSICOLOGICAL RESEARCH

For examples of ethnomusicological research, the most recent issues of the journal, *Ethnomusicology*, have been examined. The studies selected represent the wide diversity of the field but there is by no means an attempt to be inclusive of every type of study present in this journal. Bruno Nettl, former editor of the journal, says,

> . . . as musical culture changed, so did the attitude of ethnomusicologists. If a hundred (or fifty) years ago we looked for the 'traditional,' it's now conventional wisdom that traditions are invented. While we then sought to study the exotic and the 'other,' we now see that the exotic is us, and 'otherness' difficult. Once looking at music as separable and trivial, we now see it as central in culture. Ridiculed as a profession and even feared in the old days, we now find ourselves in music departments everywhere, at conferences of music history and theory, of composers, of anthropologists, historians, literary critics, political activists; and in the publications of religious or environmental or biological or gender studies, of performance analysis, archeology, narratology, popular culture, music education.[35]

The studies selected have the two characteristics which separate ethnomusicology from qualitative research: first, they have non-western musical cultures as their topics; and second, they are more concerned with the musical product than with the social context within which that product occurs. The studies are: "The Social Meanings of Modal Practices: Status, Gender, History, and Pathet in Central

---

[34]Myers, 39.

[35]Bruno Nettl, "From the Editor," *Ethnomusicology*, 44, no. 3 (Winter 2000): n.p.

Javanese Music" by Marc Perlman;[36] and "Bridging Contexts, Transforming Music: The Case of Elementary School Teacher Chihara Yoshio" by Joanna T. Pecore.[37]

Perlman begins his article with the assumption that social meanings are often encoded in easily perceptible musical features such as instrumentation, vocal quality, or ornamentation. For example, particular instruments may be associated with women and the amount or type of melodic embellishment used may serve as an index of gender, style lineage, generation, or geographical region. He posits that social meanings are not projected only by such relatively accessible musical features; they can also be conveyed through subtle differences in musical technique.

The purpose of Perlman's article is to show how certain variant modal practices in the music of the Central Javanese *gamelan* orchestra are associated with two important social distinctions in Javanese culture: center/periphery (court/village) and male/female. He argues that the variation is patterned, and arises from the interaction of the two musical principles, one "horizontal" and one "vertical," that govern multipart texture. Furthermore, the link between the interaction of these two principles and the social categories of marginality and gender is a product of colonial-era processes of change and diffusion.

His subject is the system of *pathet* ("mode") in Central Javanese *gamelan* music, as practiced in the court city of Surakarta and its environs. Perlman says,

> In this style, modal principles are expressed by the quasi-improvisational 'elaborating' parts, in particular by the *gendér barung*, a fourteen-keyed metallophone. The *gendér* part is governed by *pathet* constraints, but also must preserve a certain degree of unison with other melodic parts. The 'horizontal' priorities of *pathet* are in delicate balance with the 'vertical' priorities of interpart relations. The precise adjustment of this equilibrium carries social meaning. The balance needs to be tipped only slightly to one side (the privileging of *pathet*) to signify the mainstream (court) style. Tipped slightly to the other side (the privileging of unison), it evokes two more-or-less subordinate social categories: the peripheral (geographically marginal) and the female.[38]

---

[36]Marc Perlman, "The Social Meanings of Modal Practices: Status, Gender, History, and Pathet in Central Javanese Music," *Ethnomusicology* 42, no. 1 (Winter 1998): 45-80.

[37]Joanna T. Pecore, "Bridging Contexts, Transforming Music: The Case of Elementary School Teacher Chihara Yoshio," *Ethnomusicology*, 44, No. 1 (Winter 2000): 120–136.

[38]Perlman, 46.

He then provides a description of Central Javanese *pathet* that comes from the most prestigious style of gamelan music, that which is associated with the royal courts, and which is now transmitted through government conservatories staffed by former court musicians and their students. Scholars of Javanese music have neglected other styles of *gendér* playing such as "female" and "village." The court style is very much a male domain. It is notable that virtually the only instrument a woman could play in an otherwise all-male group has been the *gendér*.

Perlman continues with an effort to explain rather complex Javanese gender ideology and the court/village axis. The gender ideology associates men with order, control, refinement, learned knowledge; it associates women with uncontrollable disorder, untaught knowledge, and expressed emotions. Thus, the Javanese understanding of *pathet* usage in female *gendér* playing is that women lack knowledge of *pathet* because their "feelings" are in opposition to the "orderliness" of the *pathet*.

Regarding the court/village axis, Perlman explains that for Javanese musicians, the court is the source of musical value, the place of order and standards. In contrast, the village is the place of license and eccentricity. The rural/female *gendér* styles violate the urban rules of *pathet*. He then provides an extensive discussion of how this occurs.

Pecore's study is a case study that is an overview of the work of elementary school teacher, Chihara Yoshio. It explores the "dynamic interplay among historical events, perceptions of national and ethnic boundaries, and processes of musical transmission."[39] Specifically, Mr. Chihara's work is presented in conjunction with a history of the role and position of traditional music in Japan's public schools including the following: a brief description of the issues involved in bridging the contexts of the *iemoto* (headmaster) system of transmission for traditional music and Japan's public education; an overview of the *Nihonjinron* phenomenon that flourished during the 1970s; and a brief introduction to the activities of public school music teachers who were involved in presenting traditional music at that time.

Pecore states that the content of public school music education in Japan continues to be dominated by Western music while only a fraction of the core curriculum is devoted to traditional Japanese music. The *iemoto* system is the traditional pattern of passing down arts in Japan from one generation to the next. It consists of distinct schools led by the *iemoto*, or grand master, and is supported by various levels of students or apprentices. The word, *iemoto*, refers to two things: the hierarchical system of master-disciple relations and the individual who heads the system. Because notation was not used in traditional Japan, masters train apprentices through the senses rather than the intellect. Essentially, the *iemoto* passes "secrets" on to his or her disciples. Pecore shares her own experiences as a participant in the *iemoto* system demonstrating that loyalty to the master is expressed in a number of ways, including economic commitment which can be a very high cost. However,

---

[39]Pecore, 120.

any money received by the *iemoto* is of the nature of an honorarium given in thanks for an invaluable treasure received.

The *iemoto* system reflected the feudal society that was in existence at the time it flourished, during the period, 1603-1868. This, according to Pecore, is an explanation for traditional Japanese music's omission from the school curriculum: there is an inherent dissonance between the traditional music world, governed by a feudal system, and the principles of democracy, which form the basis of the modern education system.

The *Nihonjinrom* phenomenon has occurred since the late 1960s and represents a public reevaluation of the very essence of "Japaneseness" by the Japanese people as a whole. There was great interest in returning to tradition in Japan. Many music teachers became concerned with the preservation and development of traditional Japanese music. Pecore illustrates this concern by detailing the Japanese music activities of Mr. Chihara including his study of the *koto* and his founding of the Tokyo Children's Japanese Music Ensemble, and his philosophy of music teaching. He believed that through the enjoyment of Japanese music, Japanese students could get in touch with their true cultural identity.

The inclusion of Japanese music in the school curriculum did not mean the adoption of the *iemoto* system. Instead, music teachers in the schools offered students a variety of genres using methodology suitable for the group, rather than individual, context. Also, rather than spend years within the *iemoto* system, school music teachers gain their knowledge from manuals, other classroom teachers, and from a limited number of lessons with a professional teacher.

As can be seen in the brief summaries above, Perlman's study is one of a particular non-Western style of music. His article focuses on this style, including analysis of the music itself, and places the music in a social context. Pecore's study uses the details of a particular person's life to show the impact of a movement toward the inclusion of Japanese traditional music in the schools of Japan. Her study is enriched by her own participation in the *iemoto* system and her interviews with students and teachers in Japan's public schools. Both studies clearly show the characteristics of ethnomusicological research: they are about non-Western music; and they focus on the music in social context.

EXAMPLES OF QUALITATIVE RESEARCH

Qualitative research in music education is relatively new with few articles published in the major journals of the field. The articles selected were chosen from the ***Journal of Research in Music Education.*** They represent the primary interest of qualitative researchers in the social contexts of music teaching. They are: "The Development of Teaching Cases for Instrumental Music Methods Courses" by

Colleen M. Conway;[40] and "Behavioral Characteristics and Instructional Patterns of Selected Music Teachers" by Catherine Hendel.[41]

The purpose of Conway's study was to develop teaching cases for instrumental music education methods courses through analysis of current teaching practice. She documented the daily interactions, decision-making skills, and use of pedagogical content knowledge of four experienced instrumental music teachers (one elementary, two middle schools, and one high school teacher). She gathered data through observations and interviews. These data were coded into teaching case categories: curricula and objectives, program administration, recruitment and balanced instrumentation, scheduling, choosing literature, classroom management in rehearsals, motivation, assessment and grading, musicianship, and rapport with students.

Conway visited each of the three school sites for three consecutive days. The nine days included 54 hours of classroom observations, documentation of 565 teacher decisions, and 20 hours of interviews. Participant observation provided an additional perspective. She documented teacher interactions during ensemble rehearsals with an audiotape recorder while participating in the ensemble. At the end of each day, observation notes were reviewed, interview tapes were listened to, and interview questions were prepared for the next day.

The use of nonparticipant and participant observations of large and small groups plus the use of structured and unstructured interviews represented data triangulation for Conway. Triangulation is the viewing of a phenomenon through multiple lenses. It is considered an important way to address issues of validity.

The purpose of Hendel's study was to identify what good elementary music teachers do by: (a) identifying factors that contribute to effective music teaching as defined by exemplary behaviors of recognized music specialists; (b) examining the relationship of teacher-defined instructional values, which emerge through qualitative study to operationally defined characteristics of effective music instruction resulting from quantitative research; and (c) exploring the possibility that qualitative and quantitative methods of research might be complementary. She observed, audio- and videotaped, and interviewed nine experienced, elementary music specialists from three regions of the United States. In addition, she reviewed documents such as copies of lesson plans for the sessions observed and school and district curriculum guides.

---

[40]Colleen M. Conway, "The Development of Teaching Cases for Instrumental Music Methods Courses," *Journal of Research in Music Education*, 47, No. 4 (1999): 343-356.

[41]Catherine Hendel, "Behavioral Characteristics and Instructional Patterns of Selected Music Teachers," *Journal of Research in Music Education*, 43 (1995): 182-203.

Qualitative techniques included focussed and refined observations, coding analysis of field notes resulting from observations and interviews, interviews with students and teachers, and analysis of documents. These components were used in triangulation to validate each portion of the study.

Quantitative techniques were then used to analyze both audio- and videotapes. Using observation forms developed in previous research, personality components of teaching (eye contact, body movement, gestures, facial expressions, speech characteristics), components of sequential patterns in teaching (the sequential order of task presentation, student responses, and teacher reinforcement), the rate and distribution of instruction time, teaching methods, and equipment and materials used were measured or counted. Reliability for quantitative measures was computed by comparing the observations of the researcher with an independent observer and counting the number of agreements and disagreements between them. Thus, it was possible to demonstrate a percentage of agreement that was at a high level, ranging from 94% to 98% for all of the observation forms and coding of the scripted sequential patterns.

Both Conway's and Hendel's studies are reductions of their dissertations for publication in a journal.[42] It is unfortunate that these reductions cannot include the thick richness of qualitative descriptions found in their dissertations due to the space limitations of the *Journal*. For example, Hendel's dissertation includes eleven portraits, one for each of the nine teachers, one for documents and support systems, and one for student and teacher perspectives. Here, in some sixty-two pages, is where all the data, qualitative and quantitative, are discussed to characterize the teaching context.

ISSUES OF RELIABILITY AND VALIDITY

Evaluation of sources is the chief problem of ethnomusicologists and qualitative researchers. Extensive fieldwork requires all the bibliographical preparation outlined in Chapter 1, The Art of Bibliographical Control. Because the evidence gathered might be oral and not written, the collaborative efforts of anthropologists, linguists, and other experts will be invaluable to the ethnomusicologist. Often there are as many versions of a song as there are those who sing or play it. Subtleties of interpretation and meaning may escape one who has not experienced a culture over a long time period. Because of these unique problems, interdisciplinary training is often necessary to develop the expertise needed to accomplish scholarly control of data collected on site.

---

[42]Conway's dissertation was accepted at Teachers College, Columbia University in 1997; Hendel's dissertation was accepted at Louisiana State University in 1993.

An example of this may be seen in the great controversy initiated by Derek Freeman on the work of Margaret Mead in Samoa. Mead's fieldwork in Samoa during the mid-1920s was significant in that it was her first experience as a cultural anthropologist and that it was highly unusual for women to be allowed to do fieldwork in remote areas of the world.

Freeman contends that for many attendant circumstances her study that resulted in the book, *Coming of Age in Samoa*,[43] should be invalidated. Chief among his reasons is that two of her female informants were joking with her when she was questioning them about sexual behavior. Joking is a customary behavior of which Mead had quite inadequate knowledge according to Freeman. Other circumstances noted by Freeman are noted in the following excerpt from his book:

> First, she had brought with her to Samoa a fervent belief in the ideology . . . that human behavior is determined by cultural patterns. Second, her time-consuming involvement in 'doing ethnology' for the Bishop Museum had created such a severe crisis for her official research on adolescent behavior that on Ofu, she was forced to turn to [her female informants] in the hope of finding a cultural pattern that would enable her to solve . . . the problem Boas [her major professor for her dissertation] required her to investigate. Third, she had also brought with her . . . the quite false preconception . . . that she would find that premarital promiscuity was the ruling cultural pattern in Samoa. Fourth, as one of Franz Boas's dedicated followers, she wanted. . . to reach a conclusion that would gratify him and that he would find acceptable.[44]

Freeman's accusation of this legend of cultural anthropology became widely known in an article published on the front page of the *New York Times*, January 31, 1983, where it was characterized as the greatest controversy in the history of anthropology. Before her death, in 1978, she admitted that she might be proven wrong but rejected any revision of her work declaring that it must remain exactly as written. This shows her commitment to what she observed when she observed it.

It is important to note here that all research is open to disagreement and discussions of truth, reliability, and validity. Philosophical inquiry depends on the insight provided in prior assumptions. Historiography depends on decisions regarding plausibility, probability, and certainty. Qualitative research depends on triangulation techniques as seen through the eyes of the researcher. As you will see in later

---

[43]Margaret Mead, *Coming of Age in Samoa* (NY: William Morrow and Company., 1928).

[44]Derek Freeman, *The Fateful Hoaxing of Margaret Mead: A Historical Analysis of Her Samoan Research* (Boulder, CO: Westview Press, 1999),14.

chapters, quantitative research depends not only on the number of events actually observed, but also on the accuracy of the objective measures selected.

SUMMARY

This chapter is about two forms of research, ethnomusicology and qualitative research that have much in common. Both use the methods and techniques of cultural anthropology. They share intellectual roots in the philosophy of Immanual Kant that proposes that all human intellect is imbued with and limited to human interpretation and representation. Both have fieldwork as an essential component in which there are specific informants or persons who supply information. Data from this fieldwork includes recordings of musical and cultural performances, written field notes, recordings of interviews, still photographs, film and video recordings, and items acquired in the field (books, documents, musical instruments).

Although ethnomusicology is the traditionally the study of music in non-Western cultures, current scholars also study music within Western cultures. While ethno-musicologists are primarily interested in the music produced by cultures, qualita-tive researchers are more interested in the social contexts within which that music occurs.

As American scholarship in music progresses in the 21st century, we will begin to see less delineation between the methods of research. Instead, scholars are beginning to use the techniques of many research methodologies in an effort to in-crease the validity and reliability of their findings. The techniques of philosophical questioning, the application of the historiographer's internal and external criticism, and the qualitative ideas of holistic examination are invaluable to music scholars, young and old alike.

RESEARCH APPLICATIONS

1. Name ten possible ethnomusicological projects, which might be conducted in the United States.
2. Select one complete project, either a book or a dissertation, using ethnomusicological or qualitative methodologies. Read it in its entirety. Write a summary detailing the procedures and results of the research.

BIBLIOGRAPHY

Apel, Willi, ed. *Harvard Dictionary of Music*. 2nd ed. Cambridge, Mass: The Belknap Press of Harvard University Press, 1970. S.v. "Ethnomusicology" by Mantle Hood, 298-300.

Benedict, Ruth. *Patterns of Culture*. NY: The New American Library of World Literature, 1960).

Best, John W. and James V. Kahn. *Research in Education*. Boston: Allyn & Bacon, 1998.

Bogdan, Robert C. and Sari Knopp Biklen. *Qualitative Research for Education: An Introduction to Theory and Methods.* Boston: Allyn and Bacon, Inc., 1982.

Bresler, Liora and Robert E. Stake. "Qualitative Research Methodology in Music Education." In Richard Colwell, ed., *Handbook of Research on Music Teaching and Learning.* NY: Schirmer Books, 1992, 75-90.

Coppleston, Frederick. *A History of Philosophy*. Volumes IV and VI. Garden City, NY: Image Books, A Division of Doubleday & Company, Inc.

Denzin, N. K. and Y. S. Lincoln, Eds. *Handbook of Qualitative Research*. Thousand Oaks, CA: Sage, 1994.

Ellis, Alexander John. "On the Musical Scales of Various Nations." *Journal of the Society of Arts* 33 (March 27, 1885): 485.

——————. "Tonometrical Observations on Some Existing Non-Harmonic Scales." *Proceedings of the Royal Society of London* 37 (May-December 1884): 368-385.

Erickson, F. "Qualitative Methods in Research on Teaching." In Merlin C. Wittrock, ed., *Handbook on Teaching*, 3rd ed. New York: Macmillan, 1986.

Freeman, Derek. *The Fateful Hoaxing of Margaret Mead: A Historical Analysis of Her Samoan Research.* Boulder, CO: Westview Press, 1999.

Gilman, Benjamin Ives. "Zuni Melodies." *Journal of American Ethnology and Archaelogy*, ed. J. W. Fewkes 1 (1891): 65-91.

Glaser, G. A., and A. L. Strauss. *The Discovery of Grounded Theory: Strategies for Qualitative Research*. Chicago: Aldine, 1967.

Harrison, F. L. *Time, Place, and Music, an Anthology of Ethnomusicological Observation*. Amsterdam: Frits Knuf, 1973.

Hendel, Catherine. "Behavioral Characteristics and Instructional Patterns of Selected Music Teachers." *Journal of Research in Music Education*, 43 (1995): 182-203.

Hitchcock, H. Wiley and Stanley Sadie, eds. *The New Grove Dictionary of American Music*. S. v. "Ethnomusicology" by Helen Myers, v. 2, 58-62.

Hood, Mantle. *The Ethnomusicologist*. Kent, Oh: Kent State University Press, 1985.

Hood, Mantle. "Music, the Unknown." In *Musicology*, pp. 215-326. Humanistic Scholarship in America Series: The Princeton Studies, Gen. ed. Richard Schlatter. Englewood Cliffs, NJ: Prentice Hall, 1963; reprint ed., Westport, Conn. Greenwood Press, Publishers, 1974.

Hughes, E.C. "Introduction: The Place of Field Work in Social Science." In B. H. Junker, ed., *Field Work: An Introduction to the Social Sciences*. Chicago: 1960.

Krueger, P. J. "Ethnographic Research Methodology in Music Education." *Journal of Research in Music Education*, 35 (1987): 69-77.

Kunst, Jaap. *Ethnomusicology*. The Hague: Martinus Nijhoff, 1959.

Malinowski, B. *Argonauts of the Western Pacific*. NY: 1922.

Mead, Margaret. *Blackberry Winter: My Earlier Years.* NY: Kodansha International, 1995.

──────────. *Coming of Age in Samoa: A Psychological Study of Primitive Youth for Western Civilisation*. NY: William Morrow and Company, Inc., 1961.

Merriam, Alan. *The Anthropology of Music*. Evanston, IL: Northwestern University Press, 1964.

──────────. "Ethnomusicology, Discussion And Definition Of The Field." *Ethnomusicology*, 4 (1960), 107-114.

Metfessel, Milton. *Phonophotography in Folk Music*. Chapel Hill, NC: University of North Carolina Press, 1928.

Miles, M. B. and A. M. Huberman. *Qualitative Data Analysis: A Sourcebook of New Methods.* Beverly Hills, CA: Sage, 1984.

Mishler, E. G. *Research Interviewing*. Cambridge: Harvard University Press, 1986.

Myers, Helen, ed. *Ethnomusicology: An Introduction*. New York: W. W. Norton & Company, 1992.

Nettl, Bruno. *Folk and Traditional Music of the Western Continents*. Englewood Cliffs, NJ: Prentice-Hall, Inc., 1973.

──────────. *Music in Primitive Culture*. Cambridge, MA: Harvard University Press, 1956.

──────────. *Reference Materials in Ethnomusicology*. Detroit: Information Service, 1961.

──────────. *Theory and Method in Ethnomusicology*. NY: The Free Press of Glencoe, 1964.

Nettl, Bruno and Philip V. Bohlman. *Comparative Musicology and Anthropology of Music*. Chicago: The University of Chicago Press, 1991.

Patton, M. Q. *Qualitative Evaluation and Research Methods*, 2nd ed. Newbury Park, CA: Sage Publications, 1990.

Pecore, Joanna T. "Bridging Contexts, Transforming Music: The Case of Elementary School Teacher Chihara Yoshio." *Ethnomusicology*, 44, No. 1 (Winter 2000): 120-136.

Perlman, Marc. "The Social Meanings of Modal Practices: Status, Gender, History, and Pathet in Central Javanese Music." *Ethnomusicology*, 42, no. 1 (Winter 1998): 45-80.

Randal, Don M., ed. *The New Harvard Dictionary of Music*. Cambridge, MA: Belknap Press of Harvard University Press, 1986.. S. v. "Ethnomusicology" by Bruno Nettl, 291-293.

Sachs, Curt. "The Lore of Non-Western Music." *In Some Aspects of Musicology*, Eds. Arthur Mendel, Curt Sachs, and Carroll C. Pratt. NY: Liberal Arts Press,1957, 19-48.

Sadie, Stanley, ed. *The New Grove Dictionary of Music and Musicians*. 1980. S. v. "Ethnomusicology" by Barbara Krader, v. 6, 275-282.

Seeger, Charles. "An Instantaneous Music Notator." *Journal of the International Folk Music Council* 3 (1951): 103-106.

————————. "On the Moods of a Musico-Logic." *Journal of the American Musicological Society*, XIII (1960): 224-61.

————————. "Toward Universal Music Sound-Writing for Musicology." *Journal of International Folk Music Council* 9 (1957): 63.

Vansina, Jan. *Oral Tradition as History*. Madison, WN: The University of Wisconsin Press, 1985.

 **Chapter Five**

Quantitative Research: Describing Musical Events and Behavior

Chapter Five

Quantitative Research: Describing Musical Events and Behavior

As we consider all aspects of a musical score, of musical historiography, of philosophical pronouncements regarding the art of music, we may also stretch our thinking toward an actualization or realization of these ideas. How have musicians translated these ideas into musical behaviors? If music is an active as opposed to a passive art, how might we analyze that activity? How might we describe our musical interactions with musical elements?

HISTORICAL BACKGROUND FOR QUANTITATIVE RESEARCH

In 1876, G. T. Fechner proposed an approach to aesthetics "from below," or from observation of particular phenomena, rather than "from above," or by deduction from metaphysical assumptions.[1] Thus, experimental aesthetics, or the empirical study of aesthetics was born. This approach emphasizes the statistical study of individual aesthetic preferences for standardized types of objects, such as rectangles of certain sizes. Earlier, the German physicist, Hermann von Helmholtz, published what is regarded as the first music psychology text, *On the Sensations of Tone as a*

---

[1]G. T. Fechner, *Vorschule der Ästhetik*, 1876.

Physiological Basis for the Theory of Music.[2] This was followed by two volumes entitled, *Tonpsychologie*, by Carl Stumpf.[3]

In the United States, early quantitative research by music psychologist, Carl Seashore, combined the scientific, empirical research techniques of psychology and sociology with the subject matter of music.[4] The publication of Seashore's research, the advent of the first two music research journals to include quantitative research (*Journal of Music Therapy* and *Journal of Research in Music Education*), Robert Lundin's *Objective Psychology of Music*,[5] Paul Farnsworth's, *The Social Psychology of Music*,[6] and the work of Clifford Madsen and his associates[7] are milestones representing a broadening of the meaning of American musical scholarship. While there have been other contributions, these have been the most influential in terms of volume of research, text adoptions in higher education, and numbers of students who continue their efforts in research.

In Seashore's work there was a strong hereditarian bias, a belief in innate musical talent, and therefore a research thrust toward measuring musical "aptitudes." His *Psychology of Music* (1938) described experimental studies in vibrato that were conducted in his own laboratory at the University of Iowa. In 1940, Max Schoen, one of Seashore's students, published *The Psychology of Music*, a description of experimental findings through the 1930's.

———————

[2]Hermann von Helmholtz, *On the Sensations of Tone as a Physiological Basis for the Theory of Music*, trans. A. J. Ellis (New York: Dover, 1954). Originally published, 1862.

[3]Carl Stumpf, *Tonpsychologie*, v. 1 and 2 (Leipzig: Hirzel, 1883 and 1890).

[4]Carl Seashore, "Psychology in Music: The Role of Experimental Psychology in the Science and Art of Music," *Musical Quarterly*, XVI (1930): 229-237; *Psychology of Music* (New York: McGraw-Hill Book Co., Inc., 1938); *The Psychology of Musical Talent*, XVI (New York: Silver Burdett, 1919).

[5]Robert W. Lundin, *An Objective Psychology of Music* (New York: Ronald Press, 1953). 2nd ed., 1967.

[6]Paul R. Farnsworth, *The Social Psychology of Music* (Ames, Iowa: The Iowa State University Press, 1969).

[7]Clifford K. Madsen, R. Douglas Greer, and Charles H. Madsen, Jr., Eds. *Research in Music Behavior* (New York: Teachers College Press, Columbia University, 1975); Clifford K. Madsen and Charles H. Madsen, *Experimental Research in Music* (Raleigh, N.C.: Contemporary Publishing Co., 1978); Clifford K. Madsen and Randall S. Moore, *Experimental Research in Music: Workbook in Design and Statistical Tests*, rev. ed. (Raleigh, N. C.: Contemporary Publishing Co., 1978); Clifford K. Madsen and Carol A. Prickett, Eds. *Applications of Research in Music Behavior* (Tuscaloosa, AL: University of Alabama Press, 1987).

It was not until thirteen years later that another American text was published. Robert Lundin's *Objective Psychology of Music* (1953)[8] combined a cultural and relativistic outlook with a behavioral orientation. Along these lines, Farnsworth in his *Social Psychology of Music* (1969)[9] put forth the idea that music is always within some cultural context, and therefore musicians and lay persons are influenced not so much by genetic predisposition as by the culture which nurtures and shapes the music they perform, compose, and consume. Farnsworth's text remained the text of choice for a large number of universities until publication ceased.

The *Journal of Music Therapy* and the *Journal of Research in Music Education*, which began in 1952 and 1953, respectively, have made significant contributions to our scientific knowledge of how people interact with music. Music therapy is a professional field for which the goals are to teach the subject matter of music and to use music to stimulate learning in other areas. Jellison in her review of the *Journal of Music Therapy* reported an increase in the number of experimental studies published.[10] A later review by Gilbert showed another increase in the number of quantitative studies and further reported an increase in the proportion of studies focusing upon pedagogical and physical/perceptual bases for music research.[11] The most recent review of the *Journal* by Codding replicated the results reported by Jellison and Gilbert.[12]

Although music education is not a new profession, research in music education may be regarded as in its infancy. In a content analysis of the *Journal of Research in Music Education*, Yarbrough noted the predominance of quantitative research (with more descriptive research than experimental or behavioral), but also a strong presence of historical articles.[13] In both journals, published research demonstrates a primary interest in the interaction between music and people. Music therapists appear to be more action oriented in their research approaches while music educa-

---

[8]Robert W. Lundin, *An Objective Psychology of Music* (New York: Ronald Press, 1953). 2nd ed., 1967.

[9]Paul R. Farnsworth, *The Social Psychology of Music*, (New York: Holt, Rinehart, Winston, 1958), 2nd ed. (Ames, IA: Iowa State University Press, 1969).

[10]Judith A. Jellison, "The Frequency and General Mode of Inquiry of Research in Music Therapy, 1952-1972," *Bulletin of the Council for Research in Music Education*, 35 (Winter, 1973): 1-8.

[11]Janet Perkins Gilbert, "Published Research in Music Therapy, 1973-1978: Content, Focus, and Implications for Future Research," *Journal of Music Therapy*, XIV (Fall, 1979): 102-110.

[12]Peggy A. Codding, "A Content Analysis of the *Journal of Music Therapy*, 1977-85," *Journal of Music Therapy*, XXIV (Winter, 1987): 195-202.

[13]Cornelia Yarbrough, "A Content Analysis of the *Journal of Research in Music Education*, 1953-1983," *Journal of Research in Music Education*, 32 (1984): 213-222.

tors are concerned with basic and applied experimental studies as well as reflective, historical research.

More recently, the body of quantitative studies in music has been dramatically increasing through the efforts of musicians such as Clifford Madsen and psychologists such as Diana Deutsch. Madsen, who was trained as both a musician and a psychologist, is a strong advocate of strict, controlled experimental and quasi-experimental approaches to the study of observable musical behavior. He and his associates would likely lean toward the role of individuals' environments in determining the level of musicianship they might achieve. Deutsch, a cognitive psychologist, is more interested in mental schemata that control the perception of musical elements.

Thus, there appears to be a continuum proceeding from three different philosophical biases, heredity, social or cultural, and behavioral or environmental. Historically, these three biases may be seen as two psychological viewpoints that polarized music researchers and thus stimulated two quite different streams of quantitative research. One viewpoint is that of the behavioral psychologist who studies and interprets musical phenomena and behaviors in light of environmental influences, learning and achievement, and nurturing aspects. The other viewpoint is that of the cognitive psychologist who studies and interprets musical knowledge, structures, and processes through which music in its various forms may be conceptually organized and remembered.

Regardless of viewpoint, it would seem important to examine the considerable body of research from both perspectives, with attention to musical behaviors within musical settings and using a technical as well as aesthetic approach. Quantitative research in the future will likely continue to focus attention on the perception, discrimination, preference, performance, and teaching of selected musical phenomena. For example, computer searches will assist researchers in locating information regarding the perception of pitch, dynamics, tempo, style, and timbre. As expertise in the more obvious relationships among these phenomena is developed and as progress in these areas continues to be made, it will become necessary to consider interactions among musical phenomena (pitch and dynamics, tempo and style, dynamics and timbre), as well as interactions among musical behaviors (perception and preference, performance and preference, preference and teaching).

QUANTITATIVE RESEARCH AS PROCESS

Quantitative research, unlike the methodologies discussed earlier in this book, is a process whereby a particular musical phenomenon is operationally defined. This definition is then further subdivided and research proceeds by designing and implementing a series of studies regarding the phenomenon. No one study suffices in the search for truth. Sometimes a single researcher conducts a series of research studies; other times groups of researchers work on a particular problem. Each study builds upon the results of previous research.

A series of research studies concerning tempo perceptions, performances and preferences provides an illustration of this. Research in tempo discrimination has examined perception of gradual increases and decreases in tempos, in both metronomical and musical excerpts, and discrimination of tempos of musical excerpts in comparison with one another (slower than, faster than, or the same tempo). Results have demonstrated that both musicians and non-musicians perceived decreases in the tempos of metronomic beats better than increases;[14] musicians perceived an increase in the tempo of a musical excerpt by J. S. Bach more accurately than a tempo decrease, but did not perceive similarly when listening to three other compositions of differing styles and tempos;[15] and string students perceived tempo increases more accurately than decreases.[16] Thus, perception of tempo has been studied with mixed results through differing media in the context of awareness of change in tempo across time.

Using different procedures in which musical examples were presented to subjects in three or more discrete tempos (e.g., slow, moderate, fast) Wapnick concluded that subjects were better at discriminating fast tempos than slow or moderate ones.[17] When each of several musical excerpts was presented to subjects in unaltered versus faster or slower tempos, faster tempos were more correctly identified than slower ones. One of the conclusions of these studies was that the rhythmic characteristics of the musical excerpts might be the strongest influential factor in subjects' ability to discriminate tempo changes.[18] In an attempt to isolate the effect of musical

[14]Terry L. Kuhn, "Discrimination of Modulated Beat Tempo by Professional Musicians," *Journal of Research in Music Education*, 22 (1974): 270-277; Clifford K. Madsen, "Modulated Beat Discrimination Among Musicians and Non-Musicians," *Journal of Research in Music Education*, 27 (1979): 57-67.

[15]Cecelia C. Wang, "Discrimination of Modulated Music Tempo by Music Majors," *Journal of Research in Music Education*, 31 (1983): 49-55.

[16]Cecelia C. Wang and Rita S. Salzberg, "Discrimination of Modulated Music Tempo by String Students," *Journal of Research in Music Education*, 32 (1984): 123-131.

[17]Joel Wapnick, "The Perception of Musical and Metronomic Tempo Change in Musicians," *Psychology of Music*, 8 (1980): 3-12.

[18]John M. Geringer and Clifford K. Madsen, " Pitch and Tempo Discrimination in Recorded Orchestral Music Among Musicians and Non-Musicians," *Journal of Research in Music Education*, 32 (1984): 195-204; John M. Geringer and Clifford K. Madsen, "Pitch and Tempo Preferences in Recorded Popular Music," In Clifford K. Madsen and Carol A. Prickett, eds. *Applications of Research in Music Behavior* (Tuscaloosa, AL: University of Alabama Press, 1987), 3-11; Clifford K.

excerpts, Yarbrough selected two musical excerpts by Mozart and two by Chopin. One of the excerpts by Mozart and one by Chopin were judged by experts to be fast; the other excerpts by Mozart and Chopin were judged as slow. Results confirmed that indeed the unaltered tempos of the musical excerpts affected subjects' ability to discriminate tempo changes (for fast musical excerpts, all groups discriminated faster tempos better; for slow musical excerpts, all groups discriminated slower tempos better).[19]

Terry Kuhn hypothesized that there may be three potential influences on the perception of tempo: meter, melodic rhythm, and speed. In an initial study results demonstrated that ornamented versions of melodies were identified as being faster than plain versions.[20] In a subsequent two-part study, Kuhn and Booth investigated the influence of melodic activity (ornamented and plain) on the perception of tempo. Additional variables were the presence or absence of an audible steady beat and the size of tempo change. Results showed that neither an audible beat nor widely differentiated tempos affected the perception of tempo as much as melodic activity. Specifically, subjects perceived ornamented melodies to be faster.[21] In a similar study, Duke concluded that the perception of tempo is affected by melodic rhythm and that naive listeners may attend to the frequency of musical events across time rather than to beat when making determinations concerning music's relative speed.[22]

The foregoing review demonstrates some of the progress being made in systematically studying interactions among the musical behaviors of perception, performance, and discrimination of tempo. These studies proceeded from the viewpoint of musicians engaged in the daily activity of music. Their purpose, therefore, was

---

Madsen, John M. Geringer, and Robert A. Duke, "Pitch and Tempo Discrimination in Recorded Band Music Among Wind and Percussion Musicians," *Journal of Band Research*, 20 (1984): 20-29.

[19]Cornelia Yarbrough, "The Effect of Musical Excerpts on Tempo Discriminations and Preferences of Musicians and Non-musicians," In Clifford K. Madsen and Carol A. Prickett, eds. *Applications of Research in Music Behavior* (Tuscaloosa, AL: University of Alabama Press, 1987), 175-189.

[20]Terry L. Kuhn, "The Effect of Tempo, Meter, and Melodic Complexity on the Perception of Tempo," In Clifford K. Madsen and Carol A. Prickett, eds. *Applications of Research in Music Behavior* (Tuscaloosa, AL: University of Alabama Press, 1987), 165-174.

[21]Terry L. Kuhn and Gregory D. Booth, "The Effect of Melodic Activity, Tempo Change, and Audible Beat on Tempo Perception of Elementary School Students," *Journal of Research in Music Education*, 36 (1988): 140-155.

[22]Robert A. Duke. "Effect of Melodic Rhythm on Elementary Students' and College Undergraduates' Perception of Tempo." *Journal of Research in Music Education*, 37 (1989): 246-257.

to study directly preference, performance, and perception or discrimination of music within a musical context, toward the goal of improving artistic performances of pre-professional musicians. Their prior assumption seemed to be that musical behavior can be learned and can be taught. There is no overt denial of innate ability. Rather there is recognition that regardless of innate ability, the technical and artistic aspects of musicality can be and ought to be improved through informed instruction. Of foremost importance is the view of these researchers that musical behavior must be overtly observable before it can be meaningfully studied.

Another quite different approach may be seen in quantitative music research conducted by investigators who are primarily cognitive psychologists. Tracing the work by these psychologists, one is drawn into the quite disparate worlds of psychoacoustics, neurology, experimental aesthetics, psychoanalysis, music cognition, and learning or developmental studies. One may proceed from studies of the ear and hearing to the function of the brain in the perception of sound and its various characteristics, such as frequency (pitch and melody), duration (rhythm and tempo), intensity (dynamics), timbre (tone quality), and texture.[23] Experimental aesthetics, particularly as explored by Berlyne, has stimulated many studies concerning the properties of music described as complexity, novelty, and ambiguity. Attempts have been made to explore relationships among psychophysiological concepts of "arousal" or stated preferences and these properties.[24]

Cognitive psychologists stress mental representations of the stimuli and schemata that control perception and behavior. For example, Deutsch investigated the effect of non-musical interference (listening to spoken digits which had to be memorized) versus musical interference (tones not requiring memorization) on pitch retention. The finding that non-musical interference did not affect pitch retention led to her conclusion that there might be a mechanism for diminishing verbal input while musical analysis is in process.[25] Other notable studies which exemplify a cognitive approach to the quantitative study of music appear in the journal, *Music Perception*, edited by Diana Deutsch since its inception in 1984, and Deutsch's book, *The Psychology of Music*.[26]

Another example of a cognitive approach to musical learning and development is a study by Lyle Davidson concerning tonal structures of children's early songs. Using his concept of "contour schemes," which enabled him to describe the structures of children's songs before they become scalar structures, he described the

---

[23]See articles in the *Journal of the Acoustical Society of America*.

[24]D. E. Berlyne, ed., *Studies in the New Experimental Aesthetics* (Washington, D. C.: Hemisphere, 1974).

[25]Diana Deutsch, "Tones and Numbers: Specificity of Interference in Short-term Memory," *Science*, cixviii (1970): 1604.

[26]Diana Deutsch (Ed.), *The Psychology of Music* (New York: Academic Press, 1982).

tonal frame, level of pitch organization, and range of melodic motions. According to Davidson, children's tonal frames are revealed by examining whether they consistently sing songs that contain leaps within which other musical sounds are organized. Early in the children's' musical development, they may freely transpose tonal frames to any notes within their singing capacity with so little tonal stability that few pitches are repeated. The notion of melodic impulse concerns the generally rising (the first phrase of "Twinkle, Twinkle, Little Star") or falling (the second phrase of "Twinkle...") of melodic motion, which Davidson views as "something of an achievement for the young child."[27]

Thus, there are two quite different approaches to quantitative research in music, that of musicians using the techniques of psychology and that of cognitive psychologists using the subject matter of music. Whether the two will arrive at similar or different conclusions is yet to be seen. Regardless, the two approaches share a common store of quantitative research techniques.

Descriptive research methodology is used in music research when the researcher's purpose is to describe quantitatively the present facts or current conditions concerning the musical nature of a group of persons, a number of music objects, or a class of musical events. Experimental and behavioral research methodologies are used in music research to ascertain cause and effect relationships in musical behavior or a musical environment. This chapter will examine descriptive and systematic observational techniques.

DESCRIPTIVE RESEARCH

Descriptive research in music describes what is. It may involve the description, recording, analysis, and interpretations of the present nature, make up, or processes of musical phenomena. The focus is, therefore, on prevailing conditions in music or musical situations or on how a person or group behaves in a present musical situation. Typical descriptive studies in music have used survey, causal-comparative, and developmental research techniques.

As in all other modes of inquiry, the purpose of the research must be given attention first. A thorough definition of the problem under study is necessary before developing the questionnaire, survey instrument, or observation form. Often a pilot study can be helpful in further clarifying research questions that need to be answered in addressing the problem.

For example, the intent of survey data collected in music has often been to provide detailed descriptions of existing phenomena with the intent of using that data to justify current conditions and practices or to make more intelligent plans for

---

[27]Lyle Davidson, "Tonal Structures of Children's Early Songs," *Music Perception*, 2 (1985): 361-374.

improving them. After data collection, further comparisons might be accomplished in order to determine relationships to selected or established norms, standards, or criteria. Survey techniques include the use of questionnaires, interviews, controlled observations, or content analyses.

In some studies, questionnaires have been used to develop a list of music competencies for an undergraduate music education curriculum and to investigate instrumental sex-stereotyping in both children and adults. In the first mentioned study, Stegall and his colleagues sent a questionnaire to each music department in higher education institutions holding a membership in the National Association of Schools of Music. The questionnaire contained questions concerning musicianship, applied music, and music education methods. Since only 58% of the surveys were returned, field interviews were also used. The results of this survey may enable institutions to choose an undergraduate music education curriculum that will be competency-based and set a standard for certification.[28]

In the second study, results of several surveys given to children and adults by Abeles and Porter demonstrated that the clarinet, flute, and violin were considered feminine instruments, and the drum, trombone, and trumpet were considered masculine. Furthermore, results showed that it was after the third grade when students began choosing instruments associated with their sex.[29]

As was noted in the Stegall, et al., study, the questionnaire is often not enough to convince the researcher that the problem has been adequately examined. Therefore, the on-site interview is often used in a follow-up procedure. Price and Yarbrough used this combination of questionnaire and interview techniques to determine relationships among expressed opinions of composers, actual record ownership, and musical training. Music and nonmusic majors at two major universities were asked first to list their ten favorite composers and to rank them from most to least favored.

In addition, they were asked to indicate the number of years they had studied music. Finally, after the surveys had been completed, the researchers visited the students in their apartments or dormitory rooms and counted the number of records owned, categorizing them by composer. Correlation statistics were used to determine the significance of the relationship between the composers named in the survey and the number of recordings of music by those composers actually owned, and the relationship between musical training and the number of classical recordings owned. Results demonstrated a high correlation between the number of

---

[28]Joel R. Stegall, Jack E. Blackburn, and Richard H. Coop, "Administrators' Ratings of Competencies for an Undergraduate Music Education Curriculum," *Journal of Research in Music Education*, 26 (Spring 1978): 3-14.

[29]Harold F. Abeles and Susan Yank Porter, "The Sex-Stereotyping of Musical Instruments," *Journal of Research in Music Education*, 26 (Summer 1978): 65-75.

recordings reported and the recordings actually owned. Interestingly, this information might be used to validate the survey instrument, thus eliminating the necessity of the on-site interview that often requires enormous amounts of time.[30]

Descriptive methodology has also been used in music to complete case studies, correlation studies, and developmental studies. An example of case study in music is one that made an intensive investigation of factors that contributed to one person's chromesthetic responses to music. An adult female was found to consistently "see" certain colors associated with certain pitches. The technique involved controlled observations over an extended period of time.[31]

In another study, Yarbrough and Price used correlation techniques in an effort to predict performer attentiveness based upon rehearsal activity and certain carefully defined teacher behaviors. Results showed high correlations between student attentiveness and teacher eye contact, and between student attentiveness performance activity.

One of the most often cited developmental studies is one by Petzold. He wanted to identify ways in which children in elementary school (ages 6 to 12) perceive and respond to the auditory presentation of musical sounds. The project was a longitudinal study of three groups of children covering a total period of time of four, five, and six years respectively. Results of the projects are summarized in a brief article in the *Journal of Research in Music Education* and presented in detail in the full report.[32]

Descriptive studies can provide historical data for use in repertory analysis and development. Price collected data regarding orchestral repertoire programmed on main subscription series by the 34 major orchestras in the United States and Canada for the 1982-83 through 1986-87 seasons. An examination was made of the over 600 composers whose works were performed and over 10,500 programmed works. Frequency and duration of works were summarized and compared. Data demonstrated that 64 composers accounted for 8,764 works, more than 83% of the total number of works counted. The top ten composers were (in rank order) Mozart, Beethoven, Brahms, Tchaikovsky, Haydn, Richard Strauss, Mahler, Dvorak, Prokofiev, and J. S. Bach. The top ten works programmed were *Concerto in D*

---

[30]Harry E. Price and Cornelia Yarbrough, "Expressed Opinions Of Composers, Musical Training, Recording Ownership, And Their Interrelationship," In Clifford K. Madsen and Carol A. Prickett, eds., *Applications of Research in Music Behavior* (Tuscaloosa, AL: University of Alabama Press, 1987), 232-243.

[31]Paul A. Haack and Rudolf E. Radocy, "A Case Study of a Chromesthetic," *Journal of Research in Music Education*, 29 (1981): 85-90.

[32]Robert G. Petzold, "Auditory Perception by Children," *Journal of Research in Music Education*, 17 (1969): 82-87; Robert G. Petzold, Auditory Perception of Musical Sounds by Children in the First Six Grades (Madison, Wisconsin: The University of Wisconsin, 1966), Cooperative Research Project No. 1051.

major for Violin and *Symphony no. 5 in C minor* by Beethoven; *Symphony no. 8 in C major* by Schubert; *Symphony no. 2 in D major* by Brahms; *Symphony no. 3 in E-flat major, Concerto no. 4 in G major for Piano*, and *Symphony no. 7 in A major* by Beethoven; *Symphony no 1 in C minor* by Brahms, *Symphony no. 5 in E minor* by Tchaikovsky, and *Symphony no. 4 in E minor* by Brahms.[33]

SYSTEMATIC OBSERVATION

In the fields of music education and music therapy, practitioners and researchers alike are concerned with two general aspects of behavior, attention to a stimulus (music) and a response to it (composing, performing, listening, verbalizing, conceptualizing, and using music for extramusical purposes). It would seem that those music teachers and conductors who are most successful in maintaining attentive classes or performing groups, eliciting high levels of achievement or performance, and establishing favorable attitudes toward music, have several observable characteristics in common. First, they are usually highly approving. Second, they dispense approval and disapproval in a very dramatic way by maintaining eye contact, using body movement and contrasting facial expressions, and conducting in an expressive way. Finally, they are efficient users of class and rehearsal time.[34]

Through systematic observation of music classes and rehearsals, one may begin to understand the relationship between these characteristics of teacher and conductor behavior and student attentiveness, performance, and attitude. For example, did the altos miss that entrance because the conductor did not maintain eye contact, use an expressive left hand gesture, and lean towards them? Were students in that kindergarten class off-task because the music teacher made mistakes of reinforcement? Did that junior high band stay 95% on-task because the conductor was highly approving, kept the rehearsal moving at a rapid pace by changing the activity often, and used dramatic overt behavior?

Controlled observation has been used as a technique to determine patterns of instruction in music rehearsals. Verbatim typescripts of 79 experienced and inexperienced music teachers were analyzed on the basis of categories of teacher and student behavior developed and defined from prior research. Sequenced patterns of teaching labeled direct instruction in previous research were observed and counted. Results indicated that experienced teachers use more time in giving directions con-

[33]Harry E. Price, "Orchestral Programming 1982-1987: An Indication of Musical Taste," *Bulletin of the Council for Research in Music Education*, 106 (1990): 23-35.

[34]Clifford K. Madsen and Cornelia Yarbrough, *Competency-Based Music Education* (Raleigh, NC: Contemporary Publishing Co., 1985).

cerning who is to play and where they are to begin and less time in giving musical information.

When observation categories and techniques regarding sequential patterns are solidified in terms of validity and reliability, experimental techniques may be used to isolate the effects of the various patterns on the musical behavior of students.[35]

Initial research involving the use of virtual reality in music teaching and learning has shown promising findings. Virtual reality, in this line of research, is a computer simulation of real or imaginary environments that enables real time interaction with the environment. The simulation is viewed through a head mounted display equipped with a tracking device that allows the image to change in a natural way with head and body motion.

The first known study to use virtual reality in a music performance environment was a case study in 2002 that examined whether or not virtual environments could generate a sense of reality for performing musicians. Five virtual environments including a national park nature setting designed to obtain baseline measures, an empty practice room, a room with audience members, a room with a judging panel, and a room with the Director of Bands seated as if judging an audition were designed to be familiar to the subjects and expected to elicit varying levels of anxiety. Results indicated that the virtual environments did elicit physiological and psychological indications of anxiety that would likely have occurred in the same "real" world settings. Subsequent research has explored possible adaptations of virtual environments for music teaching and learning.[36]

Another more technically controlled observation technique involved EEG technology to observe the brainwaves of musicians and nonmusicians while listening to music. Wagner found that musicians produce more alpha brainwaves than nonmusicians while listening to music. This result was most interesting because alpha brainwaves are of a relatively low frequency and are associated with states of transcendental meditation. It was hypothesized that musicians would produce more beta brainwaves since they would be more attentive and therefore would be processing what they were listening to in a more informed manner than nonmusicians. However, this was not the case. This result raised many questions regarding the function of the brain while listening to music.[37]

---

[35]Cornelia Yarbrough and Harry E. Price, "Sequential Patterns of Instruction in Music," *Journal of Research in Music Education*, 37 (1989): 179-187.

[36]Evelyn K. Orman, "Effect of Virtual Reality Graded Exposure on Heart Rate and Self-reported Anxiety Levels of Performing Saxophonists," *Journal of Research in Music Education*, 51 (2003), 302-315; Evelyn K. Orman, "Effect of Virtual Reality Graded Exposure on Anxiety Levels of Performing Musicians: A Case Study," *Journal of Music Therapy*, 41 (2004), 70-78.

[37]Michael J. Wagner, "Effect of Music and Biofeedback on Alpha Brainwave Rhythms and Attentiveness," *Journal of Research in Music Education*, 23 (1975):

In addition to brainwaves researchers have examined changes in brain activity as measured by level of oxygenated blood flow using functional Magnetic Resonance Imaging (fMRI). Morrison and Demorest found no brain activation unique to culturally familiar (Western) music compared with culturally unfamiliar (Chinese) music among US-born listeners. However, listeners did demonstrate better recollection of the Western rather than the Chinese examples, a pattern the researchers have labeled an "enculturation effect." This effect was evident regardless of participants' music training, a finding replicated in subsequent behavioral research using subjects of different nationalities and ages as well as music of different traditions and levels of complexity Later fMRI research showed stronger activation associated with memory-related areas suggesting that listening to culturally unfamiliar music may demand greater neurological resources for processing. The researchers have proposed that listeners tend to accommodate culturally unfamiliar music by attempting to inappropriately interpret it according to their own culturally familiar music rule systems.[38]

Research using systematic observation methodology requires definition of music teaching and learning behaviors, development of instrumentation for measuring those behaviors, and the study of relationships among them. The next section of this chapter includes a description of the basic techniques of the methodology and the kinds of research questions the methodology best addresses. In addition, studies using the methodology and future directions for observational research in music will be discussed.

3-13.

[38]Steven J. Morrison, Steven M. Demorest, Elizabeth H. Aylward, Steven C. Cramer, and Kenneth R. Maravilla, "fMRI Investigation of Cross-Cultural Music Comprehension," *Neuroimage* 20, no. 1 (2003), 378-84; Steven M. Demorest, Steven J. Morrison, Münir N. Beken, and Denise Jungbluth, "Lost in Translation: An Enculturation Effect in Music Memory Performance," *Music Perception* 25 (2008), 213-223.; Steven J. Morrison, Steven M. Demorest and Laura A. Stambaugh, "Enculturation Effects in Music Cognition: The Role of Age and Musical Complexity," *Journal of Research in Music Education* (in press); Steven M. Demorest, Steven J. Morrison, Münir N. Beken, Laura A. Stambaugh, Todd L. Richards, and Clark Johnson, "Music Comprehension among Western and Turkish Listeners: fMRI Investigation of an Enculturation Effect," (paper presented at the 13th annual meeting of the Organization for Human Brain Mapping, Chicago, Illinois, June 10-14, 2007); Steven M. Demorest and Steven J. Morrison, "Exploring the Influence of Cultural Familiarity and Expertise on Neurological Responses to Music," *Annals of the New York Academy of Sciences* 999 (2003), 112-7.

BASIC TECHNIQUES AND
TOOLS OF SYSTEMATIC OBSERVATION

The first step in the systematic observation of music behavior is to define operationally the behavior(s) to be measured. This demands dealing only with behaviors that can be observed using one of the five senses (seeing, hearing, tasting, feeling, or smelling) and measuring these behaviors with high reliability. Behaviors must be defined such that others can read the definition, observe the behavior simultaneously with a second observer, and record the same thing. This requires specific examples of the behaviors to be observed.

For instance, if the behavior to be observed is eye contact, we might define it as "Looking at the entire group, section, individuals within the group, the music, or something other than the group, section, or individuals within the group (ceiling, floor) for at least three continuous seconds. No eye contact occurs when the teacher maintains it for less than three continuous seconds." It should be noted that value determinations, whether different types of eye contact are good or bad, are not a part of the operational definition.

Other examples of operational definitions of musical behaviors are those developed for magnitude of conductor behavior.[39] Here, magnitude was defined as "intensity of reinforcement." Drawing from behavioral literature outside the field of music allowed further expansion of the definition to include the characteristics of (1) dramatic change of pace, (2) dynamic presentation of materials, and (3) direct, personal delivery of reinforcement in order to affect student performance.[40] Transferring these ideas to conductor behavior resulted in the following operational definitions of magnitude of conductor behavior (see Figure 1):

Thus, observational methodology begins with the development of specific, detailed definitions of behaviors that singularly or in combination represent a musical and instructional concept. Once these operational definitions have been developed, one must carefully consider the measurement technique that will be used before an observation form can be designed.

Therefore, the second step in systematic observation methodology is the choice of measurement technique. These techniques include counting, time sampling, automatic recording, and continuous recording.

---

[39]Cornelia Yarbrough, "Effect of Magnitude of Conductor Behavior on Students in Selected Mixed Choruses," *Journal of Research in Music Education*, 23 (1975): 134-146.

[40]K. D. O'Leary and W. D. Becker, "The Effects of the Intensity of a Teacher's Reprimands on Children's Behavior," *Journal of School Psychology*, No. 7 (1968-1969): 8-11; K. D. O'Leary, K. F. Kaufman, R. E. Kass, and D. S. Drabman, "The Effects of Loud and Soft Reprimands on the Behavior of Disruptive Students," *Exceptional Children*, No. 38 (1970): 145-155.

FIGURE 1:
OPERATIONAL DEFINITIONS OF HIGH AND LOW MAGNITUDE

Teacher Behavior	High Magnitude	Low Magnitude
Eye Contact	Maintains with group and/or individuals throughout rehearsal.	Never looks at individuals or group. Looks at music, ceiling, or in direction of piano.
Closeness	Frequently walks or leans toward chorus or particular section.	Stands behind the music stand at all times. Music stand is always minimum of four feet from chorus.
Volume and Modulation of Voice	Volume constantly varies. Wide range of volume as well as speaking pitch. Voice reflects enthusiasm and vitality.	Volume remains clearly audible but the same approximate volume and pitch throughout rehearsal. Voice reflects little enthusiasm.
Gestures	Uses arms and hands to aid in musical phrasing. Great variety of movement. Varies size of conducting patterns to indicate phrases, dynamics, and the like.	Strict conducting pattern, never varying. Uses arms and hands for attacks and releases. Exact movements.
Facial Expressions	Face reflects sharp contrasts between approval and disapproval. Approval is expressed by grinning, laughing aloud, raising eyebrows, widening eyes. Disapproval is expressed by frowning, knitting brow, pursing lips, Narrowing eyes.	Neutral mask. No frowns. No smiles.

FIGURE 1:
OPERATIONAL DEFINITIONS OF
HIGH AND LOW MAGNITUDE—(CONTINUED)

Teacher Behavior	High Magnitude	Low Magnitude
Rehearsal Pace	Rapid and exciting. Quick instructions. Minimal talking. Less than one second between activity. Frequently gives instructions to group while they are singing.	Slow and methodical. Meticulous care and detail in instructions. Stops group to give instructions.

COUNTING BEHAVIORS

When there are only two or three behaviors to be observed, simply counting them would seem to be the most efficient way to proceed. This is most often the case in self-evaluation or music therapy case studies. Here one may want to target a few behaviors to increase or decrease. Operational definitions would be developed for each of these behaviors. The procedure would then become one of recording the number of behaviors counted over a period of minutes, days, weeks, or months. Subsequently, a reinforcement technique might be applied to attempt to change the number of times the behavior occurred. During the application of the reinforcement technique, the researcher or self-evaluator would continue counting the targeted behaviors. Finally, the reinforcement technique might be withdrawn to determine whether the change in behaviors counted could be maintained in the absence of the reinforcement technique. Of importance is the fact that counting continues throughout the self-evaluative or therapeutic study.

Numerous musical behaviors lend themselves to this technique. For example, one might count the number of rhythmic errors that occur during a performance or the number of approvals and disapprovals given by a teacher in an elementary music classroom. Music therapists might be interested in the number of times a child with cerebral palsy independently lifts his head or the number of inappropriate verbalizations of an echolalic child. Decisions regarding techniques to increase or decrease the behaviors counted require creative thought during which the characteristics of the individual (both researcher and client) must be considered.

TIME SAMPLING

The earliest observational research in music focused on the reinforcement component, approvals and disapprovals, in music teaching. As the concept of reinforcement was explored, researchers targeted eight different behaviors that might demonstrate that concept. These behaviors included academic approval, academic disapproval, social approval, social disapproval, and mistakes of academic or social, approval or disapproval. They were then defined operationally such that two observers could independently agree upon having observed them.

The Teacher Observation Form was then developed to count the number of approvals and disapprovals using a time sampling technique consisting of an observation interval and a recording interval.[41] This technique prescribed that the observer should observe a teacher for fifteen seconds and then record what was observed (approvals, disapprovals, and mistakes of reinforcement) for five seconds. This procedure continued for approximately 17 minutes, or the length of the observation form.

Extending Madsen & Madsen's observational approaches, a Choral Rehearsal Observation form (see Figure 2) was designed to time sample the number of approvals, disapprovals, instructional instances, group and sectional performance; and the number of students who were off-task;[42] and another form was developed to sample Music Conductor behavior (see Figure 3) such as activity (instruction, singing along with the group, teaching while the group is performing), body movement (approach, departure, stationary), conducting gestures (strict, expressive, none), eye contact (group, individual, music, other), facial expressions (approval, disapproval, neutral), speech speed (steady, hesitant, repetitive), voice pitch (low, variable, high), and voice volume (soft, normal, loud).[43]

Observation procedures for these forms are similar to those outlined for the Teacher Observation Form. However, for these forms, behavior is sampled four times per minute instead of three. Therefore, the observe interval is 10 seconds and the record interval is 5 seconds. The Music Conductor Observation Form was designed for use with videotape, thus allowing for repeated viewings.

---

[41]Charles H. Madsen, Jr. and Clifford K. Madsen, *Teaching/Discipline: A Positive Approach for Educational Development*, 3rd Ed. (Raleigh, NC: Contemporary Publishing Co., 1981).

[42]Madsen and Yarbrough, 57.

[43]Madsen and Yarbrough, 61.

Figure 2:
Choral Rehearsal Observation Form

CHORAL REHEARSAL OBSERVATION FORM:

Student Activity; Student On/Off-Task; Teacher Response

Observer ______ School ______
Reliability Observer ______ Teacher ______
Number in Group ______ Group Name ______
Time: Start ______ End ______ Selection(s) ______
Page ______ of ______ Observe/Record Interval ______

INTERVALS

Line	# of Ss	OBSERVE 1	RECORD 2	OBSERVE 3	RECORD 4	OBSERVE 5	RECORD 6	OBSERVE 7	RECORD 8	Comments
1			N P - S A T B / A D I / Ⓐ Ⓓ S		N P - S A T B / A D I / Ⓐ Ⓓ S		N P - S A T B / A D I / Ⓐ Ⓓ S		N P - S A T B / A D I / Ⓐ Ⓓ S	
2			N P - S A T B / A D I / Ⓐ Ⓓ S		N P - S A T B / A D I / Ⓐ Ⓓ S		N P - S A T B / A D I / Ⓐ Ⓓ S		N P - S A T B / A D I / Ⓐ Ⓓ S	
3			N P - S A T B / A D I / Ⓐ Ⓓ S		N P - S A T B / A D I / Ⓐ Ⓓ S		N P - S A T B / A D I / Ⓐ Ⓓ S		N P - S A T B / A D I / Ⓐ Ⓓ S	
4			N P - S A T B / A D I / Ⓐ Ⓓ S		N P - S A T B / A D I / Ⓐ Ⓓ S		N P - S A T B / A D I / Ⓐ Ⓓ S		N P - S A T B / A D I / Ⓐ Ⓓ S	
5			N P - S A T B / A D I / Ⓐ Ⓓ S		N P - S A T B / A D I / Ⓐ Ⓓ S		N P - S A T B / A D I / Ⓐ Ⓓ S		N P - S A T B / A D I / Ⓐ Ⓓ S	
6			N P - S A T B / A D I / Ⓐ Ⓓ S		N P - S A T B / A D I / Ⓐ Ⓓ S		N P - S A T B / A D I / Ⓐ Ⓓ S		N P - S A T B / A D I / Ⓐ Ⓓ S	
7			N P - S A T B / A D I / Ⓐ Ⓓ S		N P - S A T B / A D I / Ⓐ Ⓓ S		N P - S A T B / A D I / Ⓐ Ⓓ S		N P - S A T B / A D I / Ⓐ Ⓓ S	
8			N P - S A T B / A D I / Ⓐ Ⓓ S		N P - S A T B / A D I / Ⓐ Ⓓ S		N P - S A T B / A D I / Ⓐ Ⓓ S		N P - S A T B / A D I / Ⓐ Ⓓ S	

TOTALS:

N intervals ______
P intervals ______
Section intervals ______
(SATB combinations)
______ ______
______ ______

Reliability ______

A ______
Ⓐ ______
D ______
Ⓓ ______

I ______
S
Other ______

Reliability ______

% off-task ______
% on-task ______
Reliability ______

Observation forms have also been developed for use in basic conducting technique courses. Figures 4 and 5 show forms that enable conducting students to self-assess accuracy (+) or inaccuracy (-) of beat pattern, tempo, style, dynamics, eye contact (see Figure 4), preparations, releases, and cueing (see Figure 5).[44]

Basic Conducting Observation Form A may be used to evaluate time sampled conducting behavior with a 10 second observe and 5 second record interval or to evaluate each measure of music conducted. Basic Conducting Observation Form B is designed to provide an opportunity to evaluate each occurrence of a preparation, release, and cue.

AUTOMATIC RECORDING

Automatic observation of the accuracy of the musical task presentation and student response has been accomplished using Macintosh computer systems, MIDI, an analog to digital converter, and Performer[45] software. Figure 6 shows MIDI data from a pitch-matching study which explored the ability of inaccurate singers to match descending minor thirds sung by male, female, and child singers. In this illustration, we see the pitches sung by the female and male models.

The computer data obtained (using Performer software) for each of the two models is displayed in three columns (see Figure 6). From left to right, the first column indicates beginning time for each note sung, expressed in terms of the measure number, which beat in the measure, and the "tick" on which the note began (480 ticks comprise a quarter note in a metronomic context); the second column expresses the pitch name of each note that was sung; and the third column represents the exact duration of each note sung in units of full beats (480 ticks) and/or fractions of beats, the first numbers representing the beats and the second number representing "ticks."

For purposes of this observation technique, correct and incorrect notes sung were observed in column two; durations were computed from the data in column three. To describe the correct pitch content of the data set for each model, the total duration for all pitches in each MIDI data set were summed; then the durations for all G's and E's appearing in the correct order were summed; and finally, the G plus E durations were divided by the total duration to achieve a percentage of time during which correct pitches were sung in the correct order.

---

[44]Madsen and Yarbrough, 116-117.
[45]Mark of the Unicorn, 1989.

FIGURE 3:
MUSIC CONDUCTOR OBSERVATION FORM

Observer _____   Teacher _____   School _____

Reliability Observer _____   Number in Group _____   Selection(s)_____

Time: Start _____   End _____   Date _____   Page _____ of _____

		Activity	Body Movement	Conducting Gesture	Eye Contact	Facial Expression	Speech Speed	Voice Pitch	Voice Volume
LINE 1	1	I SP TP	A D S	S E None	G I M O	A D N	S H R	L V H	S N L
	2	I SP TP	A D S	S E None	G I M O	A D N	S H R	L V H	S N L
	3	I SP TP	A D S	S E None	G I M O	A D N	S H R	L V H	S N L
	4	I SP TP	A D S	S E None	G I M O	A D N	S H R	L V H	S N L
LINE 2	5	I SP TP	A D S	S E None	G I M O	A D N	S H R	L V H	S N L
	6	I SP TP	A D S	S E None	G I M O	A D N	S H R	L V H	S N L
	7	I SP TP	A D S	S E None	G I M O	A D N	S H R	L V H	S N L
	8	I SP TP	A D S	S E None	G I M O	A D N	S H R	L V H	S N L
LINE 3	9	I SP TP	A D S	S E None	G I M O	A D N	S H R	L V H	S N L
	10	I SP TP	A D S	S E None	G I M O	A D N	S H R	L V H	S N L
	11	I SP TP	A D S	S E None	G I M O	A D N	S H R	L V H	S N L
	12	I SP TP	A D S	S E None	G I M O	A D N	S H R	L V H	S N L
LINE 4	13	I SP TP	A D S	S E None	G I M O	A D N	S H R	L V H	S N L
	14	I SP TP	A D S	S E None	G I M O	A D N	S H R	L V H	S N L
	15	I SP TP	A D S	S E None	G I M O	A D N	S H R	L V H	S N L
	16	I SP TP	A D S	S E None	G I M O	A D N	S H R	L V H	S N L
LINE 5	17	I SP TP	A D S	S E None	G I M O	A D N	S H R	L V H	S N L
	18	I SP TP	A D S	S E None	G I M O	A D N	S H R	L V H	S N L
	19	I SP TP	A D S	S E None	G I M O	A D N	S H R	L V H	S N L
	20	I SP TP	A D S	S E None	G I M O	A D N	S H R	L V H	S N L
LINE 6	21	I SP TP	A D S	S E None	G I M O	A D N	S H R	L V H	S N L
	22	I SP TP	A D S	S E None	G I M O	A D N	S H R	L V H	S N L
	23	I SP TP	A D S	S E None	G I M O	A D N	S H R	L V H	S N L
	24	I SP TP	A D S	S E None	G I M O	A D N	S H R	L V H	S N L
LINE 7	25	I SP TP	A D S	S E None	G I M O	A D N	S H R	L V H	S N L
	26	I SP TP	A D S	S E None	G I M O	A D N	S H R	L V H	S N L
	27	I SP TP	A D S	S E None	G I M O	A D N	S H R	L V H	S N L
	28	I SP TP	A D S	S E None	G I M O	A D N	S H R	L V H	S N L
LINE 8	29	I SP TP	A D S	S E None	G I M O	A D N	S H R	L V H	S N L
	30	I SP TP	A D S	S E None	G I M O	A D N	S H R	L V H	S N L
	31	I SP TP	A D S	S E None	G I M O	A D N	S H R	L V H	S N L
	32	I SP TP	A D S	S E None	G I M O	A D N	S H R	L V H	S N L

Mannerisms (foot tapping, bouncing, facial tick, overuse   _____
  of certain words, clapping hands, finger snapping,
  touching face, hair, glasses with hands, mouthing words,   _____
  adjusting clothing, etc,):
  Also list frequency of occurrence.   _____

Comments: _____

_____

FIGURE 4:
BASIC CONDUCTING OBSERVATION FORM A

Name _____ Date _____ Rel. Observer _____

Selection _____ Meter(s)_____

	Int.	Beat Pattern	Tempo	Dynamics	Style	Eye Contact
1	1	+ −	+ −	+ −	+ −	+ −
	2	+ −	+ −	+ −	+ −	+ −
	3	+ −	+ −	+ −	+ −	+ −
	4	+ −	+ −	+ −	+ −	+ −
2	5	+ −	+ −	+ −	+ −	+ −
	6	+ −	+ −	+ −	+ −	+ −
	7	+ −	+ −	+ −	+ −	+ −
	8	+ −	+ −	+ −	+ −	+ −
3	9	+ −	+ −	+ −	+ −	+ −
	10	+ −	+ −	+ −	+ −	+ −
	11	+ −	+ −	+ −	+ −	+ −
	12	+ −	+ −	+ −	+ −	+ −
4	13	+ −	+ −	+ −	+ −	+ −
	14	+ −	+ −	+ −	+ −	+ −
	15	+ −	+ −	+ −	+ −	+ −
	16	+ −	+ −	+ −	+ −	+ −
5	17	+ −	+ −	+ −	+ −	+ −
	18	+ −	+ −	+ −	+ −	+ −
	19	+ −	+ −	+ −	+ −	+ −
	20	+ −	+ −	+ −	+ −	+ −
6	21	+ −	+ −	+ −	+ −	+ −
	22	+ −	+ −	+ −	+ −	+ −
	23	+ −	+ −	+ −	+ −	+ −
	24	+ −	+ −	+ −	+ −	+ −
7	25	+ −	+ −	+ −	+ −	+ −
	26	+ −	+ −	+ −	+ −	+ −
	27	+ −	+ −	+ −	+ −	+ −
	28	+ −	+ −	+ −	+ −	+ −
8	29	+ −	+ −	+ −	+ −	+ −
	30	+ −	+ −	+ −	+ −	+ −
	31	+ −	+ −	+ −	+ −	+ −
	32	+ −	+ −	+ −	+ −	+ −

TOTALS:

Beat Patterns +____ −____ % correct_____

Tempo +____ −____ % correct_____

Dynamics +____ −____ % correct_____

Style +____ −____ % correct_____

Eye Contact +____ −____ % correct_____

RELIABILITY: Agreements +_____ Disagreements −_____

% Disagreements _____

FIGURE 5:
BASIC CONDUCTING OBSERVATION FORM B

NAME _____ DATE _____ RELIABILITY OBSERVER _____

SELECTION _____ METER _____

Int.	Preparation — Eye Contact	Body Mvt.	Gesture	Release — Eye Contact	Body Mvt.	Gesture	Eye Contact	Body Mvt.	Gesture
1	+ −	+ −	+ −	+ −	+ −	+ −	+ −	+ −	+ −
2	+ −	+ −	+ −	+ −	+ −	+ −	+ −	+ −	+ −
3	+ −	+ −	+ −	+ −	+ −	+ −	+ −	+ −	+ −
4	+ −	+ −	+ −	+ −	+ −	+ −	+ −	+ −	+ −
5	+ −	+ −	+ −	+ −	+ −	+ −	+ −	+ −	+ −
6	+ −	+ −	+ −	+ −	+ −	+ −	+ −	+ −	+ −
7	+ −	+ −	+ −	+ −	+ −	+ −	+ −	+ −	+ −
8	+ −	+ −	+ −	+ −	+ −	+ −	+ −	+ −	+ −
9	+ −	+ −	+ −	+ −	+ −	+ −	+ −	+ −	+ −
10	+ −	+ −	+ −	+ −	+ −	+ −	+ −	+ −	+ −
11	+ −	+ −	+ −	+ −	+ −	+ −	+ −	+ −	+ −
12	+ −	+ −	+ −	+ −	+ −	+ −	+ −	+ −	+ −

TOTALS

Preparation
Eye Contact: + _____ − _____ _____%+
Body Mvt.: + _____ − _____ _____%+
Gesture: + _____ − _____ _____%+

Cueing
Eye Contact: + _____ − _____ _____%+
Body Mvt.: + _____ − _____ _____%+
Gesture: + _____ − _____ _____%+

Release
Eye Contact: + _____ − _____ _____%+
Body Mvt.: + _____ − _____ _____%+
Gesture: + _____ − _____ _____%+

Reliability
Eye Contact: + _____ − _____ _____%+
Body Mvt.: + _____ − _____ _____%+
Gesture: + _____ − _____ _____%+

Thus, data obtained represented time spent singing correct pitches or duration of pitch accuracy. Not surprisingly, results demonstrated that inaccurate singers could more easily match the female model than the male model.[46]

Other research, using this kind of MIDI data, has compared dynamics and articulation of keyboard performances. A measurement of dynamics is achieved by reading the MIDI data indicating the velocity of keystroke. The scale of measurement is from one to 64 with the smaller number indicating a slower velocity of keystroke resulting in a softer dynamic level, and the larger number indicating a faster velocity of keystroke resulting in a louder dynamic level.

Articulation (staccato, legato, and so forth) is measured by reading the numbers representing duration. Results have shown that graduate and undergraduate piano majors can imitate a model's articulation quite well, but they have great difficulty in imitating dynamics. Research continues along these lines using children who are studying piano and comparing different teaching methods to improve performance of dynamics.[47]

Another type of automated recording is that using a Continuous Response Digital Interface (CRDI) to a computer. Madsen and his associates in the Center for Music Research at Florida State University have pioneered the use of this device to study operant music preferences. The CRDI uses a potentiometer enclosed in a protective case and mounted into a piece of Plexiglas. The potentiometer is fitted with a knob and pointer with a guide mechanism such that it may be moved left and right on an arc of 250 degrees. The CRDI pointer is positioned above an evaluative response overlay. Thus, subjects can listen to a musical excerpt and simultaneously twist the knob moving it along a continuum from 0 (negative response) to 250 (positive response). This mechanism is further connected to an interface which translates incoming voltage from an analog to a digital representation ranging from 0 - 250 degrees; that is, placement of the pointer along the dial sends a corresponding voltage which is then converted to a numerical rating. These numerical ratings are automatically recorded by computer for subsequent analysis.[48]

---

[46]Cornelia Yarbrough, Georgia Green, Wilma Benson, and Judy Bowers, "Inaccurate Singers: An Exploratory Study of Variables Affecting Pitch Matching," *Bulletin of the Council for Research in Music Education*, 107 (1991): 23-34.

[47]Michael Sharp, "Relationships Among Model Performances and Performances by Piano Majors: Articulation and Dynamics in Selected Bach Fugal Excerpts, Unpublished Dissertation, Louisiana State University, 1982; Cornelia Yarbrough, Donald Speer, and Sharon Parker, "Perception and Performance of Dynamics and Articulation Among Young Pianists," *Bulletin of the Council for Research in Music Education*, 118, 33-44.

[48]Clifford K. Madsen, "Measuring Musical Response," *Music Educators Journal*, 77 (November 1990): 26-28.

FIGURE 6:
MIDI DATA FROM FEMALE AND MALE VOCAL MODELS

	Beginning	Pitch	Duration
Female Model:	4|1|157	F#4	0|012
Total Duration = 903 ticks	4|1|169	G4	0|109
Duration of G = 401	4|1|283	G4	0|075
Duration of E = 320	4|1|360	G#4	0|022
Percentage Correct - 79.84	4|1|384	G4	0|043
	4|1|427	G#4	0|037
	4|1|465	G4	0|053
	4|2|039	G#4	0|029
	4|2|068	G4	0|053
	4|2|121	G#4	0|030
	4|2|151	G4	0|011
	4|2|162	F#4	0|014
	4|2|177	G4	0|057
	4|2|296	F4	0|024
	4|2|320	E4	0|302
	4|3|142	F4	0|014
	4|3|159	E4	0|018
Male Model:	3|2|453	G3	0|169
Total Duration = 827 ticks	3|3|190	G3	0|035
Duration of G = 280	3|3|238	F#3	0|052
Duration of E = 363	3|3|290	G3	0|076
Percentage Correct = 77.75	3|3|421	E3	0|042
	3|4|000	E3	0|142
	3|4|144	D#3	0|036
	3|4|180	E3	0|056
	3|4|244	D#3	0|036
	3|4|280	E3	0|059
	3|4|339	D#3	0|036
	3|4|375	E3	0|043
	3|4|418	D#3	0|024
	3|4|444	E3	0|021

Results from Madsen's early research using the CRDI while subjects listened to a 20 minute excerpt from Act I of Puccini's *La Boheme* demonstrated that subjects' aesthetic experiences did group at certain points throughout the excerpt. These experiences were relatively short (15 seconds) preceded by a period of concentrated focus of attention, and generally followed by an "afterglow" ranging from 15 seconds to several minutes. All subjects reported having at least one aesthetic experience and also that movement of the dial roughly approximated their experiences. Aesthetic experiences for subjects seemed to cluster at many of the same places in the music with one collective peak experience that was represented by the highest and lowest dial movements. This innovative measurement technique certainly holds much promise for future research.[49]

CONTINUOUS RECORDING

Systematic observation techniques have been used in music research to isolate and define components of an adaptation of the direct instruction model for teaching. The earliest model for direct instruction defined interactive units of teaching in which the sequential order of events, or pattern of instruction, was of paramount importance. Specifically, the pattern began with the teacher's presentation of the task to be learned, followed by student interaction with the task and the teacher, and solidified by immediate praise or corrective feedback related to the task presented.[50]

As can be seen in Figure 7, sequential patterns of instruction in music have been identified, components of those patterns have been operationally defined, and sub-categories of each component have been developed and defined. Thus, verbal interactions among teachers and students can now be observed and analyzed.[51]

---

[49]Madsen, Clifford K., Ruth V. Brittin, and Deborah A. Capperella-Sheldon. "An Empirical Method for Measuring the Aesthetic Response the Aesthetic Experience to Music." *Journal of Research in Music Education*, 41 (1993): 57-69.

[50]W. C. Becker, S. Englemann, and D.R. Thomas, *Teaching: A Course in Applied Psychology* (Chicago: Science Research Associates, 1971).

[51]Harry E. Price, "An Effective Way to Teach and Rehearse: Research Supports Using Sequential Patterns," *Update: Applications of Research in Music Education*, 8 (Fall-Winter 1989): 242-246; Cornelia Yarbrough and Harry E. Price, "Prediction of Performer Attentiveness Based on Rehearsal Activity and Teacher Behavior," *Journal of Research in Music Education*, 29 (1981): 209-217; Cornelia Yarbrough and Harry E. Price," Sequential Patterns of Instruction in Music," *Journal of Research in Music Education*, 37, (1989): 179-187; Cornelia Yarbrough, Harry E. Price, and Judy Bowers, "The Effect of Knowledge of Research on Rehearsal Skills

One of the most recent observational techniques is that of scripting entire re-hearsal periods, categorizing each activity, and timing or counting each occurrence of every activity. This technique has been used extensively to study sequential patterns in teacher/student interactions. The script contains the words spoken by the teacher and describes student responses. The idea is to create a script resembling that of a dramatic play. Additional information can then be added to the script such as the codes defined in Figure 7 and the number of seconds that each coded segment of script lasts.

RELIABILITY

The observation techniques described in the previous pages require a special tech-nique for the measurement of observation reliability called interobserver agreement. This is due to the fact that if reliable measurement procedures are not used, it might be possible for the behavior to remain stable while the recording of the behavior changes. Conversely, it might be possible for the behavior to change while the record of it remains unchanged.

Interobserver agreement provides added confidence that it is indeed the behavior that has changed from one condition to another, and that the behavior has been adequately defined. The formula used for the computation of interobserver agree-ment is the number of agreements between two independent observers divided by the number of agreements plus disagreements. This results in a percentage of observer agreement. Agreement of less than 70% is considered unacceptable.[52] Should this occur, observers may need retraining or the observation instrument may need revision. When a reliable measurement technique has been achieved, data can be gathered concerning the occurrence of the operationally defined behavior(s) over time, and the method of reporting data can be designed.

SUMMARY

The descriptive branch of quantitative research includes the approaches of ques-tionnaires, surveys, and systematic observation. Results of these approaches are numbers grouped into categories that have been derived through operational defini-tions. These numbers may be frequencies, ranks, or intervals. At the present time,

---

and Teaching Values of Experienced Teachers," *Update: Applications of Research in Music Teaching* (Spring-Summer, 1991): 17-20.

[52]Observation forms presented in this book have been used and revised many times before reaching the final product. Average agreement among observers using these forms exceeds 80%.

FIGURE 7:
OPERATIONAL DEFINITIONS OF SEQUENTIAL PATTERNS OF INSTRUCTION IN MUSIC

Teacher Presentations (1)

1a - academic musical task presentation (talking about musical or performance aspects, including modeling by teacher or piano and questioning)

1d - direction (giving directions regarding who will, or where to sing/play; counting beats, usually ending in "ready, go"; questioning)

1s - social task presentation (presenting rules of behavior)

1o - off-task statement (unnecessary and irrelevant comments such as talking to oneself)

Student Responses (2)

2p - performance (entire ensemble or sections performing)

2v - verbal (ensemble members asking or answering a question, or making a statement)

2nv - nonverbal (ensemble members nodding heads, raising hands, or moving in response to teacher instruction)\par

Reinforcement (3)

3a - verbal academic or social approval (positive statement about student performance or social behavior)

3d - verbal academic or social disapproval (negative statement about student performance or social behavior)

Specific - exact feedback containing musical information

Nonspecific - vague feedback containing no musical information

Sequential Patterns:

Complete - Presentation of Task (1) - Student Response (2) - Reinforcement (3)

        1a - 2 - 3a specific
        1a - 2 - 3d specific
        1d - 2 - 3a specific
        1d - 2 - 3a nonspecific
        1d - 2 - 3d nonspecific
        1a - 2 - 3a nonspecific
        1a - 2 - 3d nonspecific

Incomplete - Presentation of Task (1) - Student Response (2)

        1a - 2
        1d - 2

descriptive tools are used in combination to give a broader view of the problem under investigation.

Systematic observation begins with thorough definition of observable, measurable behaviors. Observational techniques have been developed such that data can be collected during a session or afterwards using audio- or videotape. Both continuous and time-sampled protocols have been developed and are available.

In addition to observational collection of data, other descriptive techniques such as questionnaires and surveys remain viable alternatives for the illumination of current behavior and opinions. However, these techniques, unlike systematic observation, are not useful in determining cause and effect relationships. Observation tools are reliable and valid dependent measures for use in behavioral or experimental designs. In addition, practitioners will find them useful in recording and changing inappropriate as well as appropriate musical behaviors.

The primary practitioners of observational methodology are music educators and therapists. Researchers and teachers from these groups are interested in techniques to effect change in learning and behavior. Therefore, the systematic observation of behavior becomes merely the first step in a continuing process of observe, record, treat, evaluate, observe, record, treat, evaluate, and so forth.

The technology and knowledge available to us today will enable those who choose research as their applied performing area to revolutionize the way we teach and learn music. Through technology, musicians have an opportunity now as never before to put innovation and creativity to work in expanding and revising the knowledge we now have about music and musical behaviors. It is time for us to study how we form our musical ideas, how we communicate them, how we translate them into musical behaviors, and the effect of our musical behaviors upon listeners. Systematic observational methodology will be an exciting avenue for gifted musician-scholars of the future.

Beyond practical concerns of the educator and therapist, more formal designs are necessary to isolate cause and effect relationships between variables subsumed under the categories of teaching and learning. For the conduct of these more controlled investigations, we must study experimental modes of inquiry.

RESEARCH APPLICATIONS

1. Make a videotape of yourself performing in recital, playing in your lesson, practicing, conducting a rehearsal, or doing any other musical behavior. Design a time-sampled observation form to measure your behavior by
   a. Creating and operationally defining categories and specific behaviors within those categories;
   b. Using the form to analyze your videotape;
   c. Summarizing the data collected;
   d. Discussing your results; and
   e. Suggesting revisions for your form. Use observation forms in this chapter as models and read the referenced pages in *Competency-Based Music Education* by Madsen and Yarbrough.

BIBLIOGRAPHY

Abeles, Harold F. and Susan Y. Porter. "The Sex-Stereotyping of Musical Instruments*." Journal of Research in Music Education* 26 (Spring 1978): 65-75.

Becker, W. C., S. Englemann, and D. R. Thomas. *Teaching: A Course in Applied Psychology*. Chicago: Science Research Associates, 1971.

Berlyne, D. E., ed. *Studies in the New Experimental Aesthetics*. Washington, D.C.: Hemisphere, 1974.

Codding, Peggy A. "A Content Analysis of the *Journal of Music Therapy*, 1977-85." *Journal of Music Therapy*, XXIV (Winter, 1987): 195-202.

Davidson, Lyle. "Tonal Structures of Children's Early Songs. *Music Perception* 2 (1985): 361-374.

Demorest, Steven M., Steven J. Morrison, Münir N. Beken, and Denise Jungbluth. "Lost in Translation: An Enculturation Effect in Music Memory Performance." *Music Perception* 25 (2008), 213-223.

Demorest, Steven M., Steven J. Morrison, Münir N. Beken, Laura A. Stambaugh, Todd L. Richards, and Clark Johnson. "Music Comprehension among Western and Turkish Listeners: fMRI Investigation of an Enculturation Effect." Paper presented at the 13th annual meeting of the Organization for Human Brain Mapping, Chicago, Illinois, June 10-14, 2007.

Deutsch, Diana (Ed.). *The Psychology of Music*. NY: Academic Press, 1982.

——————. "Tones and Numbers: Specificity of Interference in Short-Term Memory." *Science*, cixviii (1970): 1604.

Duke, Robert A. "Effect of Melodic Rhythm on Elementary Students' and College Undergraduates' Perception of Tempo." *Journal of Research in Music Education*, 37 (1989): 246-257.

Farnsworth, Paul R. *The Social Psychology of Music*. Ames, IO: The Iowa State University Press, 1969.

Fechner, G. T. *Vorschule der Ásthetik*. 1876.

Geringer, John M. and Clifford K. Madsen. "Pitch and Tempo Discrimination in Recorded Orchestral Music Among Musicians and Non-Musicians." *Journal of Research in Music Education* 32 (1984): 195-204.

——————. "Pitch and Tempo Preferences in Recorded Popular Music*." In Applications of Research in Music Behavior*, ed. Clifford K. Madsen and Carol A. Prickett, 3-11. Tuscaloosa, AL: University of Alabama Press, 1987.

Gilbert, Janet Perkins. "Published Research in Music Therapy, 1973-1978: Content, Focus, and Implications for Future Research. *Journal of Music Therapy*, XIV (Fall, 1979): 102-110.

Haack, Paul A. and Rudolf E. Radocy. "A Case Study of a Chromesthetic." *Journal of Research in Music Education*, 29 (1981): 85-90.

Hall, R. V. and R. Van Houten. *Behavior Modification: The Measurement of Behavior*. Austin, TX: Pro-Ed, 1983.

Helmholtz, Hermann von. *On the Sensations of Tone as a Physiological Basis for the Theory of Music*. Trans. A. J. Ellis. NY: Dover, 1954.

Hitchcock, H. Wiley and Stanley Sadie, eds. *The New Grove Dictionary of American Music*. S. v. "Psychology of Music" by George L. Duerksen, v. 3, 649-650.

Jellison, Judith A. "The Frequency and General Mode of Inquiry of Research in Music Therapy, 1952-1972." *Bulletin of the Council for Research in Music Education*, 35 (Winter, 1973): 1-8.

Kuhn, Terry L. "Discrimination of Modulated Beat Tempo by Professional Musicians." *Journal of Research in Music Education* 22 (1974): 270-77.

Kuhn, Terry L. and Gregory D. Booth. "The Effect of Melodic Activity, Tempo Change, and Audible Beat on Tempo Perception of Elementary School Students," *Journal of Research in Music Education*, 36 (1988): 140-155.

Lundin, Robert W. *An Objective Psychology of Music*. NY: Ronald Press, 1953; 2nd ed, 1967.

Madsen, Charles H., Jr. and Clifford K. Madsen. *Teaching/Discipline: A Positive Approach for Educational Development*, 3rd ed. (Raleigh, NC: Contemporary Publishing Co., 1981.

Madsen, Clifford K. "Measuring Musical Response." *Music Educators Journal*, 77 (November 1990): 26-28.

——————. "Modulated Beat Discrimination Among Musicians and Non-Musicians." *Journal of Research in Music Education*, 27 (1979): 59-67.

Madsen, Clifford K., Ruth V. Brittin, and Deborah A. Capperella-Sheldon. "An Empirical Method for Measuring the Aesthetic Response the Aesthetic Experience to Music." *Journal of Research in Music Education*, 41 (1993): 57-69.

Madsen, Clifford K., John M. Geringer, and Robert A. Duke. "Pitch and Tempo Discrimination in Recorded Band Music Among Wind and Percussion Musicians." *Journal of Band Research* 20 (1984): 20-29.

Madsen, Clifford K., R. Douglas Greer, and Charles H. Madsen, Jr., Eds. *Research in Music Behavior*. NY: Teachers College Press, Columbia University, 1975.

Madsen, Clifford K. and Charles H. Madsen, Jr. *Experimental Research in Music*. Raleigh, NC: Contemporary Publishing Co., 1978.

Madsen, Clifford K. and Randall S. Moore. *Experimental Research in Music: Workbook in Design and Statistical Tests*. Raleigh, NC: Contemporary Publishing Co., 1978.

Madsen, Clifford K. and Carol A. Prickett, Eds. *Applications of Research in Music Behavior*. Tuscaloosa, AL.: University of Alabama Press, 1987.

Madsen, Clifford K. and Cornelia Yarbrough. *Competency-Based Music Education*. Raleigh, NC: Contemporary Publishing Co., 1985.

Morrison, Steven J., Steven M. Demorest, Elizabeth H. Aylward, Steven C. Cramer, and Kenneth R. Maravilla. "fMRI Investigation of Cross-Cultural Music Comprehension." *Neuroimage* 20, no. 1 (2003), 378-84.

Morrison, Steven J., Steven M. Demorest and Laura A. Stambaugh. "Enculturation Effects in Music Cognition: The Role of Age and Musical Complexity." *Journal of Research in Music Education* (in press).

O'Leary, K. D. and W. D. Becker. "The Effects of the Intensity of a Teacher's Reprimands on Children's Behavior." *Journal of School Psychology*, No. 7 (1968-1969): 8-11.

O'Leary, K. D., K. F. Kaufman, R. E. Kass, and D. S. Drabman. "The Effects of Loud and Soft Reprimands on the Behavior of Disruptive Students." Exceptional Children, No. 38 (1970): 145-155.

Orman, Evelyn K. "Effect of Virtual Reality Graded Exposure on Anxiety Levels of Performing Musicians: A Case Study." *Journal of Music Therapy*, 41 (2004): 70-78.

Orman, Evelyn K. "Effect of Virtual Reality Graded Exposure on Heart Rate and Self-reported Anxiety Levels of Performing Saxophonists." *Journal of Research in Music Education*, 51 (2003): 302-315.

Petzold, Robert G. "Auditory Perception by Children." *Journal of Research in Music Education* 17 (1969): 82-87.

——————. *Auditory Perception of Musical Sounds by Children in the First Six Grades*. Madison, Wisconsin: The University of Wisconsin, 1966, Cooperative Research Project No. 1051.

Price, Harry E. "An Effective Way to Teach and Rehearse: Research Supports Using Sequential Patterns." *Update: Applications of Research in Music Education*, 8 (Fall-Winter 1989): 242-246.

——————. "Orchestral Programming 1982-1987: An indication of Musical Taste." *Bulletin of the Council for Research in Music Education*, 106 (1990): 23-36.

Price, Harry E. and Cornelia Yarbrough. "Expressed Opinions of Composers, Musical Training, Recording Ownership, and Their Interrelationship." In *Applications of Research in Music Behavior* ed. Clifford K. Madsen and Carol A. Prickett, 232-243. Tuscaloosa, AL: University of Alabama Press, 1987.

Seashore, Carl. "Psychology in Music: The Role of Experimental Psychology in the Science and Art of Music." *Musical Quarterly* XVI (1930): 229-237.

——————. *Psychology of Music*. NY: McGraw-Hill Book Co., Inc., 1938.

——————. *The Psychology of Musical Talent*. NY: Silver Burdett, 1919.

Sharp, Michael. "Relationships Among Model Performances and Performances by Piano Majors: Articulation and Dynamics in Selected Bach Fugal Excerpts." Unpublished Dissertation, Louisiana State University, 1988.

Stegall, Joel, Jack E Blackburn, and Richard H. Coop. "Administrators' Ratings of Competencies for an Undergraduate Music Education Curriculum." *Journal of Research in Music Education* 26 (Spring 1978): 3-14.

Stumpf, Carl. *Tonpsychologie*, v. 1 and 2. Leipzig: Hirzel, 1883 and 1890.

Wagner, Michael J. "Effect of Music and Biofeedback on Alpha Brainwave Rhythms and Attentiveness." *Journal of Research in Music Education*, 23 (1975): 3-13,

Wang, Cecelia C. "Discrimination of Modulated Music Tempo by Music Majors." *Journal of Research in Music Education* 31 (1983): 49-55.

Wang, Cecelia C. and Salzberg, Rita. "Discrimination of Modulated Music Tempo by String Students." *Journal of Research in Music Education* 32 (1984): 123-131.

Wapnick, Joel. "The Perception of Musical and Metronomic Tempo Change in Musicians." *Psychology of Music* 8 (1980): 3-12.

Yarbrough, Cornelia. "A Content Analysis of the Journal of Research in Music Education: 1953-1983." *Journal of Research in Music Education* 32 (1984): 213-222.

——————————. "The Effect of Magnitude of Conductor Behavior on Students in Selected Mixed Choruses. *Journal of Research in Music Education* 23 (1975): 134-146.

——————————. "The Effect of Musical Excerpts on Tempo Discriminations and Preferences of Musicians and Non-Musicians." In *Applications of Research in Music Behavior* ed. Clifford K. Madsen and Carol A. Prickett, 175-189. Tuscaloosa, AL: University of Alabama Press, 1987.

Yarbrough, Cornelia, Georgia Green, Wilma Benson, and Judy Bowers. "Inaccurate Singers: An Exploratory Study of Variables Affecting Pitch Matching. *Bulletin of the Council for Research in Music Education*, 107 (1991): 23-34.

Yarbrough, Cornelia and Harry E. Price. "Prediction of Performer Attentiveness Based on Rehearsal Activity and Teacher Behavior. *Journal of Research in Music Education* 29 (1981): 209-217.

——————————. "Sequential Patterns of Instruction in Music." *Journal of Research in Music Education* 37 (1989): 179-187.

Yarbrough, Cornelia, Harry E. Price, and Judy Bowers. "The Effect of Knowledge of Research on Rehearsal Skills and Teaching Values of Experienced Teachers." *Update: Applications of Research in Music Teaching*, (Spring-Summer, 1991): 17-20.

Yarbrough, Cornelia, Donald Speer, and Sharon Parker. "Perception and Performance of Dynamics and Articulation Among Young Pianists." *Bulletin of the Council for Research in Music Education*, 118, 33-44.

Chapter Six

Statistical
Concepts

 **Chapter Six**

Statistical
Concepts

An introduction to quantitative research in music must include a basic overview of statistical concepts. An understanding of the logic of statistical analysis including how the analysis informs the researcher is important not only to those who plan to use quantitative techniques but also to those who will be reading quantitative studies.

While researchers in other modes of inquiry focus on individual, and often unique, cases for intensive study, quantitative researchers seek to generalize their results to a broader population. In other words, one of the goals of quantitative research is to determine whether the results of a study of thirty individuals or events will generalize to all other similar individuals or events.

SAMPLING

In planning the procedural aspects of quantitative research, one must be concerned with choosing the *population* to be studied, the choice of instrumentation for measurement, and the reliability and validity of that instrument. When one speaks of a population, one is referring to everyone or everything in that classification; the population of professional musicians includes every musician who is paid for his/her performance, composition, or teaching. On the other hand, a *population sample* refers to a portion of the entire population; professional musicians playing in the top thirty professional symphony orchestras in the United States represent a population sample of all professional musicians. Obviously, if one were able to study an entire population, one could simply describe it using summarizing statistics such as percentages, averages, and so forth.

However, we often want to *generalize* the results we obtain from a sample to an entire population. Therefore, we must first insure random selection of that sample; secondly, we must create a sample of sufficient size; and thirdly, we must *control for bias* in the selection of the sample. *Random selection* may be accomplished by assigning a number to each unit (person or thing) in the population to be studied. After each unit has a number, a table of random numbers, which may be found in most statistics books, can be used to assign every unit a new number depending upon how its number comes up from the table of random numbers. The larger the size of the sample, or the more units studied, the more confidence one can have in generalizing from the way the units studied behaved to all other units in the population from which the sample was randomly selected.

Although sample size is critical in all quantitative research, it is especially so when using the survey technique in descriptive methodology. When questionnaires are mailed, for example, the return rate is often less than half of the original mailing. Therefore, it becomes necessary to initiate a second and sometimes a third or fourth mailing to insure a valid sample size. Sample bias may occur when units are selected (albeit randomly) from one geographic area, age group, sex, occupation, race, ethnic group, and so forth. It may be important to insure equal representation across these various categories.

INSTRUMENTATION

Instrumentation needed for dependent measures is often the most important aspect of quantitative research. Before beginning the research process, consideration should be given to how subjects will respond (questionnaire, interview, performance, attitude survey, perception, discrimination, for example), how that response will be recorded, and how it will be analyzed subsequently. Often a pilot study is conducted in order to solve problems in instrumentation before beginning the main study. The development of computers, samplers, and music software is rapidly replacing oscilloscopes, audio generators, stroboscopes, tuners, and adjustable intonation keyboards as components in experimental research in music laboratories.[1] Nonetheless, active tryouts of any instrumentation should be a requirement for both experienced and inexperienced music researchers.

---

[1]Clifford K. Madsen and Charles H. Madsen, Jr., *Experimental Research in Music* (Raleigh, N.C.: Contemporary Publishing Co., 1980), pp. 108-112; Joel Wapnick, "The Use of Computers and Samplers in Music Research," Paper presented at Research in Music Behavior Symposium, Logan, Utah, April, 1987.

RELIABILITY AND VALIDITY

Elements of control, including *reliability* and *validity*, should be employed and reported as part of the procedures of the research study. *Reliability* is the degree to which one obtains the same result with a measuring device when the same variable is measured twice (or more). Reliability must always be obtained for controlled observations. In observational research and in research requiring performance ratings, two or more independent observers (judges) count (rate) carefully defined categories of behavior. Although there are statistical tests for the computation of reliability,[2] one of the most conservative ways is to count each time the observers (judges) agree and each time they disagree. To obtain the percentage of agreement, divide the number of agreements by agreements plus disagreements; then, multiply the result by 100. This will result in a percentage of agreement between/among judges or observers.

Validity is more difficult to ascertain.[3] It is the degree to which a test, questionnaire, survey, or other measurement, measures what it purports to measure. Sources of invalidity can be both *internal* and *external*. Regarding internal validity, Campbell and Stanley discuss variables, which if not controlled, might produce effects not related to the question under study: history, maturation, testing, instrumentation, statistical regression, sample bias, and mortality. Instrumentation and sample-bias have been discussed previously. History concerns the specific events occurring between the first and second measurements and the independent variable. Maturation refers to the passage of time including growing older or hungrier or more tired. Testing refers to the effects of the first testing on the scores of a second testing. Statistical regression refers to the possibility that (a) subjects scoring high on a first testing may, through regression toward the mean, score lower on the second testing; and (b) subjects scoring low on a first testing may score higher on the second testing because of the same regression toward the mean, phenomenon. Mortality refers to the loss of subjects through attrition and, perhaps, death. External validity issues revolve around questions concerning the generalizability of the data to other settings or populations. This question may never be completely answerable.[4]

---

[2]Pearson Product Moment, Spearman Rank Correlation Coefficient, Kendall Coefficient of Concordance, for example.

[3]A nationally known tests and measurements expert who is senior author of a major general achievement test remarked to this author that, "Only God knows validity."

[4]Donald T. Campbell and Julian C. Stanley, *Experimental and Quasi-Experimental Designs for Research* (Chicago: Rand McNally College Publishing Co., 1973), pp. 5-18.

LEVELS OF MEASUREMENT

Having operationally defined and stated a problem and selected an appropriate instrument for measurement, one should think through the analysis of the data one will collect before beginning the research procedure. In the analysis of the results of a descriptive or observational study, both qualitative and quantitative issues should be considered in interpreting and reporting the data. The first consideration should be the question to which the researcher sought an answer. The next consideration should be the data (the numbers) to be used in the analysis. Data may be gathered from many different sources (pitch deviation in cents, frequency of correct and incorrect responses, minutes practiced per day, judges ratings of performances, number of distractions during practice sessions, degree of enjoyment of a particular piece of music, to name but a few) resulting in a multitude of data points. The kinds of numbers generated will depend on the measurement level selected. Madsen and Madsen state:

> There are four types of measurement scales used in experimentation: (1) nominal, (2) ordinal, (3) interval, and (4) ratio. The nominal or 'naming' scale is used solely for classification, for example, flat-sharp, good-bad, large, improvement...For example, a large chorus is easily classified nominally into soprano, alto, tenor, or bass...
>
> The ordinal scale not only allows comparisons of equality and differences but also permits the rank ordering of members of a group or events...The assignment of orchestral parts within a section on the basis of assessed proficiency (auditions) is an excellent example of ordinal scaling by the conductor...
>
> An interval scale permits measurements of equality and differences of intervals and also greater-than and less-than measurements...The chromatic scale on the equal-tempered piano represents interval scaling at its best, that is, C# is to D as D is to D#, and so on. An interval scale does not need an absolute zero point; however, the distances between points on the scale are of known size (common examples are the metronome, thermometer, and calendar). An interval scale is perhaps the strongest scale that can be used for most experimental research in music...
>
> The ratio scale has all of the above characteristics but also has an absolute zero point. This allows values to be doubled, tripled, etc. Some apparatuses for measuring pitch and duration (for example, Strobocohn, electric clock) represent possibilities for ratio scaling, for

example, stroboscopic analysis of pitch in plus or minus cent deviations and timings of durational rhythmic patterns...[5]

Thus, data collected may describe the frequency of occurrence of specific categories of behavior or events, the rank order of those behaviors or events, or the magnitude of them. Figure 8 compares the different levels of measurement and presents a concrete example of a similar research question answered by collecting data within each of these levels of measurement.

FIGURE 8:
LEVELS OF MEASUREMENT IN MUSIC DATA ANALYSIS

Nominal	Ordinal	Interval
Frequency	Ranks	Magnitude
How many?	More Than, Less Than Better Than, Worse Than	How Much?
Within Classified Categories	Comparisons of Quality Distance, or Differences	Distance, Duration
Number of Pitches Played Sharp, In-Tune, Flat by Violinists and Cellists	Frequencies Ranked OR Deviations Ranked	Each pitch measured with pitch extractor to determine how many cents deviation from target pitch.

DECISIONS REGARDING SIGNIFICANCE

Quantitative studies rely on statistical tests to determine whether data collected are significantly different from chance or random occurrence. The raw data are

---

[5]Clifford K. Madsen and Charles H. Madsen, Jr. *Experimental Research in Music* (Raleigh, NC: Contemporary Publishing Co., 1980) 70-71.

subjected to a statistical test chosen on the basis of the type of data collected (nominal, ordinal, interval, or ratio), the size of the sample, and the number of factors to be compared. The researcher chooses an *alpha level* for declaring the data non-significant or significant.

The researcher usually sets an alpha level prior to running a statistical test. Choice of an alpha level (for example, alpha = .05 or .01), indicates how many times out of one hundred it is probable that the data occurred by chance alone (for example, .05 = five times out of a hundred; .01 = one time out of a hundred). The setting of an alpha level is particularly important where consequences of the study are potentially dangerous or deadly. Perhaps when testing a possibly deadly drug, an alpha level of .0001 would be more acceptable than .05. In other words, a quantitative researcher might say that results of the drug tests showed a probability of less than .0001 that a consumer would die upon taking the drug.

Several other factors must be considered in the decision regarding significance or nonsignificance of a statistical value. Choosing the highest level of measurement, (intervallic or ratio) and conducting many observations (size of *n*) may insure the least amount of error in the final decision regarding the significance of the statistic.

Statistical test formulas compare the numbers that have been observed to numbers in some theoretical distribution (for example, the *chi* square distribution, the Mann-Whitney *U* distribution, the normal curve distribution). A theoretical distribution describes what statistical values would occur by chance alone given a certain level of measurement, size of *n* (number of observations), alpha level, and degrees of freedom (*n* - 1 or *k* - 1).

Practical Example: Nominal Level

Here are some practical examples. The following data set contains cent deviation scores from a pitch performance test taken by singers (*n* = 10) and violinists (*n* = 10). If these subjects were exactly on pitch, their deviation scores would be zero; if flat, the score would be a minus something; if sharp, a plus. Thus, the data represent a ratio scale with an absolute zero point (no deviation), and with greater than (sharp) and lesser than (flat) comparisons (see Table 1).

This data set can be analyzed initially by simply counting the number of singers and violinists who played sharp and the number who played flat. Thus, the analysis of the data set occurs at the nominal level of measurement. The following outline represents the steps generally followed in quantitative research:

TABLE 1:
CENT DEVIATION SCORES OF SINGERS AND VIOLINISTS

Singers	Violinists
50	- 10
40	6
100	20
35	22
10	25
8	- 6
- 25	- 20
- 10	5
- 6	8
20	12

Hypothesis: There will be no significant difference between the number of singers and violinists who play sharp and the number who play flat. Alpha level = .05.

Procedure: Twenty students (singers and violinists) were asked to play or sing a single pitch, A = 440 Hz. Cent deviations were measured using a Korg tuner. The number of students playing sharp and flat were counted.

Results: From the twenty performances counted, fourteen played sharp and six played flat. These data were analyzed using the chi-square statistical test[6] as follows:

[6]Sidney Siegel, *Non Parametric Statistics for the Behavioral Sciences* (NY: McGraw-Hill Book Co., 1956), 42-47.

	Sharp	Flat
Expected (E)	10	10
Observed (O)	14	6

$$\begin{aligned} x^2 &= \sum [(O\text{-}E)^2 \div E] \\ &= [(14\text{-}10)^2 \div 10] + [(6\text{-}10)^2 \div 10] \\ &= (16 \div 10) + (16 \div 10) \\ &= 1.60 + 1.60 \\ &= 3.20 \end{aligned}$$

df = 2 - 1 = 1

Significance level: alpha = .05

Conclusion: Reference to the *Chi* Square Table (available in most statistics books) reveals that a *chi* square value of 3.20 with *df* = 1 is not significant. Therefore the observed data would have occurred by chance alone more than five times out of one hundred. In order to be significant at the 05 level, the value of chi square would have to be equal to or greater than 3.84. Thus, we must conclude that singers' and violinists' flat and sharp performances of A = 440 Hz. were not significantly different from what might have occurred by chance alone.

PRACTICAL EXAMPLE: ORDINAL LEVEL

Next, the same data set can be analyzed at the ordinal level of measurement. Singers and violinists will be considered as two independent groups and data analyzed using the Mann-Whitney *U* statistic to determine differences between their performances of A = 440 Hz.:

Hypothesis: There will be no significant differences between singers' and violinists' performances of A = 440 Hz.

Procedure: Twenty students (singers and violinists) were asked to play or sing a single pitch, A = 440 Hz. Cent deviations were measured using a Korg tuner. These performances were rank ordered from sharpest (100 cents) to flattest (- 25 cents).

Test: A Mann-Whitney U test was chosen because there
                   were two independent groups, small group size,
                   and ordinal level of measurement. Alpha = .05
                   with $n1$ = 10 singers; $n2$ = 10 violinists.

Results: Scores = the ranks assigned to cent deviations for
                   singers (Group 1) and violinists (Group 2).

TABLE 2:
CENT DEVIATION SCORES AND
RANKS OF SINGERS AND VIOLINISTS

Singers	R1	Violinists	R2
50	2	-10	17.5
40	3	6	13
100	1	20	7.5
35	4	22	6
10	10	25	5
8	11.5	-6	15.5
-25	20	-20	19
-10	17.5	5	14
-6	15.5	8	11.5
20	7.5	12	9
	$\sum R1 = 92$		$\sum R2 = 118$

Thus, the first step in computing the Mann-Whitney U statistic was to
record the scores of both groups. Next the scores were ranked (taking both
groups together and averaging the ranks of tied scores) giving rank 1 to the
sharpest deviation (100 cents) and the rank of 20 to the flattest deviation
(-25 cents). Next the ranks for each group were summed with R1 = sum
of the ranks for Group 1 and R2 = sum of the ranks for Group 2.

Using the statistical formula we computed the U values for both R1 and R2 in order to find the smaller of the two U values:

$U = n1n2 + [n1(n1 + 1) \div 2] - R1$ $U = n1n2 + [n2(n2 + 1) \div 2] - R2$
    $= (10)(10) + [(10)(10+1) \div 2] - 92$ $= (10)(10) + [(10)(10+1) \div 2] - 118$
    $= 100 + 55 - 92$ $= 100 + 55 - 118$
    $= 63$ $= 37$

Thus, the obtained value for the smallest $U = 37$. Next we checked the appropriate Mann-Whitney U Table (available in most statistics books) for the critical value of U at alpha $= .05$ and $n1 = 10$, $n2 = 10$. Given these criteria, the critical value of $U = 27$.

Conclusion: Since the critical value of $U=27$ is less than the obtained value of $U=37$, we must accept the hypothesis of no significant difference. Therefore, we must conclude that singers do not perform A = 440 Hz. significantly flatter or sharper than violinists.

PRACTICAL EXAMPLE: INTERVAL OR RATIO LEVEL

Finally this data set can be analyzed at the interval or ratio level of measurement. Here relationships to the normal curve must be considered (see Figure 9). The curve is symmetrical with the mean in the exact center and the total area under the curve representing 100%. We can observe that in consideration of standard scores such as IQ, GRE, standard deviations, and Z scores, the mean of a normal distribution is zero. Note that 34.13% of the area of the curve lies between the mean and plus one standard deviation, 34.13% lies between the mean and minus one standard deviation, 13.59% lies between plus one standard deviation and plus two standard deviations, 13.59%, between minus one standard deviation and minus two standard deviations, and so forth.

If we had a large group of people responding to a musical question in such a way that the resulting level of measurement was interval or ratio, then it might be possible to achieve a normal distribution. If this happened, 34.13% of the scores would fall between the mean and plus one standard deviation, 34.13% would fall between the mean and minus one standard deviation, 13.59% would fall between plus one standard deviation and plus two standard deviations, and so forth.

---

[7]Madsen and Madsen, *Experimental Research in Music*, 102.

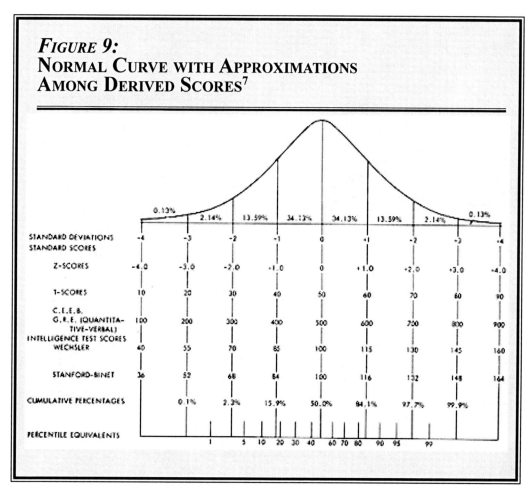

FIGURE 9:
NORMAL CURVE WITH APPROXIMATIONS
AMONG DERIVED SCORES[7]

An interval scale of measurement permits comparisons of equality and differences. These comparisons are possible since the distances between points on this scale are known (for example, measurements by a metronome or thermometer). A ratio scale of measurement is stronger because in addition to the possibility of intervallic measurement, a ratio scale has an absolute zero point. Most ratio levels of measurement are achieved through the use of sophisticated apparatuses such as electric timers, voice spectrographs, and tuners indicating cent deviations.

First, it is important to convert each cent deviation score for each singer and violinist into a standard score so to determine where each score lies in a theoretical, normal distribution (see Table 3). To do this, a grand mean (M) is computed by adding every score (x) and dividing the result by the total number of scores (in this case, 20). The sum of the scores of the singers and violinists is 438. (Note that when adding these scores to obtain a grand mean, minus signs are ignored. At this point, we are not interested in direction of deviation. We are only interested in magnitude of deviation.) Dividing 438 by 20, we achieve the grand mean (M) of 21.9.

To convert each individual score into a standard (Z) score, (1) subtract the grand mean (M) from each individual score ($x - M$, see columns 2 and 5 for these results);

TABLE 3:
**COMPUTATION OF NORMAL DISTRIBUTION OF CENT DEVIATION
SCORES OF SINGERS AND VIOLINISTS**

Singers	$x - M$	$(x - M)^2$	Z
50	28.1	789.61	.96
40	18.1	327.61	.62
100	78.1	6,099.61	2.68
35	13.1	171.61	.45
10	-11.9	141.61	.41
8	-13.9	193.21	-.48
- 25	-46.9	2,199.61	-1.61
- 10	-31.9	1,017.61	-1.09
- 6	-27.9	778.41	-.96
20	-1.9	3.61	-.06

Violinists	$x - M$	$(x - M)^2$	Z
-10	-31.9	1,017.61	-1.09
6	-15.9	252.81	.55
20	-1.9	3.61	-.06
22	.1	.01	.003
25	3.1	9.61	.11
-6	-27.9	778.41	-.96
-20	-41.9	1,755.61	-1.44
5	-16.9	285.61	-.58
8	-13.9	193.21	-.48
12	- 9.9	98.01	-.34

(2) square the resulting difference (see columns 3 and 6); (3) sum the (16,117); (4) compute the standard deviation by dividing 16,117 by N-1, or 19, and take the square root of the result (29.12); (5) obtain a Z score for each singer's and violinist's deviation score by dividing the number representing x-M (the difference between the observed score and the grand mean) by the standard deviation (29.12).

For example, the Z score for the first Singer is 28.1 divided by 29.12 equals .96. This means that this singer's deviation from the average of all singers and violinists taking this pitch discrimination test is almost one standard deviation out of tune from equi-temperament. Another way of describing this singer's score would be to say that the 50 cent sharp deviation is about one standard deviation from the average cent deviation for the twenty singers and violinists taking the test. Take a pencil and place the Z scores for all singers and violinists on the normal curve (Figure 11) so that the distribution of the scores becomes clearer. Remember that minus values should be places to the left of the mean and plus values to the right. Having done this, answer the question of whether the scores form a normal distribution or not.

The purpose of this example is not to test an hypothesis but merely to experience some descriptive techniques using ratio level of measurement. Significance tests that are appropriate under the assumption of a normal distribution, an interval or ratio level of measurement, and a large number of observations are t tests and analyses of variance (also known as F tests or ANOVAs). These tests are more sophisticated and complex and, therefore, may not be appropriate for introductory experiences.

SUMMARY

As has been demonstrated, statistical analyses of this data set answered three very different questions. First, at the nominal level of measurement, we determined whether the number of flat and sharp performances by singers and violinists could have occurred by chance alone. Since our hypothesis, that there would be no significant difference between what would have been expected by chance alone and what we observed was accepted there was nothing further to discuss. If we had rejected our hypothesis, data might have indicated some sort of trend in terms of whether violinists and singers played more sharp A's or more flat A's. Secondly, at the ordinal level of measurement, we determined whether singers were sharper or flatter than violinists. Our hypothesis of no significant difference between their performances was accepted. Finally, at the ratio level of measurement, we did not answer the question of whether the magnitude of cent deviation from A = 440 Hz. was significantly greater for singers or violinists. However, in the computation of Z scores, it became clear that the 20 scores did not represent a normal distribution.

RESEARCH APPLICATIONS

1. Describe any musical idea or behavior numerically at the nominal level of measurement. Do this by counting and categorizing. Use the example of nominal data analysis as a reference and model. Include the following in your report: Hypothesis, Procedure, Statistical Test, Level of Significance, Results, and Conclusions. Requirements: (a) at least two categories; (b) $N = 30$ with a final count of more than 5 in each category (to achieve this you may have to increase the N).

2. Describe any musical idea or behavior numerically at the ordinal level of measurement. Do this by ranking the responses or scores of subjects. Use the example of ordinal data analysis as a reference and model. Include the following in your report: Hypothesis, Procedure, Statistical Test, Level of Significance, Results, and Conclusions. Requirements: (a) at least two groups, and (b) an N of 20 with $n1 = 10$ and $n2 = 10$.

3. Describe any musical idea or behavior numerically at the interval or ratio level of measurement. Do this by measuring musical behavior with a timepiece, metronome, a tuner measuring cent deviations, a decibel meter, centimeters, and so forth. Use the example of interval data analysis as a reference and model. If you can, go beyond a description of the mean, standard deviation, and standard scores by computing a t statistic or an F statistic (see any parametric statistics textbook). Include the following in your report: Presentation of data in table form; Description of what the data represents; Procedure for collecting data; Computational procedures for grand mean, standard deviation, and Z scores; Results; and Conclusions.

BIBLIOGRAPHY

Campbell, D. T. and J. C. Stanley. *Experimental and Quasi-Experimental Designs for Research*. Chicago: Rand McNally, 1963.

Madsen, Clifford K. and Madsen, Charles H., Jr. *Experimental Research in Music*. Raleigh, NC: Contemporary Publishing Co., 1978.

Madsen, Clifford K. and Randall S. Moore. *Experimental Research in Music: Workbook in Design and Statistical Tests*. Raleigh, NC: Contemporary Publishing Co., 1978.

Siegel, Sidney. *Non-Parametric Statistics for the Behavioral Sciences*. NY: McGraw-Hill Book Company, 1956.

Wapnick, Joel. "The Use of Computers and Samplers in Music Research." Paper presented at Research in Music Behavior Symposium, Logan, Utah, April, 1987.

Chapter Seven

The Logic of Experimental Design
in Music Research

 **Chapter Seven**

The Logic of Experimental Design in Music Research

In the preceding chapters we have discussed at length the processes of deductive and inductive analysis and synthesis. Philosophers construct a premise and critically analyze it using formal principles of deductive logic. Qualitative researchers use their observations to determine hypotheses rather than set them *a priori*. Conversely, in descriptive and observational methodology, a null hypothesis (one stating that there will be no significant differences in the occurrence of one category of behavior versus another) is constructed regarding the objects or situations under observation. Philosophers use model and contrary examples to rationalize their premises or the antithesis of them. Qualitative researchers develop a rich description of what they have observed and what they have been told by informants, adding their own interpretations of the information. Quantitative researchers count the occurrence of carefully defined behaviors or situations, thereby converting events into numbers which can then be summarized. Interpretation of the data is also appropriate in this mode of inquiry.

Although many quantitative research studies are purely descriptive in nature, many also go another step by attempting to change the behavior that has been observed. This requires more sophisticated knowledge of the principles of logic, more rigorous operational definitions of variables under study, and judicious application of statistical analysis to results.

BEHAVIORAL AND STATISTICAL DESIGNS

Experimental research in music begins with the assumption that musical behavior is lawful, or in other words, that there is a functional relationship between cause (independent variable) and effect (dependent variable). Having made this assumption, each experimental research design represents an endeavor to manipulate an independent variable to test or isolate the effect of that manipulation on the dependent variable. For example, a pianist might assume that there is a functional relationship between the fingering of a particular scale passage (independent variable) and the accuracy of the performance of that scale (dependent variable). To determine if that relationship is functional the independent variable may be manipulated by altering the fingering of the scale. The effect of this manipulation would be determined by the accuracy of subsequent performance of the scale.[1]

There are two methods of experimentation in music, behavioral and statistical. The logic of behavioral design is that of continuous measurement over time with subjects serving as their own controls. The logic of statistical design involves discrete measurement of samples from varied or counterbalanced time periods or conditions. Behavioral experimentation is concerned with individual changes; statistical, with group changes.

In statistical design one is concerned with how many subjects are being studied. In behavioral design, the number of subjects is not so crucial since each individual case is of utmost importance. Statistical experimenters are interested in generalizing the results of experiments to larger populations; this explains their interest in a large N (number of subjects). Behavioral experimenters often are not interested in generalizing the results of experiments to larger populations; they believe that the behavior of each individual or group is under unique environmental control.

Statistical analysis involves comparisons of samples. Measurements are taken on discrete entities. Each group measurement or observation (O) may be compared with every other group measurement using the same dependent variable. If the differences are great enough, assumptions are made about the effect of the independent variable (X).

Appropriate analysis for behavioral design generally takes the form of graphic analysis. Continuous lines connecting points illustrate a relationship between variables and a predictable as well as environmental change over intervals of time.

Quantitative researchers in music have in the past used behavioral and statistical methods of experimentation. Music therapists have made the chief contributions in behavioral design. Some studies employ complete reversal designs with graphic analysis and may involve either a single subject or a group of subjects.[2] The logic

---

[1]C. K. Madsen and Cornelia Yarbrough, "The Effect of Experimental Design on the Isolation of Dependent and Independent Variables." In **Research in Music Behavior**, eds. C. K. Madsen, R. D. Greer, and C. H. Madsen, Jr. (New York: Teachers College Press, 1975), 226-243.

[2]L. P. Hauck and P. L. Martin, "Music As a Reinforcer in Patient-Controlled Time-Out," **Journal of Music Therapy**, 7 (1970): 43-53; H. Jorgenson, "Effect of Contingent Preferred Music in Reducing Two Stereotyped Behaviors of a Profoundly

of complete reversal designs is reflected in the graphic analyses showing the effect of baseline (data collected before the independent variable is introduced), introduction of the independent variable, return to baseline (withdrawal of the independent variable), and reintroduction of the independent variable. Musicians may readily identify with the form of the behavioral complete reversal design: A (baseline), B (introduction of the independent variable), A (return to baseline), B (reintroduction of the independent variable).

Other behavioral studies use multiple independent variables altering the return to baseline. For example, the behavioral designs, ABCADA, ABCDA, and ABA (known as an incomplete reversal design) have appeared in music therapy research literature.[3]

An example of a complete reversal design with a group (as opposed to individual) experiment may be found in a study by Purvis.[4] In this study, three groups worked arithmetic problems for five sessions. One group had rock-dance music as a background for working problems; another had rock-listening music as a background; and the third had no music. The design outline for the five sessions was as follows:

Retarded Child," *Journal of Music Therapy*, 8 (1971): 139-145; H. Jorgenson and M. K. Parnell, "Modifying Social Behaviors of Mentally Retarded Children in Music Activities," *Journal of Music Therapy*, 7 (1970): 83-87; B. J. Morgan and O. R. Lindsley, "Operant Preference for Stereophonic over Monophonic Music," *Journal of Music Therapy*, 3 (1966): 135-143; M. Rieber, "The Effect of Music on the Activity Level of Children," *Psychonomic Science*, 3 (1969): 325-326; A. L. Steele, "Music Therapy: An Effective Solution to Problems in Related Disciplines," *Journal of Music Therapy*, 8 (1971): 131-139.

[3]For the design, ABCADA, see A. L. Steele, "Effects of Social Reinforcement on the Musical Preference of Mentally Retarded Children," *Journal of Music Therapy*, 4 (1967): 57-62; for the design, ABCDA, see S. Baird, "A Technique to Assess the Preference for Intensity of Musical Stimuli in Young Hard-of-Hearing Children," *Journal of Music Therapy*, 6 (1969): 6-11; For the design, ABA, see J. M. Johnson and L. L. Phillips, "Affecting the Behaviors of Retarded Children with Music," *Music Educators Journal*, 57 (1971): 45-46; For other studies using these designs, see Charles E. Furman, *Effectiveness Of Music Therapy Procedures: Documentation Of Research And Clinical Practice* (Washington, D. C.: National Association for Music Therapy, 1988) and Clifford K. Madsen and Carol A. Prickett, *Applications of Research in Music Behavior* (Tuscaloosa, AL.: University of Alabama Press, 1987).

[4]J. Purvis, "The Effect of Rock Music on the Arithmetic Performance of Sixth-Grade Children," (Master's Thesis, Florida State University, 1971).

Group I	A	B	A	A	B
Group II	A	C	A	C	A
Group III	A	A	A	A	A

where: A (baseline) = number of arithmetic problems worked

B (first independent variable) = rock-dance music as background

C (second independent variable) = rock-listening music as background

In this design two groups undergo a modified complete reversal pattern while a third group serves as a control. This is similar to a multiple-baseline design in that behavior measured but not treated within the multiple-baseline design actually acts as a control condition to isolate the precise effect of the intervening independent variable.[5] It should be noted that the number of arithmetic problems worked is counted both during baseline (A) and during treatment (B and C); another way to state this is that measurement is continuous rather than discrete.

Experimental studies in music that have used statistical designs have generally involved pre- and posttests as well as multiple groups. Most basic statistical designs involve two groups, one experimental (experiencing the independent variable, X, as well as the dependent variable, O) and one control (experiencing only the dependent variable, O). An example of this design may be found in a study by Madsen and Madsen[6] outlined as follows:

Group 1	O	X	O
Group 2	O		O

where: O = vocal pitch accuracy

X = reinforcement

Close examination reveals one of the principal differences between behavioral and statistical designs. A behavioral design employs continuous measurement over time:

---

[5]Madsen and Yarbrough, 1975.

[6]C. K. Madsen and C. H. Madsen, Jr., "Selection Of Music Listening Or Candy As A Function Of Contingent Versus Non-Contingent Reinforcement And Scale Singing," *Journal of Music Therapy*, 9 (1972): 190-198.

```
A   B      A     B
       or
O   OX     O     OX
```

A statistical design samples measurement from varied and (or) counterbalanced time periods:

```
O   X    O
O        O
```

In other words, behavioral experimentation emphasizes measurement throughout all experimental conditions of behavioral change, whereas statistical experimentation emphasizes a static measurement to assess the effect of discrete temporal treatments.

MILL'S FIVE METHODS OF EXPERIMENTAL INQUIRY

To begin to understand the logical basis of experimental research, we will start with a discussion of Mill's canons of logic. John Stuart Mill, an English philosopher, believed that mere observation could not do much to advance scientific knowledge. To determine the true cause of an event requires not only verification of that event through observational methodology, but also the elimination of alternative possibilities. The exploration of alternative possibilities and thus the determination of cause and effect relationships require methods of experimental inquiry.

Mill gives five methods of experimental inquiry. The first two methods are those of agreement and disagreement, respectively. The canon, or regulating principle, of the *method of agreement* states that "if two or more instances of the phenomenon under investigation have only one circumstance in common, the circumstance in which alone all the instances agree is the cause (or effect) of the given phenomenon." The canon of the *method of disagreement* states that if we consider a case in which the phenomenon under investigation occurs and a case in which it does not occur and if we find that the two cases have all circumstances in common save one, which is present only in the former case, this one circumstance is the cause. Both methods are obviously methods of elimination, the first stating that whatever *can* be eliminated is not connected to the occurrence of the phenomenon under investigation, and the second stating that whatever *cannot* be eliminated is so connected. Mill then combines these methods of agreement and disagreement for the third experimental method, the *joint method*.

The canon of the fourth experimental method, the *method of residues*, states, "Subduct from any phenomenon such part as is known by previous inductions to be the effect of certain antecedents, and the residue of the phenomenon is the effect of the remaining antecedents." The fifth method is that of *concomitant variations*. It is used in cases where experimental variation is not practicable. Its principle is that whatever phenomenon varies whenever another phenomenon varies in a given manner is either a cause of this phenomenon or its effect or connected with it through some causal fact. For example, if we find that variations in the moon's position are always followed by corresponding variations in the tides, we may conclude that the moon is the cause, total or partial, which determines the tides or that they are both the result of some as yet unidentified cause. Obviously, we are not able to remove the moon to see what happens in its absence.[7]

The purpose of formal experimental design based upon the guiding principles of logic is to control for possible threats to validity. As discussed in Chapter 6, these include history, maturation, testing regression, mortality, sample bias, instrumentation, and the ability to generalize to other similar populations or samples. To illustrate both the logical principles outlined by Mill and techniques for the control of threats to validity, it is necessary to carefully examine an example of complex design issues.

In 1975, Madsen and Yarbrough completed an experiment that addressed the effect of experimental design on the isolation of dependent and independent variables.[8] The Solomon Four Group statistical design formed the basis for the total design of this experiment.[9] This design is essentially a pretest-posttest control group design (where O = pre- or posttest and X = treatment):

Group I	O	X	O
Group II	O		O

with the addition of one other experimental and one other control group, both lacking the pretest:

Group III	X	O
Group IV		O

[7]Frederick Coppleston, S.J., *A History of Philosophy*, v. VIII (Garden City, NY: Image Books, 1985), 50-92; John Stuart Mill, *A System of Logic*, Book III, Chapter 8 (NY: Harper and Brothers, 1873); C. K. Madsen and C. H. Madsen, Jr., *Experimental Research in Music* (Raleigh, NC: Contemporary Publishing Co., 1978), 51-52; C. K. Madsen and R. S. Moore, *Experimental Research in Music: Workbook in Design and Statistical Tests* (Raleigh, NC: Contemporary Publishing Co., 1978), 13-16.

[8]C. K. Madsen and Cornelia Yarbrough, 1975.

[9]D. T. Campbell and J. C. Stanley, *Experimental and Quasi-Experimental Designs for Research* (Chicago: Rand McNally, 1963).

In the above design, subjects can either be (a) randomly assigned to one of four groups; or (b) assigned to one of the four groups after results of the pretest have been calculated. Proper assignment of subjects to groups is very important, because it is helpful when the pretest scores of each group are equivalent. If a very large number of subjects are available, random assignment should result in group equivalency. If a small number of subjects is available, assignment on the basis of pretest scores is the easiest route to take.

The Solomon Four Group design illustrates Mill's *Joint Method* (*Method of Agreement* and *Method of Disagreement*). Groups I and II share the administration of pre- and posttests, but both do not receive treatment. The treatment is eliminated for Group II. The process of elimination continues for Group III which has the presentation of treatment followed by posttest in common with Group I, but does not receive the pretest. Group IV has the posttest in common with Group II, but does not receive the pretest. Thus, whatever *can* be eliminated is not connected to the occurrence of the phenomenon; and what *cannot* be eliminated is so connected.

Next a behavioral design with a control group was added to the Solomon Four Group design:

```
Group V    A    B    A    B
Group VI   A    A    A    A
```

This represented a complete reversal design where continuous dependent measures (baseline or A) were taken throughout the experiment both within the experimental group (group getting B) and in a control group (group not getting B). While baseline continued in the control group, a complete reversal (ABAB) was put into effect in the experimental group. Here, also, Mill's *Joint Method* is the logical basis. Not only is the treatment (B) withdrawn and replaced in Group V, but it is also the one thing not held in common with Group VI.

At this point, the experimental design included both a behavioral complete reversal design with a control group as well as a Solomon Four Group statistical design. Thus, the experimental design was as follows:

```
Group I     O    X    O              Statistical Aspect
Group II    O         O
Group III        X    O
Group IV              O

Group V     A    B    A    B         Behavioral Aspect
Group VI    A    A    A    A
```

where: O   =   total minutes practiced and
                    rating of productivity during
                    practice
          X and B =   distraction index (number of
                    off-task thoughts during
                    practice sessions)

Finally, after using the above and other experimental design we may know more about specific factors and what parts of a phenomenon they affect. Mill's *Method of Residues* proposes that when the specific factors causing certain parts of a given phenomenon are known, the remaining parts of the phenomenon must be caused by the remaining factors. For example, if there are no significant differences among the Groups which received treatment; if these same Groups practiced an equal amount of time with equal productivity ratings; and, regardless, all Groups had significantly different performance scores; then, something other than treatment, practice, and productivity caused differences in performance scores.

Research in music will benefit greatly from carefully planned and well-executed experimentation. However, one should remember that the design and subsequent manipulation of variables exists in order to isolate the effect of the variables in question. Clear, operational definitions of both dependent and independent variables coupled with a logical approach to the design is essential before commencing with the procedural aspects of the experiment.

STATISTICAL DESIGN APPLICATION

In planning the procedural aspects of statistical designs one must be concerned with choosing the population sample to be studied, the instrumentation for measuring the effect of the independent variable, the experimental environment, and the reliability and validity of the dependent measures (see Chapter 6). The following example is based on the experiment conducted by Madsen and Yarbrough.[10] It illustrates the detail and precision necessary to complete an experimental project.

Subjects were selected from the population of a large southern university. Members of the Psychology of Music and Behavior Modification in Music classes served as subjects. In addition, each class member randomly selected three other music students who had the same applied instrument and were within their classification (freshman, sophomore, junior, senior, graduate). The following instructions were given to class members:

---

[10]C. K. Madsen and Cornelia Yarbrough, 1975.

Step 1:   Each participant lists all other students within the School of
                 Music who perform on the same instrument as the class
                 member. Piano and voice choose only one class level.

Step 2:   List names and give each name a number of 1 - .

Step 3:   Get a telephone directory, open up any page and, taking the
                 last digit(s) of telephone numbers, assign every name a new
                 number depending upon how its number comes up from the
                 directory, e.g., your number 8 (Step 2) might come up as new
                 number 1, etc.

Step 4:   Start with number 1 and find your subjects, then ask them to
                 participate in your experiment. You need three others plus
                 yourself. If your first-ordered subjects have already been
                 chosen, then go to the next names in order and ask them—
                 continue until you get three who will participate.

Step 5:   Give subjects written instructions.

Thus, 120 subjects were randomly selected and assigned to one of four groups
(n = 30). Figure 10 depicts the experimental treatment for each group in the study.
Note that the dependent variable is a time log (O) and the independent variable is a
distraction index (X).

FIGURE 10:
SOLOMON FOUR-GROUP DESIGN

	2 weeks	2 weeks	2 weeks
Group I	Time Log O1	Distraction Index X	Time Log O2
Group II	Time Log O3		Time Log O4
Group III		Distraction Index X	Time Log O5
Group IV			Time Log O6

FIGURE 11:
APPLIED MUSIC PRACTICE TIME LOG

Subject # _____   Group # _____
Instrument _____
Class _____   Name _____
Age _____   Sex _____

Rating Scale

1. Absolutely nonproductive   6. Moderately productive
2. Extremely nonproductive   7. Mostly productive
3. Mostly nonproductive   8. Very productive
4. Not very productive   9. Extremely productive
5. Somewhat productive   10. Absolutely productive

Week of (circle)   10-16,   17-23,   24-30,   31-6,   7-13,   14-20,   21-7,   28-5

Monday	Tuesday	Wednesday	Thursday	Friday	Saturday	Sunday	Total Min.	Aver. Min.

Comments: _____

_____

_____

_____

_____

Two-week Total Averages

Total 10-16 + 17-23 _____

Total 24-30 + 31-6 _____

Total 7-13 + 14-20 _____

Total 21-27 + 28-5 _____

GRAND TOTAL _____

Subjects were asked to keep a record of their practice time by the use of time logs. Each time log represented the number of minutes practiced for one week. Also, space was provided for ratings of the productivity of each practice session on a scale from one to ten. Minutes practiced were totaled and practice ratings were averaged each week for a period of six weeks (see Figure 11).[11]

The following instructions were given to each subject:

> You are asked to participate in a very important experiment that is designed to ascertain effective applied music practice. Please fill out the attached forms concerning your applied music practice. BE AS ACCURATE AS POSSIBLE, listing the exact times you start and stop practicing including small breaks (two or three minutes). Also, place a number from 1 to 10 (1 is low, 10 is high) in the bottom space on the box indicating how effective you judge the sessions to have been for the day. Thus, for each day please provide for the experimenter a precise record of (1) how much you practiced and (2) how worthwhile you judge the session(s) to have been.

Spaces were provided for recording as many as four practice sessions per day. Days on which there was no practice were not rated.

In addition, subjects in Groups I and III were to keep a distraction index, which is a record of every time a subject was not on task to practicing. Each subject was told to mark the distraction index every time s/he thought of something other than practicing (see Figure 12).[12]

---

[11]*Ibid*, 240.
[12]*Ibid*, 241.

FIGURE 12:
DISTRACTION INDEX FOR APPLIED MUSIC PRACTICE

Subject's Name _____ Group # _____

Week of (circle) 10-16, 17-23, 24-30, 31-6, 7-13, 14-20, 21-7, 28-5

A distraction should be marked whenever you think of something other than the practice material. When this occurs, mark the card immediately and then get back to work immediately.

(1) With each distraction (thought, general off-task, interruption, mind wandering while still performing, etc.) make a mark on the sheet
(2) After marking the sheet get back to work immediately.

DISTRACTIONS   Day _____

Total _____

DISTRACTIONS   Day _____

Total _____

DISTRACTIONS   Day _____

Total _____

DISTRACTIONS   Day _____

Total _____

DISTRACTIONS   Day _____

Total _____

DISTRACTIONS   Day _____

Total _____

DISTRACTIONS   Day _____

Total _____

DISTRACTIONS   Day _____

Total _____

DISTRACTIONS   Day _____

Total _____

WEEKLY TOTAL

Class members assisting in the experiment were responsible for their subjects' reliability. Subjects were told that it was not important how long they practiced; it was important that they record their practice time honestly and accurately. Class members were given reliability check sheets for each of their subjects and were told to make three checks per week per subject. Reliability was computed by dividing the number of "yes" checks by the number of "yes" plus "no" checks.

In the analysis of the results of a statistical study, both qualitative and quantitative issues should be considered in interpreting and reporting the data. The first consideration should be the question to which the researcher sought an answer. It is expected that an experimental design exercises enough control to isolate the variable of interest. However, one must remember that any analysis, numerical or inferential, should not be extracted from the design pattern. Instead, the relationships of dependent and independent variables should be carefully thought through, the function of control groups considered, and finally the appropriate statistical or behavioral formats selected.

The next consideration should be the data (the numbers) to be used in the analysis. Data collected in this study were minutes practiced, number of distractions during practice sessions, and average ratings of practice sessions. Understanding the analysis of data collected as the result of the implementation of this statistical design might be facilitated by first recalling the Solomon Four Group design used in this study (see Figure 13) where O = total minutes practiced and rating of productivity during practice and average ratings of each practice session and X = distraction index (number of distractions). Comparisons can then be discussed by referring to Figure 13.

FIGURE 13:
STATISTICAL COMPARISONS AND PROJECTED RESULTS

Data Points	Statistical Test	Expected Results
1) O1 vs. O3 vs. O4 vs. O6	One-Way ANOVA	NS
2) O2 vs. O5	t-test	NS
3) O2 + O5 vs. O4 + O6	t-test	S
4) O2 - O1 vs. O4 - O3	t-test on gain scores	S
5) O1 vs. O2 vs. O3 vs. O4 vs. O5 vs. O6	One-Way ANOVA followed by multiple -range test	S

The first comparison looks at O (minutes practiced, for example) without having received the independent variable (X). The appropriate statistical test would be the one-way analysis of variance, which essentially compares more than two columns of numbers to determine whether there is a significant difference among, in this case, the four columns. The result one might expect is that of no significant difference since the independent variable (X) has not been received.

The second comparison looks at O after receiving X. Here the appropriate statistical test would be the t-test that compares two columns of numbers to determine whether there is a significant difference between the columns. Here the result one might expect is again that of no significant difference. Since the two groups representing the O's we are comparing are different in that one group was pretested and the other was not, a significant difference between the O's which are the object of comparison would indicate that subjects who were pretested learned from the pretest and not necessarily from X, a validity problem.

The third comparison looks at the sum of the O's after X versus the sum of the O's (at the same time period) not receiving X. Here one would expect a significant difference between the O's receiving X and those not receiving X.

The fourth comparison looks at the two groups receiving O at the beginning of the experiment and at the end. The beginning scores are subtracted from the final scores and gain scores are compared again using a t-test. One would expect a significant difference between the gain scores of the group receiving X and those of the group not receiving X.

The final comparison looks at every O with the expectation of a significant difference. Since the one-way analysis of variance indicates a significant difference but does not indicate which pairs of O's are significantly different from one another, further analysis using a multiple range test is necessary. A multiple range test is performed after a statistical test; it compares more than two columns (in this case) to determine which two column-pairs are significantly different from one another. If there are no design validity problems, one would expect the multiple range test to show a significant difference between, for example, O1 and O2, O2 and O4, O4 and O5, O2 and O6, O5 and O6, and O3 and O5. All other pairs of O should not be significantly different.

The above represents the simplest possible logical comparisons for analysis purposes. Of course, more complex analyses might be devised to determine possible interactions between or among O's and X's and comparisons would have to be duplicated to study changes in ratings of practice productivity. However, a basic understanding of the importance of design in the isolation of cause and effect relationships is the goal of this exercise.

BEHAVIORAL DESIGN APPLICATION

Sometimes it may be more useful to analyze the results of a study by charting the change in the dependent measures across time. To study the effects of behavioral self-assessment procedures on the acquisition of basic conducting techniques, Madsen and Yarbrough graphed the progress of the class as a whole across one semester. Eight aspects of conducting technique were operationally defined (beat pattern, tempo, style, dynamics, eye contact, preparations, releases, and cueing), observation forms were developed for student use, and specific procedures for learning were developed. Students were videotaped conducting a pretest in which they were told to demonstrate the eight aspects of conducting technique. They then conducted three videotaped practica. For the initial practicum, they observed only preparations, beat patterns, eye contact, tempo, and releases; for the second practicum, an additional two categories, dynamics and cueing were observed; for the third practicum, one more category was added, that of style. Beginning with the fourth practicum, the music to be conducted was changed and the procedure just outlined was repeated. In this way the student was encouraged to build conducting technique through successive approximations and through behavioral self-assessment of progress. Following the sixth practicum, a posttest was recorded and evaluated to determine whether the student was able to transfer the skills learned to a new situation.

The following graph (see Figure 14) shows the percentages of correct responses for the pre- and posttests and for each practicum. It demonstrates the effectiveness of the successive approximations approach with behavioral self-assessment. At the pretest, students were achieving below 40% correct in every category of conducting technique. The graph clearly illustrates the categories assigned for initial practice and the result of above 40% correct for all five categories assigned. With the addition of two categories in the second practicum, students achieved above 50% correct in seven categories; and for the third practicum, above 70% correct in all eight categories. The graph shows that when the music was changed for the fourth practicum, students were able to transfer what they had learned for five of the categories, but were less successful for the remaining three. As they progressed through the fifth and sixth practica to the posttest, it is apparent that they were successful in achieving a high rate of accuracy in conducting technique.[13]

The complexities of the foregoing statistical and behavioral design applications are immense. It is the complexity of even simple experiments that alternately confuse, delight, and intimidate the musician interested in research in music behavior. It would appear that many musicians go through life in awe of experimental designs and proper statistical analysis. Yet one only has to seek out several eminent

---

[13]Clifford K. Madsen and Cornelia Yarbrough, *Competency-Based Music Education* (Raleigh, NC: Contemporary Publishing Co., 1985), 96-123.

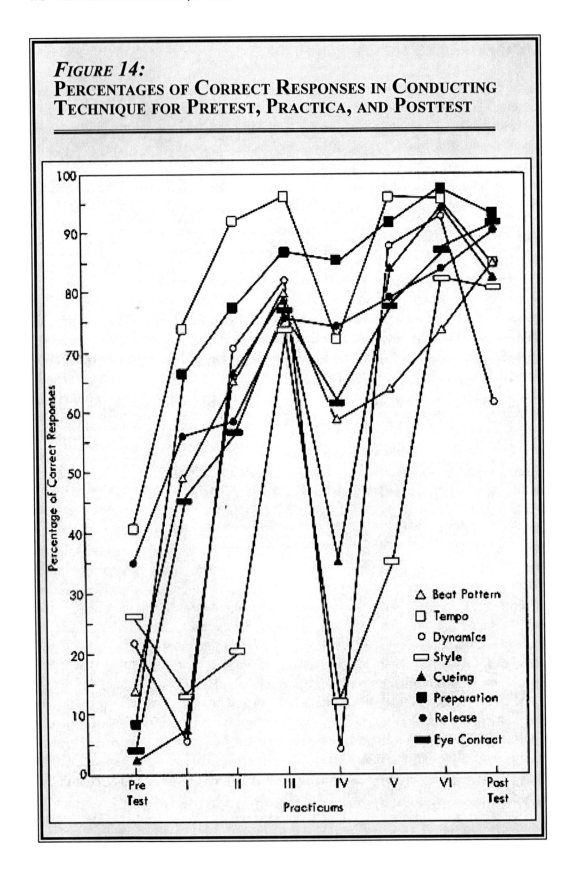

FIGURE 14:
PERCENTAGES OF CORRECT RESPONSES IN CONDUCTING TECHNIQUE FOR PRETEST, PRACTICA, AND POSTTEST

authorities or sit on an editorial board to realize that there are many appropriate as well as inappropriate evaluations possible concerning almost all experiments. However, one should remember that the design and subsequent manipulation exists in order to isolate the effect of the variables under question, not as a vehicle to be argued and debated in the pursuit of intellectual gamesmanship, to correct sloppy methodology, or in any other way to serve the *process* at the exclusion of the *product*.

WRITING TECHNIQUES FOR QUANTITATIVE STUDIES

Articles reporting the results of experimental studies in music generally include a title page, an abstract, an introduction, the method, results, discussion, and references. The style manual used is that of the American Psychological Association.[14]

The title of an experimental study usually names both the independent and dependent variables. For example, the title, "The effect of videotape feedback techniques on performance, verbalization, and attitude of beginning conductors," identifies "videotape feedback" as the independent variable (treatment) and "performance, verbalization, and attitude" as dependent variables (those representing the data collected). In addition to the title, a title page contains the author's name and institutional affiliation, date, and the running head (optional).

Following the title page is an abstract of about 150 words. The abstract is a brief, comprehensive summary of the contents of the article. It should begin with the words, "The purpose of this study was ..." It should continue with, for example, "Subjects ($N = 20$) were randomly assigned to one of two groups: an experimental group that ...; and a control group that ... Finally, the abstract should end with a statement beginning with "Results demonstrated that ..." A good abstract is succinct, accurate, and quickly comprehensible.

The introduction of the paper contains the rationale for studying the problem, a review of literature, and a clear statement of the problem or purpose of the study. It begins with the title and author centered on the page. The first paragraph should state the rationale behind the study and should end with one sentence stating the specific purpose of it, as in "Therefore, the purpose of this study was ..." Of course, the rationale may take more than one paragraph, but it should be specific and brief.

Following the rationale and one-sentence statement of the purpose, a review of literature should be presented. The literature reviewed should be closely related to the problem under study. It may be appropriate to state the results or procedures of studies reviewed. In addition, the review should demonstrate the logical continuity

---

[14]*Publication Manual of the American Psychological Association*, 5th ed. (Washington, D. C.: American Psychological Association, 2001).

between previous and present research. It is important that the review contain only studies using quantitative methodology. Other articles (philosophical, historical) may be cited in the rationale or statement of the problem sections.

The next section should describe the method used in completing the experiment. It might include an explanation of how subjects were selected, a description of subjects, experimental design, definitions of dependent and independent variables, experimental environment, equipment, and so forth. Enough detailed description should be provided so that the reader can evaluate the appropriateness of the procedures, the reliability and validity of the results, and replicate the study if they so desire. In other words, the method section should describe *what* was done and *how* it was completed.

Following the methods section, are the results of statistical analyses. These may range from simple, descriptive statistics such as mean, mode, median, standard deviation, percentages, or frequencies, to more complex statistical tests such as factorial analyses and analyses of variance. First, the main results or findings should be briefly stated. Then the data should be reported in sufficient detail to support the conclusions. Discussion of the findings is not appropriate in this section.

Because clarity and economy are the aims of scientific writing, tables that provide exact values and illustrate main effects are the most effective medium for reporting data. However, individual scores or raw data should be omitted from the final report. The information reported in table form should be accompanied by text explaining the salient aspects of the table.

A discussion of the results is the concluding section of an experimental article. Here it is important to revisit the review of literature and compare results cited there to those in the present study. In addition, this section can be used to make recommendations for future study and to speculate regarding why results were as they appeared. A list of references appears at the end of the article. Only works cited may appear in this list.

SUMMARY

Quantitative research in music requires the transformation of musical information, ideas, and behavior into numerical data. It is often useful to describe musical phenomena by counting its occurrence. Detailed definition of the phenomena under study must precede the description of it. This definition must be operational; what is being described must be observable.

After an operational definition has been satisfactorily achieved and after the musical behavior has been observed and counted, it is often desirable to apply some sort of treatment to that behavior in order to isolate the cause of the behavior or effect of the treatment. When some treatment is applied and measurement of the cause and effect of the treatment occurs, the methodology is labeled experimental.

Experimental methodology requires the statement of an hypothesis, the estab-
lishment of a logical procedural design, reliable and valid dependent measures, and
appropriate statistical or graphic analyses. It should be recognized that not all problems lend themselves to experimental study. In addition, many musical phenomena
should be studied using a variety of methodologies and modes of inquiry.

We perceive, discriminate, perform, and prefer music in seemingly complex
ways. Ambiguities and paradoxes regarding human responses to music both confuse and delight experienced researchers. Realizing that as musicians we operate
within different and often conflicting modes of inquiry as we interact with music,
we should accept the fact that knowledge of our art may involve many different
and conflicting approaches to it. Continuing scrutiny of music from all available
viewpoints cannot help but bring us to a better understanding of our relationship to
music within our culture.

RESEARCH APPLICATIONS

1. State a null hypothesis regarding some aspect of musical behavior (i.e., performance, perception, discrimination, preference, teaching). Review at least 10 quantitative studies relative to your hypothesis. Then choose one of the following two designs:
   a. Behavioral: Measure baseline behavior(s) of one or more subjects for at least five days. When baseline has become stable, begin treatment for at least five days, but no more than ten. At the end of this initial treatment period, return to baseline. Finally, reinstitute treatment procedures.
   b. Statistical: Randomly assign 20 people to one of two groups: an experimental group and a control group. Give all subjects a pre- and a posttest. Submit the experimental group to a treatment in an attempt to change their musical behavior. Compare the pre- and posttest scores of the experimental group receiving treatment to the control group not receiving treatment. In your first attempt you may feel more comfortable using descriptive statistics to analyze your results. More sophisticated analysis can be applied to the data as progress is made in expertise. Finally, describe and discuss your results.

2. .Write an article describing the research project conducted in #1. The article should include the following sections: Statement of the problem including the null hypothesis; review of literature (at least 10 studies); procedures (selection of subjects, equipment, environment, independent and dependent variables, etc.); results; discussion relating your results to those outlined in the review of literature; and references.

BIBLIOGRAPHY

Baird, S. "A Technique to Assess the Preference for Intensity of Musical Stimuli in Young Hard-of-Hearing Children." *Journal of Music Therapy* 6 (1969): 6-11.

Campbell, D. T. and J. C. Stanley. *Experimental and Quasi-Experimental Designs for Research*. Chicago: Rand McNally, 1963.

Coppleston, Frederick. *A History of Philosophy*, v. VIII. Garden City, NY: Image Books, 1985.

Furman, Charles E. *Effectiveness of Music Therapy Procedures: Documentation of Research and Clinical Practice*. Washington, D. C.: National Association for Music Therapy, 1988.

Hauck, L. P. and P. L. Martin. "Music As a Reinforcer in Patient-Controlled Time-Out." *Journal of Music Therapy*, 7 (1970): 43-53.

Hitchcock, H. Wiley and Stanley Sadie, eds. *The New Grove Dictionary of American Music*. S. v. "Psychology of Music" by George L. Duerksen, v. 3, 649-650.

Johnson, J. M. and L. L. Phillips. "Affecting the Behaviors of Retarded Children with Music." *Music Educators Journal*, 57 (1971): 45-46.

Jorgenson, H. "Effect of Contingent Preferred Music in Reducing Two Stereotyped Behaviors of a Profoundly Retarded Child." *Journal of Music Therapy*, 8 (1971): 139-145.

Jorgenson, H. and M. K. Parnell. "Modifying Social Behaviors of Mentally Retarded Children in Music Activities." *Journal of Music Therapy*, 7 (1970): 83-87.

Lundin, Robert W. *An Objective Psychology of Music*. NY: Ronald Press, 1953; 2nd ed, 1967.

Madsen, Clifford K., R. Douglas Greer, and Charles H. Madsen, Jr., Eds. *Research in Music Behavior* NY: Teachers College Press, Columbia University, 1975.

Madsen, Clifford K. and Madsen, Charles H., Jr. *Experimental Research in Music*. Raleigh, NC: Contemporary Publishing Co., 1978.

——————. "Selection of Music Listening or Candy as a Function of Contingent Versus Non-Contingent Reinforcement and Scale Singing." *Journal of Music Therapy* 9 (1972): 190-98.

Madsen, Clifford K. and Randall S. Moore. *Experimental Research in Music: Workbook in Design and Statistical Tests*. Raleigh, NC: Contemporary Publishing Co., 1978.

Madsen, Clifford K. and Carol A. Prickett, Eds. *Applications of Research in Music Behavior*. Tuscaloosa, AL.: University of Alabama Press, 1987.

Madsen, Clifford. K. and Cornelia Yarbrough. *Competency-Based Music Education*. Raleigh, NC: Contemporary Publishing Co., 1985.

——————. "The Effect of Experimental Design on the Isolation of Dependent and Independent Variables." In *Research in Music Behavior*, pp. 226-243. Ed.

by C. K. Madsen, R. D. Greer, and C. H. Madsen, Jr.   NY: Teachers College Press, 1975.

Mill, John Stuart.   *A System of Logic*, Book III, Chapter 8. NY: Harper and Brothers, 1873.

Morgan, B. J. and O.R. Lindsley. "Operant Preference for Stereophonic over Monophonic Music*." Journal of Music Therapy* 3 (1966): 135-143.

Ogden, R. M. *The Psychology of Art.* NY: C. Scribner's & Sons, 1938.

Opper, J. *Science and the Arts: A Study in Relationships from 1600-1900.* Rutherford, N. J.: Fairleigh Dickinson University Press, 1973.

Publication Manual of the American Psychological Association, 5th ed. Washington, D. C.: American Psychological Association, 2001.

Purvis, J. "The Effect of Rock Music on the Arithmetic Performance of Sixth-Grade Children." Master's Thesis, Florida State University, 1971.

Radocy, R. E. and J. David Boyle. *Psychological Foundations of Musical Behavior.* Springfield, IL: Charles C. Thomas Books, 1979.

Rieber, M. "The Effect of Music on the Activity Level of Children." *Psychonomic Science* 3 (1969): 325-326.

Schneider, E. H. and Cady, Henry L. *Evaluation and Synthesis of Research Studies Relating to Music Education.* Cooperative Research Project E-016. Item Ed 010 298 in ERIC Document Reproduction Service. Cleveland, OH: Bell and Howell, Co., 1965.

Schoen, Max. *The Psychology of Music.* NY: Ronald Press Co., 1940.

Seashore, Carl. *In Search of Beauty in Music.* NY: Ronald Press Co., 1947.

—————————. "Psychology in Music: The Role of Experimental Psychology in the Science and Art of Music." *Musical Quarterly* XVI (1930): 229-237.

—————————. *Psychology of Music.* NY: McGraw-Hill Book Co., Inc., 1938.

—————————. *The Psychology of Musical Talent.* NY: Silver Burdett, 1919.

Siegel, Sidney. *Non-Parametric Statistics for the Behavioral Sciences.* NY: McGraw-Hill Book Company, 1956.

Steele, A. L. "Music Therapy: An Effective Solution to Problems in Related Disciplines." *Journal of Music Therapy*, 8 (1971): 131-139.

—————————. "Effects of Social Reinforcement on the Musical Preference of Mentally Retarded Children." *Journal of Music Therapy*, 4 (1967): 57-62.

Stumpf, Carl. *Tonpsychologie*, v. 1 and 2. Leipzig: Hirzel, 1883 and 1890.

Valentine, C. W. *The Experimental Psychology of Beauty.* London: 1962.

Appendices

 **Appendix A**

General Reference
Bibliographies

T he most important general reference guide is the one edited by Eugene P. Sheehy.[1] Bibliographical control is not complete until this work has been consulted. The following annotated list from Sheehy and Balay's supplement is a highly selective one. The *Guide* has five main divisions: A. General Reference Works; B. The Humanities; C. Social and Behavioral Sciences; D. History and Area Studies; and E. Science, Technology and Medicine. Most of the references listed below have been selected from the General Reference Works and Humanities divisions. Call numbers have been provided; of course, these numbers may differ to varying degrees among libraries.

BIBLIOGRAPHIES OF BIBLIOGRAPHIES

Besterman, T. *A World Bibliography of Bibliographies.* 4th ed., rev. and enl. Lausanne, Switzerland: Societas Bibliographisa, 1965-66, 5 vols. Z 1002 T67
A classified bibliography of separately published bibliographies of books, manuscripts, and patent abridgements. International in scope. The 4th edition records bibliographies published through 1963, with some later additions.

---

[1] Eugene P. Sheehy, Ed., *Guide to Reference Books*, 10th ed (Chicago: American Library Association, 1986); Robert Balay, Ed., *Guide to Reference Books: Covering Materials from 1985-1990*, supplement to the 10th ed (Chicago: American Library Association, 1992). Call No. Z 1035.1 S 43

Bibliographic Index: A Cumulative Bibliography of Bibliographies, 1937 -. NY: The H. W. Wilson Co., 1938-. Z 1002 B595

An alphabetical subject arrangement of separately published bibliographies and bibliographies included in books and periodicals. About 2600 periodicals, including many in foreign languages, are now examined regularly. It is a valuable supplement to Besterman.

BIBLIOGRAPHIES

Cumulative Book Index. NY: The H. W. Wilson, Co.,1898-. Z 1219 M78

Indexes books in the English language. Subject headings conform to LCSH. Published monthly with a bound cumulation each year, thus is more current than Books in Print.

Books in Print. NY: R. R. Bowker Co., 1969-. Z 1215 P972

Author, Subject, and Title indexes. Annual with a mid-year supplement.

Books Out-of-Print. NY: R. R. Bowker Co., 1983 -.

U. S. Copyright Office. Catalog of Copyright Entries, 1891-1946. Washington: Government Printing Office, 1891 -. LC 3.6

Issues covering 1978 were the last to be published in paper. The catalog is now published only on microfiche. Includes information on copyrights of books, pamphlets, sound recordings, music, etc.

LIBRARY CATALOGS

National Union Catalog. Washington, D. C.: Library of Congress. Z881 A1 C32

This is an author and main entry catalog (with cross references but not added entries) of books and other materials for which Library of Congress printed cards were available in (1) the Library of Congress (as cards had not been printed for all the Library's books, the catalog is not a complete record of the Library's holdings, but does represent a large percentage; (2) many government department libraries; and (3) various libraries throughout the country, as a result of the cooperative cataloging program. Information given is detailed and highly accurate.

British Museum, Department of Printed Books. ***General Catalogue of Printed Books.*** London: Trustees of the British Museum, 1959-66 (vol. 1, 1965), 263 vols. Z921 B87

The catalog is a complete record of the printed books in the library of the British Museum (now the British Library), which have appeared from the 15th century to the end of 1955, in all languages except the Oriental. For the most part, it is an author catalog only. There are currently two supplements, one for the years 1956-1965 and another for the years, 1966-1970.

British Library. *General Catalogue of Printed Books.* London: British Museum Publications, Ltd., 1978. 13 vols. Z921 B87
   Nearly 600,000 entries for works cataloged 1971-1975. Continued with a supplement for the years 1976-1982.

Berlin, Preussische Staatsbibliothek. *Berliner Titeldrucke; fünfjahrs Katalog, 1930/34-1935/39.* Berlin: Staatsbibliothek, 1935-40. Z929 B5 M15
   Lists works published 1930-39 cataloged in more than 100 German libraries.

Paris, Bibliothèque Nationale. *Catalogue général des livres imprimés: Auteurs.* Paris: Impr. Nationale, 1900-81, 231 vols. Z927 P2
   An alphabetical author catalog. In addition to its comprehensive coverage of French publications, the catalog is particularly strong in other Romance-language and classical materials.

Rome, Centro Nazionale per il Catalogo Unico delle Biblioteche Italiane e per le Informazioni Bibliografiche. *Primo catalog collettivo delle biblioteche italiane.* Rome: 1962-79, vols. 1-9 (in progress).
   A first effort toward a national union catalog for Italy. The annotation in Sheehy states that, "Progress on the catalog was seriously delayed as a result of the Florence flood of 1966, and survival of numerous Florentine copies reported in at least the first six volumes is open to question."

BIOGRAPHY

American Council of Learned Societies. *Dictionary of American Biography.* NY: Scribner, 1928-. E176 D56
   Includes noteworthy persons of all periods who lived in the territory now known as the United States, excluding British officers serving in America after the colonies declared their independence. Does not include living persons.

Who's Who in America. Chicago: Marquis Who's Who, 1899/1900 - .E663 W56

Who's Who in American Women. CT 3260 W5

Who's Who Among Black Americans. Detroit: Gale Research, Inc., 1975-76 - . E185 .96 W52

Who Was Who in America. Chicago, Marquis Who's Who. E663 W54

MICROFORMS

Guide to Microforms in Print. Westport, CT: Microform Review, 1978-. Englewood, Colorado: Microcard Editions, 1961 - . AAS8519

This guide has author, title, and subject indexing and provides a cumulative annual listing of microform title, comprising books, journals, newspapers, government publications, archival material, collections, and other projects (excepting dissertations and theses) which are currently available from micropublishing organizations throughout the world.

ANCIENT, MEDIEVAL, AND RENAISSANCE MANUSCRIPTS

Braswell, Laurel Nichols. *Western Manuscripts from Classical Antiquity to the Renaissance: A Handbook.* NY: Garland, 1981. Z105 B73
An annotated bibliography which is a guide to the study of early Western manuscripts. Includes sections on incipits, paleography, diplomatics and archives, illumination, music, codicology textual criticism, bibliographies and reference works. Indexed.

Briquet, Charles Moïse. *Les filigranes. Dictionnaire historique dés marques du papier dés leur apparition vers 1282 jusqu'en 1600.* Ed. by Allan Stevenson. Amsterdam: Paper Publications Soc., 1968.
Contains reproductions of more than 16,000 watermarks and a selective and annotated bibliography.

Cappelli, Adriano. *The Elements of Abbreviation in Medieval Latin Paleography.* Translated by David Heimann and Richard Kay Lawrence, Kansas: University of Kansas Libraries, 1982. Z111 C36
An alphabetical list of abbreviations given both in manuscript facsimile and in printed letters followed by the words for which they stand.

Gaskell, Phillip. *A New Introduction to Bibliography*. Winchester, UK: St. Paul's Bibliographies, 1995. Z116.A2 G27 1995

Gravell, Thomas L. and Miller, George. *A Catalogue of American Watermarks, 1600-1835.* NY: Garland, 1979. TS 1115 G7
Identifies more than 700 watermarks, giving location of the manuscript, place and date of use, and a reproduction of the watermark.

Ker, Neil Ripley. *Medieval Manuscripts in British Libraries.* Oxford: Clarendon Press, 1969-1983.
Provides information about manuscripts written before 1500, in Latin or a Western European language.

Scriptorium; Revue international des études relatives aux manuscrits. Anvers: Standaard Boekhandel, 1947 -. Z108 S35
Includes current bibliographies of manuscript studies and facsimile editions.

COPYRIGHT

Johnston, Donald F. *Copyright Handbook*. 2nd ed. NY: Bowker, 1982. KF2994
  J63
  Explains the 1976 Copyright Act and reports on legal developments that have
  taken place since it took effect at the beginning of 1978.

Appendix B

Basic Music
Bibliographical Tools

The references listed here are selected for the most part from Duckles and Reed.[2] Only the most basic of reference materials has been included. For additional and more specific sources, consult Duckles and Reed, a valuable tool that should be in every music scholar's library.

DICTIONARIES, ENCYCLOPEDIAS, HISTORIES, AND CHRONOLOGIES

Besseler, Heinrich, and Max Schneider. *Musikgeschichte in Bildern*. Leipzig: Deutscher Verlag für Musik, 1964 - . ML 89 M9
A multivolume example of musical iconography containing numerous plates (images incorporating some reference to music), with commentary, a bibliography, chronological tables, and indexes.

Blume, F., ed. *Die Musik in Geschichte und Gegenwart: Allgemeine Enzyklopädie der Musik.(MGG)*. 17 vols. Kassel, Germany: Basel: Bärenreiter-Verlag, 1949-1986. ML100 B48
A comprehensive music reference work of the highest scholarly merit. In German, but international in scope and coverage. Articles contributed by specialists throughout the world. Gives complete listings of composers works and detailed monographs. The work continues in two Ergänzungs Banden, 1973-79 and a Register Band published in 1986. The Ergänzungs Banden both supplement

---

[2]Vincent H. Duckles and Ida Reed, *Music Reference and Research Materials*, 5th ed. (NY: Schirmer Books, 1997).

and correct information in the first 14 volumes. The Register Band, edited by Elisabeth Heckmann and Harald Heckmann is an extensive index.

Cary, Tristram. *Dictionary of Musical Terminology*. New York: Greenwood Press, 1992. ML 102 E4 C37

A 1-volume encyclopedia of music technology, with over 6,00 copiously illustrated main entries and 200 subsidiary ones, emphasizing electronic instruments and computer music, with some traditional instruments, with helpful quotations from acknowledged experts.

Eisler, Paul E. *World Chronology of Music History*. Dobbs Ferry, NY: Oceana Publications, 1972 - . 6 vols. to date. At completion to be 8-10 vols. ML 161 .E4

Hitchcock, H. Wiley and Stanley Sadie, eds. *The New Grove Dictionary of American Music*. NY: Grove' Dictionaries of Music, 1986. 4 vols. ML 101 U6 N48

Covers American music and musicians including detailed coverage of popular styles and genres. Numerous descriptions of uniquely American musical instruments. Historical sketches of musical publishers.

Kaufmann, Walter. *Selected Musical Terms of Non-Western Cultures: A Notebook-Glossary*. Warren, MI: Harmonie Park Press, 1990. ML 108 K37

Kernfeld, Barry. *The New Grove Dictionary of Jazz*. New York: Grove's Dictionary of Music, 1988. 2 vols. ML 102 J3 N48

The largest dictionary of jazz ever published; it contains the broadest coverage and gives detailed attention to all periods and styles of jazz from many countries.

Lowenberg, A. *Annals of Opera, 1597-1940*. 3rd ed. rev. Totowa, NJ: Rowman and Littlefield, 1978. ML102.06 L6 1943

Chronological listing of operas by dates of first performance, including (with a few exceptions) only works known to have been produced. The list is limited to older operas that are extant and modern ones that have created interest outside their countries of origin. Each entry includes composer's name, original title of the work, English translation for all languages except German, French, and Italian. Librettist identified; place and date of first performance given.

Marcuse, Sibyl. *Musical Instruments; A Comprehensive Dictionary*. NY: Norton, 1964. ML 102.15 M37

Intended to serve English readers as Sachs' Real Lexicon (see entry below) does German. World coverage, although incomplete with respect to non-European and folk instruments.

Marcuse, Sibyl. *A Survey of Musical Instruments*. 1st ed. NY: Harper & Row, 1975. ML 460 M365 S94.

The New Oxford History of Music. London: Oxford University Press, 1954-1990. 10 vols. ML 160 N44

A multivolume history of music, each volume of which is a composite work made up of contributions by scholars of international repute, edited by a specialist in the period and usually containing an extensive bibliography. An accompanying set of LP recordings, The History of Music in Sound (RCA Victor LM 6015-6016, 6029-6031, 6037, 6057, 6092, 6146, and 6153, 22 discs in 10 vols.) was issued 1954-57 accompanied by 10 vols. Of extensive notes in pamphlet form, thoroughly documenting the works.

Randel, Donald. M. *New Harvard Dictionary of Music.* Cambridge, Mass.: Belknap Press of Harvard University Press, 1986. ML 100 R3

The standard one-volume reference work in English for non-biographical information. The emphasis is on the historical approach and on Western art music, although there is some coverage of non-Western and popular musics.

Riemann, Hugo. *Riemanns Musik-Lexikon.* 12th ed. Edited by Wilibald Gurlitt. New York: Schott Music Corporation, 1959-75. 5 vols. ML 100 R 52

An international dictionary of music, covering all times and places and incorporating achievements of German musical scholarship.

Sachs, Curt. *Real-Lexicon der Musikinstrumente.* NY: Dover Publications, 1964. ML 102 .I5 S2

A technical and historical dictionary of instruments of all periods and countries. Names of instruments and parts of instruments in some 120 languages and dialects - European, African, and Asian. Locations of examples in instrument collections.

Sadie, S., Ed. *New Grove Dictionary of Music and Musicians.* Washington, D. C.: Grove's Dictionaries of Music, 1980. 20 vols. ML 100 N48

This is the standard comprehensive music encyclopedia in English and is directed toward the interests of music scholars rather than informed amateurs and performers. It contains entries on music history, theory, and practice, instruments and terms. The longer biographical entries include lists of works and extensive bibliographies. Entries are signed.

Sadie, S., Ed. *New Grove Dictionary of Musical Instruments.* Washington, D. C.: Grove's Dictionaries of Music, 1984. 3 vols. ML 102 .I5 N48

Sadie, Stanley, and Christine Bashford. *The New Grove Dictionary of Opera* . New York: Grove's Dictionaries of Music, 1992. ML 102 O6 N5

Covers composers, singers, conductors, librettists, designers, producers, directors, dancers, choreographers, patrons, and impresarios. Also includes entries on operas, opera houses, national opera traditions, and opera-related terms.

GUIDES TO MUSICAL SCHOLARSHIP

Colwell, Richard, ed., *Handbook of Research on Music Teaching and Learning.* NY: Schirmer Books, 1992.

Contains chapters on methodology and extensive reviews of the extant literature on a variety of topics.

Harrison, Frank L., Mantle Hood, and Claude V. Palisca. *Musicology.* Englewood Cliffs, NJ: Prentice-Hall, 1963. Reprinted by Greenwood Press, Westport, CT, 1974. ML 3797 .H27 M9

Three expansive, thoughtful essays on the place of musicology in the world of learning that represent a milestone in the history of the discipline.

Madsen, Clifford K., and Charles H. Madsen, Jr. *Experimental Research in Music.* Englewood Cliffs, NJ: Prentice-Hall, 1970. Reprinted by Contemporary Pub. Co., Raleigh, NC, 1978. MT 1 .M13

A research manual that explores techniques of experimental research in music and the quantitative aspects of scholarship.

Madsen, Clifford K., and Cornelia Yarbrough. *Competency-Based Music Education.* Englewood Cliffs, NJ: Prentice-Hall, 1980. Reprinted by Contemporary Pub. Co., Raleigh, NC, 1985. MT 1 M127

Contains a chapter on systematic behavioral observation complete with observation forms and instruction.

Myers, Helen. *Ethnomusicology: An Introduction.* NY: W. W. Norton, 1992. ML 3799 E82

An overview of the current state of ethnomusicology including a historical overview of the field, discussions on theory and method, discussions of fieldwork, analysis, biology of music making, gender, ethics of fieldwork, and preservation of world musics.

Phelps, Roger P, Ronald H. Sandoff, Edward C. Warburton, and Lawrence Ferrara, and Thomas Goolsby. *A Guide to Research in Music Education.* 5th ed. Metuchen, NJ: The Scarecrow Press, Inc., 2005. MT1 .P5

Covers bibliography and research procedures and techniques, including bibliographical references.

Poultney, David. *Studying Music History; Learning, Reasoning, and Writing about Music History and Literature.* 2nd ed. Englewood Cliffs, NJ: Prentice-Hall, 1995.

Pruett, James W., and Thomas P. Slavens. *Research Guide to Musicology.* Chicago, IL: American Library Association, 1985. ML 113 .P83

A comprehensive exposition of the development of the discipline including a substantial bibliography. Emphasis is on historical musicology, music theory and performance practices.

Rainbow, Edward L. and Hildegard C. Froehlich. *Research in Music Education: An Introduction to Systematic Inquiry.* NY: Schirmer Books, 1987.

BIOGRAPHY

Baker, Theodore. ***Baker's Biographical Dictionary of Musicians***. 8th ed. revised by Nicolas Slonimsky. NY: Schirmer Books, 1992. ML 105 B16
The most authoritative and extensive one-volume biographical dictionary in English. It focuses mainly upon musicians "in the world of 'art music.'"

Bull, Storm. ***Index to Biographies of Contemporary Composers.*** NY: Scarecrow Press, 1964 - 87. 3 vols. ML 105 B9
Indexes sources of information for about 8000 composers.

Historical Records Survey. District of Columbia. ***Bio-bibliographical Index of Musicians in the United States of America from Colonial Times.***   2nd ed.   Sponsored by the Board of Commissioners of the District of Columbia. Washington, D. C.: Music Section, Pan American Union, 1956. ML 106 U3 H6
Bio-bibliographical index of musicians in the United States of America from colonial times.

Cummings, David M. ***International Who's Who in Music and Musicians' Directory (in the Classical and Light Classical Fields).*** 14ᵗʰ ed. Cambridge, England: International Who's Who in Music, 1994. ML 106 G7 W44
Résumés of about 8000 musicians, musicologists, music critics, managers, publishers, librarians, and others in the field. Includes addresses of the subjects. Emphasis on western European and western hemisphere figures. International lists of organizations with addresses by various categories: orchestras, competitions, libraries, conservatories, etc.

BIBLIOGRAPHIES OF MUSIC LITERATURE [GENERAL]

Brockman, William S. Music: ***A Guide to the Reference Literature.*** Littleton, CO: Libraries Unlimited, Inc., 1987. ML 113 B85
Annotations for 558 music reference works, principally in English, giving a current look at the field.

Darrell, Robert D. ***Schirmer's Guide to Books on Music and Musicians; a Practical Bibliography.*** NY: G. Schirmer, 1951. ML 113 D3

Diamond, H. J. ***Music Analyses: An Annotated Guide to the Literature***. NY: G. Schirmer, 1991. ML 128 A7 D5
The 4,600 citations in this work were gleaned from more than 750 books, 100 periodicals, and 400 dissertations.

Gerboth, W. ***An Index to Musical Festschriften and Similar Publications***. NY: W. W. Norton, 1969. ML 128 M8 G4.

The most comprehensive treatment of music Festschriften available. Arranged in three parts: A. Under the name of the individual or institution honored; B. Subject listing of more than 2,700 articles; C. Author and secondary-subject index.

Harris, Ernest E. ***Music Education: A Guide to Information Sources***. Volume 1 of Education Information Guide Series. Francesco Cordasco, Series Editor. Detroit, MI: Gale Research Company, 1978. ML 19 H37

Arranged in 74 sections, titles are divided into five categories: generalia, music in education, subject matter areas, uses of music, and multimedia and equipment. There are appendices listing library holdings and music periodicals.

Marco, Guy A. and Sharon Paugh Ferris. ***Information on Music: A Handbook of Reference Sources in European Languages.*** Littleton, CO.: Libraries Unlimited, 1975 - 84. 3 vols. ML 113 M33

An annotated guide to music reference works with the intention of providing comprehensive access to information about music. Each entry provides complete bibliographic information, an LC classification, references to other guides to music reference and research materials, and an introduction. There are indexes to names and titles, and to subjects.

Megget, Joan. M. ***Music Periodical Literature: An Annotated Bibliography of Indexes and Bibliographies.***. Metuchen, NJ: Scarecrow Press, 1978. ML 128 P24 M43

Covers more than 250 indexes to music periodicals in general works and works devoted to the subject of music. Provides a bibliography of lists of periodicals and a guide to the literature of the history of music periodicals. Indexes of subjects and titles.

Mixter, Keith. E. ***General Bibliography for Music Research***. 2nd ***ed***. Detroit: Information Coordinators, 1975. ML 113 M595 G4

Contains references to general bibliographical tools that may be helpful for research in North American and European music.

Nettl, Bruno. ***Reference Materials in Ethnomusicology***. 2nd ed., revised. Detroit: Information Coordinators, 1967. ML 128 M8 N5

A narrative and critical discussion of the leading reference works in the field, organized in terms of the structure of the discipline.

Notes, the Quarterly Journal of the Music Library Association, 1948 - . ML 27 U5

Provides the largest available source of reviews of music and its literature as well as substantial listings of the same.

Vinquist, M. and Zaslaw, N. ***Performance Practice; a Bibliography***. NY: W. W. Norton, 1971. ML128 L3V55

First appeared as issue 8 (1969) of Current Musicology; supplemented in issue 10 (1970), issue 12 (1971), and issue 15 (1973. Excluding these supplements, the bibliography includes about 1200 entries of both primary and secondary sources. International in scope, the book includes a bibliography of performance practice bibliographies.

BIBLIOGRAPHIES OF MUSIC LITERATURE
[CURRENT OR ANNUAL]

Arts and Humanities Citation Index. Philadelphia: Institute for Scientific Information, 1976 - Z 5931 A78
Three times a year with the last issue being cumulative for the year. Citation index; Source index; Corporate index; Permuterm index; Guide and Journal index; vols. for 1980-1989 issued in more than 3 vols.

Bibliographia Musicologica, a bibliography of music literature. Utrecht: Joachimsthal, 1970-76. 9 vols. ML 113 B535
An international bibliography of books about music, listed alphabetically by author, with a subject index. The listings give publisher, pagination, and include current reprints, facsimile editions, and revised editions.

Humanities Index. NY: The H. W. Wilson, Co., 1974-. AI 3 H8
Supersedes Social Sciences and Humanities Index. a cumulative index to English language periodicals. Among the music periodicals indexed are the Journal of the American Musicological Society, Current Musicology, Music and Letters, The Music Review, The Musical Quarterly, Notes, Opera, and Opera News. Many of the music periodicals indexed in this index are also indexed in InfoTrac, a CD-ROM periodical index.

BIBLIOGRAPHIES OF MUSIC LITERATURE
[DISSERTATIONS]

Adkins, Cecil and Alis Dickinson, Eds. *Doctoral Dissertations in Musicology.* Philadelphia: American Musicological Society, 1990. Supplements, 1991 - . ML 128 M8 A4
Entries provide University Microfilm numbers, *Dissertation Abstracts* reference numbers, and RILM numbers,

Gordon, R. "Doctoral Dissertations in Music and Music Education, 1957-63." *Journal of Research in Music Education*, 12, 1-112. ML 1 J6

Gordon, R. "Doctoral Dissertations in Music and Music Education, 1963-67." *Journal of Research in Music Education*, 16, 87-218. ML 1 J6

Gordon, R. "Doctoral Dissertations in Music and Music Education, 1968-71." *Journal of Research in Music Education*, 20, 2-185. ML 1 J6

Larson, W. S. "Bibliography of Research Studies in Music Education, 1949-56." *Journal of Research in Music Education*, 5, 64-225. ML 1 J6

BIBLIOGRAPHIES OF MUSIC [GENERAL]

Music in Print Series. Philadelphia: Musicdata, 1974. 6 vols. and annual supplements   ML 113 M874

Volumes 1 and 2 with supplements contain listings of choral music in print; volume 3, organ music; volume 4, vocal music; volume 5, orchestral music; and volume 6, string music.

U. S. Copyright Office. *Catalog of Copyright Entries: Music*. Washington, D. C.: Government Printing Office, 1947-. LC 3.6/5: pt. 5

Cites all music deposited for copyright in the U. S. whether published in the U. S. or elsewhere. Arranged by title with index to names of composers, authors, editors, compilers, arrangers, and so forth. Beginning in 1978 the catalog appears on microfiche.

U. S. Library of Congress. *Library of Congress Catalog, Music and Phonorecords, a Cumulative List of Works Represented by Library of Congress Printed Cards*. Washington, D. C.: The Library of Congress, 1954-72. Z881 A1 C328

Current music accessions, printed or sound recordings, of the Library of Congress and of libraries participating in its cooperative cataloging program. Includes purchased current or retrospective materials and a selection of recent copyright deposits. Entries are reproduced from the library's printed cards. Semi-annual with annual cumulation.

American Society of Composers, Authors and Publishers. *ASCAP Symphonic Catalog*, 3rd ed. NY: R. R. Bowker, 1977. ML128 O5 A55

Alphabetical listing, by composers and arrangers, of symphonic literature controlled by ASCAP. Entries give instrumentation, duration, publisher. List of publishers' addresses.

BIBLIOGRAPHIES OF MUSIC
[EARLY MUSIC IN MODERN EDITIONS]

Heyer, A. H. *Historical Sets, Collected Editions, and Monuments of Music*. 3rd ed. Chicago: American Library Association, 1980. 2 vols. ML113 H52

An indispensable guide to editorial work in the field of early music. Approximately 1,300 entries in this edition. Detailed listings of the contents of sets. Numerous cross references. Comprehensive index of composers, editors, titles. The only guide to the contents of the collect scholarly editions of scores cataloged in the M2's and M3's.

Hill, George R. and Norris L. Stephens. *Collected Editions, Historical Series and Sets, and Monuments of Music*. Berkeley, CA: Fallen Leaf Press, 1997. ML 113 H 55

This work does not completely replace Heyer's work (see above) which will remain indispensable for some older material not included here. Fulfils the need to update Heyer's work because the rate of publication of scholarly editions of music has greatly increased in the last thirty years.

BIBLIOGRAPHIES OF MUSIC
[PRIMARY SOURCES OF EARLY MUSIC, MANUSCRIPTS AND PRINTED BOOKS]

The British Union Catalogue of Early Music Printed Before the Year 1801. Ed. by Edith B. Schnapper. London: Butterworths Scientific Publications, 1957. 2 vols. ML 116 B7
A major reference tool for work with early printed sources of music. These volumes provide the key to sources in British libraries. Brief bibliographical entries.

Eitner, R. *Biographisch-bibliographische Quellen-Lexikon der Musiker und Musikgelehrten der christlichen Zeitrechnung bis zur Mitte des 19.* Leipzig: Breitkopf & Hartel, 1898-1904, 10v. ML 105 E36
Although this work is out-of-date and much of the information is incorrect, it is still valuable for the identification of works no longer extant as it precedes two world wars which resulted in much damage to European library collections. The International Inventory of Musical Sources (RISM) has replaced it as a key to the sources of early music.

CATALOGS OF MUSIC LIBRARIES
AND COLLECTIONS

Boston Public Library. *Dictionary catalog of the music collection of Boston Public Library.* Boston, MA.: G. K. Hall and Co., 1972, 20 v.

British Museum, *Department of Manuscripts. Catalogue of Manuscript music in the British Museum, by A. Hughes-Hughes.* London, 1906-09, 3 v. ML 136 L8 B72

British Museum. Department of Printed Books. *Catalogue of Printed Music Published Between 1487 and 1800 Now in the British Museum.* By Barclay Squire. London, 1912. 2 vols. ML 136 LB B71

International Association of Music Libraries. Commission of Research Libraries. *Directory of Music Research Libraries, Including Contributors to the International Inventory of Musical Sources (RISM).* By Rita Benton. Iowa City: University of Iowa, 1967-72, 3 v. ML 12 B45

New York Public Library, Music Division. ***Dictionary Catalog of the Music Collection, New York Public Library.*** Boston: G. K. Hall, 1965, 33 v. ML136 N5 N573

JAZZ AND POPULAR MUSIC

Feather, Leonard. ***The Encyclopedia of Jazz.*** New York: Horizon Press, 1960. ML 3561 J3 E55
Introductory essays on the history, sociology, and structure of jazz; biographies of jazz musicians, outlining their careers and summarizing their recording activities. Followed by The Encyclopedia of Jazz in the Sixties (ML 105 F35) and The Encyclopedia of Jazz in the Seventies (ML 105 F36; co-authored by Ira Gitler).

Havlice, P. P. ***Popular Song Index.*** Metuchen, NJ: The Scarecrow Press, Inc., 1975. ML 128 S3 H4
Three supplements covering publications to 1989. Indexes to folk songs, pop tunes, spirituals, children's songs, sea chanties, and blues in several hundred song anthologies published since 1940.

Mattfeld, J. ***Variety music cavalcade, 1620-1961; a chronology of vocal and instrumental music popular in the United States.*** 3rd ed. Englewood Cliffs, NJ: Prentice-Hall, Inc., 1971. ML 128 V7 M4
A chronological bibliography of American popular music, with parallel social and historical events listed for each year.

Shapiro, N. ***Popular Music: An Annotated Index of American Popular Songs.*** NY: Adrian Press, 1964-84, 9 v. ML120 U5 S5
A selective annotated list of the significant popular songs of the 20th century.

Stambler, I. ***Encyclopedia of Pop, Rock, and Soul.*** Rev. ed. NY: St. Martin's Press, 1989. ML 102 P66 S8
Preceded by three essays on the genres, the dictionary consists mostly of biographical entries, with a few terms and trends defined or discussed. There are articles on films and musicals included. Lists of winners of various prizes. Bibliography.

Stambler, I. and Landon, G. ***Encyclopedia of Folk, Country, and Western Music.*** 2nd ed. NY: St. Martin's Press, 1983. ML 102 F66 S7
Contains biographical entries to performers and groups. Appendices include special articles. Also, award listings and a selective discography. Bibliography.

DISCOGRAPHIES

Clough, F. F. and Cuming, G. J. *The World's Encyclopedia of Recorded Music.*
London: The London Gramophone Corp. in association with Sidgwick &
Jackson, 1952. 4 supplements. ML156.2 C6

Schwann Opus. Santa Fe, NM: Stereophile, 1991 - . ML 156 .2 O68
Currently a quarterly publication listing currently available classical recordings
on CD and cassette tape.

Schwann Spectrum.   Santa Fe, NM: Stereophile, 1991 - .
A quarterly publication listing currently available popular CD, LP record, and
cassette tape.

 **Appendix C**

Selected Serials in Music and Related Fields

MUSIC SERIALS

American Choral Review – ML 1 A36
American Music – ML 1 A497
American Music Teacher – ML 1 A5
American Record Guide – ML 1 A725
American String Teacher – Ml 27 U5 A8356
The Black Perspective in Music – ML 3556 B6
British Journal of Music Education – ML 5 B 6898
Bulletin of the American Musicological Society, 1936-41
Bulletin of the Council for Research in Music Education – M1 C684x
The Choral Journal – ML 1 C656
Clavier – ML 1 C79
Ethnomusicology – ML 1 E864
Galpin Society Journal ML5 G26
The Gramophone – ML 5 G65
High Fidelity – ML1 H45
High Fidelity and Musical America – ML1 H452x
Instrumentalist – ML 1 I714
Journal of American Instrument Society – ML1 A527
Journal of the American Musicological Society – ML 27 U5 83363
Journal of Band Research – ML 1300 J46
Journal of Historical Research in Music Education
Journal of the International Folk Music Council – ML 26 I544
Journal of Musicology – ML 1 J 693
Journal of Musicological Research – ML 5 M 6415

Journal of Music Theory – ML 1 J86
Journal of Music Therapy – ML 1 J685
Journal of Renaissance and Baroque Music (1946-47; in 1948 it became Musica Disciplina) – ML 5 M722
Journal of Research in Music Education – ML 1 J6
Journal of the Society of Arts – AS 122 R69
Moravian Music Journal – ML 1 M192
Music and Letters – ML 5 M64
Music Clubs Magazine – ML 1 N14
Music Educators Journal – ML 1 M985
Music Journal – ML 1 M276
Music Library Association Notes – ML 27 U5 M695
Music News – ML 1 M27
Music Perception – ML1 M2735
Music Review – ML 5 M657
Music Sound Output – ML 3469 M89
Music Teachers National Association, Proceedings – ML 27 U5 M8
Music Therapy, Yearbooks of the NAMT
Musica Disciplina – ML 5 M722
Musical Courier – ML 1 M43
Musical Quarterly – ML 1 M725
NACWPI Journal – ML 27 U5 N17
National Association of Teachers of Singing – ML 27 U5 N2652
NAJE Educator – ML 1 N124
Opera – ML 5 061
Opera Notes – ML 5 061
School Musician, Director and Teacher – ML 1 S36
The Strad – ML 5 S89
Tempo – ML 5 T317

SERIALS IN RELATED FIELDS

American Annals of the Deaf - HV 2510 . A5
American Journal of Occupational Therapy – RM 735 A1 A5
American Journal of Physical Medicine – RM 735 A1 03
American Journal of Psychiatry – RC 312 A52
American Journal of Psychology – BF 1 A5
American Journal of Psychotherapy – RC 321 A54
American Journal of Sociology – HM 1 A7
American Psychologist – RC 467 A53
American Sociological Review – HM 1 A75

Archives of General Psychiatry – RC 321 A66
Archives of Neurology – RC 321 A67
Archives of Otolaryngology – RF 1 A7
Behavioral Science – BF 1 B45
Behavior Research and Therapy – BF 1 B4
Brain – RC 321 A1 B7
British Journal of Educational Psychology – LB 1051 A2 B7
British Medical Journal – R 31 B93
Child Development – HQ 750 A1C
Comparative Psychiatry – RC 454.4 .M87
Contemporary Psychology – BF 1 C53
Diseases of the Nervous System – RC 321 D5
Education – L11 E2
Education of the Visually Handicapped – HV 1571 1523
Educational and Psychological Measurement – BF 1 E3
Elementary School Journal – L11 E6
Exceptional Children – LC 3951 J6
International Journal of Social Psychiatry – RC 321 I58
Journal of Abnormal Psychology – RC 321 J7
Journal of the Acoustical Society of America – QC 221 A4
Journal of Aesthetics and Art Criticism – N1 J6
Journal of Aesthetic Education – N1 J58
Journal of American Ethnology and Archaeology – E 51 .F43
Journal of American Folklore – GR 1 J8
Journal of the American Medical Association – R15 A48
Journal of Applied Behavior Analysis – BF 636 A1 J6
Journal of Applied Psychology – BF 1 J55
Journal of Clinical Psychology – RC 321 J74
Journal of Consulting Psychology – BF 1 J 575
Journal of Education – L11 J5
Journal of Educational Psychology – LB 1951 A2 J6
Journal of Educational Research – L 11 J75
Journal of Experimental Child Psychology – BF 721 J64
Journal of Experimental Education – L11 J77
Journal of Experimental Psychology – BF 1 J6
Journal of General Psychology – BF 1 J64
Journal of the History of Ideas – B 1 J75
Journal of Neurology and Psychiatry – RC 321 J833
Journal of Personality – BF 1 J66
Journal of Personality and Social Psychology – RC 321 J7
Journal of Physical Education, Recreation, and Dance – GV 201 J6
Journal of Psychology – BF 1 J67

Journal of Rehabilitation – HD 7255 A2 N35
Journal of School Psychology – LB 3013.6 J6
Journal of Social Issues – HN 51 J6
Journal of Social Psychology – HM 251 A1 J6
Journal of Special Education – LC 4001 J6
Journal of Speech and Hearing Disorders – RC 423 J68
Nature
Neurology – RC 321 A47
New Biology – GH 1 N57
Occupational Therapy and Rehabilitation
Perceptual and Motor Skills – BF 311 P36
Proceedings of the Royal Society – Q 41 E21
Psychiatric Quarterly – RC 321 N52
Psychoanalytic Quarterly – BF 173 A2P7
Psychoanalytic Review – BF 1 P5
Psychological Bulletin – BF 1 P75
Psychological Monographs – RC 331 P79
Psychological Reports BF 21 P843
Psychological Review – BF 1 P7
Psychology in the Schools – LB 1101 P75
Psychology Today – BF 1 P82
Quarterly Journal of Experimental Psychology – QP 351 E95234
Recreation – GV 421 R5
Renaissance Quarterly – CB 361 R45
Saturday Review – Z 1219 S25
Science – Q 1 S35
Scientific Monthly – Q 1 S817
See and Hear – LB 1043
Social Forces – HN 51 S5
Sound – QP 460 B74
Southern Folklore Quarterly – GR 1 S65
Southwestern Journal of Anthropology – GN 1 S64
Young Children – LB 1140 A1 J6

 **Appendix D**

Library Classification Systems

The Dewey Decimal Classification, first published in 1876 by Melvil Dewey, provides for the classing of published materials under ten major headings:

000	General Works
100	Philosophy and Religion
200	Religion
300	Social Sciences
400	Philology
500	Natural Sciences
600	Applied Sciences and Technology
700	Fine Arts and Recreation
800	Literature
900	History, Geography, Biography

Music entries are assigned numbers from 780 through 789. The following are representative examples:

780.01	Research
781	General Principles (Theory of Music) and techniques
782	Dramatic music and production of musical drama
783	Sacred Music
783.026	Sacred Music-Christianity
784	Voice and vocal music

784.105	Appreciation (analytical and program notes)
785	Instrumental ensembles and their music
785.066	Orchestra
786	Keyboard instruments and their music
786.109	Historical and geographical treatment
787	String instruments and their music
787.1	Violin
788	Wind instruments and their music
788.7	Oboe and English horn
789	Percussion, mechanical, electrical instruments
789.1	Membranophones
789.913	Catalogs, lists, critical appraisal of recordings.

The Dewey classification system has been replaced in many academic libraries by the Library of Congress system published in 1902. The system is:

A   General Works-Polygraphy
B   Philosophy-Religion
C   History-Auxiliary Sciences
D   History and Topography (except America)
E-F America
G   Geography-Anthropology
H   Sociology
I   Vacant, left for expansion
J   Political Science
K   Law
L   Education
M   Music
N   Fine Arts
N   Fine Arts
P   Language and Literature
Q   Science
R   Medicine
S   Agriculture-Plant and Industry
T   Technology
U   Military Science
V   Naval Science
W, X,
Y   Vacant, left for expansion
Z   Bibliography and Library Science

Music entries are classified under three broad subheadings: M for Music (scores); ML for Literature of Music; and MT for Music Theory, Musical Instruction and Study. Some large subdivisions within each of these areas are:

M 5	- 1459	Instrumental Music
M 1495	- 2199	Vocal Music
ML 159	- 3790	History and criticism
ML 1100	- 1354	Chamber and orchestral music, band (military music
ML 3800	- 3920	Philosophy, physics, psychology, esthetics
MT 40	- 67	Composition, rhythm, melody, harmony, counterpoint
MT 170	- 810	Instrumental technics; for organ, piano, string, wind, and plectral instruments
MT 820	- 949	Singing and voice culture
MT 855	- 883	Special technics; chanting, sight singing, choral singing

Each of these is further divided into small topics.

 **Index**

Author Index

A
Abeles, H.F. 47, 111, 132
Apel, W. 55, 56, 80, 98
Aristotle 31, 37, 42, 47
Aristoxenus 27

B
Bacon, F. 21, 67, 68, 69, 82, 88, 98
Barzun, J. 2, 20, 68
Baumgarten, A. 28, 47
Becker, W.C. 116, 127, 132, 134
Benedict, R. 77, 78, 98
Bent, I. 33, 47, 50
Berlyne, D.E. 39, 47, 109, 132
Biklen, S.K. 82, 85, 87, 88, 98
Boas, F. 77, 78, 95
Bogdan, R.C. 82, 85, 87, 88, 98
Boyle, J.D. 178
Bragg, G. 5, 6
Bresler, L. 78, 98
Britain, H. 29, 47
Brittin, R.V. 127, 133

C
Campbell, D.T. 141, 153, 162, 177
Capperella-Sheldon, D. 49, 127, 133
Chase, G. 59, 73
Codding, P.A. 105, 132
Conway, C.M. 93, 94
Coppleston, F. 78, 98, 162, 177
Crawford, R. 58, 59, 60, 73

D
Darwin, C. 77
Davidson, L. 20, 109, 110, 132
Demorest, S.A. 115, 132, 133, 134
Densmore, F. 81
Deutsch, D. 106, 109, 132
Duckles, V.H. 8, 9, 20, 56, 57, 187
Duke, R.A. 108, 132, 133

E
Edison, T.A. 80
Elliott, D. 28, 48
Ellis, A.J. 38, 48, 83, 84, 98, 104, 133

F
Farnsworth, P. 34, 104, 105, 132
Fechner, G.T. 48, 103, 132
Fewkes, J.W. 80, 84, 98
Fiske, H. 44, 48
Freeman, D. 95, 98
Furman, C.H. 159, 177

G
Geringer, J.M. 107, 108, 132, 133
Graff, H.F. 2, 20, 68
Greer, R.D. 104, 133, 158, 177, 178
Gurney, E. 29, 48

H
Hall, R.V. 132
Hanslick, E. 29, 38, 48
Harrison, F.L. 53, 54, 55, 73, 98, 190
Hegel, G. 28, 48, 77
Heller, G.N. 58, 73
Helmholtz, H. 38, 48, 84, 103, 104, 133
Hendel, C. 93, 94, 98
Hitchcock, H.W. 20, 58, 59, 60, 73, 98, 133, 177, 188
Hood, M. 36, 80, 81, 84, 98, 99, 190

J
Jellison, J.A. 105, 133
Johnson, D. 56, 64, 65, 73, 115, 132, 159, 177
Jorgenson, H. 158, 159, 177

K
Kant, I. 28, 77, 78, 96
Kuhn, T.L. 28, 48, 107, 108, 133

L
Langer, S. 35, 49
LeBlanc, A. 39, 49
Locke, J. 30, 32, 49
Lundin, R.W. 104, 105, 133, 177

M
Madsen, C.H., Jr. 104, 119, 140, 153, 158, 162, 177
Madsen, C.K. 28, 34, 49, 50, 104, 106, 119, 121, 127, 132, 140, 153, 158, 162, 177
Malinowski, B. 77, 78, 86, 99
Mead, M. 77, 95, 98, 99
Mendel, A. 38, 48, 64, 73, 100
Merriam, A. 36, 81, 99
Meyer, L.B. 35, 39, 49
Mill, J.S. viii, 49, 161, 162, 163, 164, 178
Moore, R.S. 34, 104, 133, 153, 162, 177
Morrison, S.J. 115, 132, 133, 134

N
Nettl, B. 55, 79, 89, 99, 100, 192

O
O'Leary, K.D. 116, 134
Orman, E.K. xiv, 114, 134

P
Palisca, C.V. 57, 59, 63, 66, 190
Patton, M.Q. 86, 99
Pecore, J.T. 90, 91, 92, 100
Perlman, M. 90, 91, 92, 100
Petzold, R.G. 112, 134
Plato 27, 30, 31, 32, 34, 42, 43, 49
Price, H.E. xiv, 50, 111, 112, 113, 114, 127, 134, 135
Prickett, C.A. xiv, 50, 104, 107, 108, 112, 132, 133, 134, 135, 159, 177
Pythagoras 27, 31

R
Radocy, R.E. 112, 132, 178
Randal, D.M. 35, 49, 74, 100

 **Index**

Subject Index

LaVergne, TN USA
12 July 2010
189196LV00001B/5/P